THE HEAD
of the
SNAKE

A NOVEL

Dick Carlsen

authorHOUSE®

AuthorHouse™
1663 Liberty Drive
Bloomington, IN 47403
www.authorhouse.com
Phone: 1 (800) 839-8640

This is a work of fiction. All of the characters, names, incidents, organizations, and dialogue
in this novel are either the products of the author's imagination or are used fictitiously.

Published by AuthorHouse 10/22/2018

ISBN: 978-1-5462-6306-7 (sc)
ISBN: 978-1-5462-6305-0 (e)

Library of Congress Control Number: 2018911866

Print information available on the last page.

Any people depicted in stock imagery provided by Getty Images are models,
and such images are being used for illustrative purposes only.
Certain stock imagery © Getty Images.

This book is printed on acid-free paper.

Because of the dynamic nature of the Internet, any web addresses or links contained in
this book may have changed since publication and may no longer be valid. The views
expressed in this work are solely those of the author and do not necessarily reflect the
views of the publisher, and the publisher hereby disclaims any responsibility for them.

This book is for Krista and Carl. You are loved.

ACKNOWLEDGEMENTS

Smithsonian Answer Book – Snakes; Zug and Ernst; Smithsonian Books, Smithsonian Institution, Washington, D.C.; 2004; Page 124.

John Gottman/Christopher Dollard – Gottman Institute; Marriage Study.

City of Virginia Beach Public Library, Great Neck Branch, Library staff, with particular thanks to LaVoreen Terrey and McPherson West.

Steve White, Navy Region Mid-Atlantic, IT Staff, a former colleague, for his continued assistance in helping me navigate the IT world.

My wife, Cathy, for her review and comments.

PREAMBLE

A mortally wounded snake dies quickly; however, nerve reflexes may cause muscle twitches for several hours after death, resulting in spasmodic movements of the jaw. Because of the lingering nerve reflexes, even a dead venomous snake is dangerous. A Florida man died after a bite from the decapitated head of a canebrake rattlesnake.

2000
PROLOGUE

There's a parable that goes something like this – picture yourself living on a pretty, tree-lined street. Pretend that your neighbor's "problems", as well as yours, could have tangible, physical qualities and could be placed curbside for all the neighbors to see. Upon "seeing" the neighbor's problems, you would want no part of any of those problems and would quickly, gladly pull yours back into the house and keep them, secure in the realization that you could deal with them and that you wanted no part of other people's problems.

My name is Dave Pedersen, and I'm just an easygoing, incurable romantic guy that had the misfortune to marry the wrong person. My marital and divorce problems with my ex-wife were the exception to the above parable, with no question about it. Other people would happily retain their money issues, problems raising the kids, the auto accident, even severe health issues that turn lives around and put victims in that downward spiral of a life without purpose or happiness. Me? Take the viper ex-wife and please get her the hell out of my life. I can shed the skin of her lunatic, vicious episodes a hundred times and not be fully, uncompromisingly free of the pain and anguish she caused in my life. There is not a strong enough soap to clean my body, nor an elixir to cleanse my soul and vanquish the memories that cling to my psyche like flies to flypaper.

The long ago television program about New York City, The Naked City, opened each episode with the attention-grabbing statement that there were eight million stories in that city. Well, my ex-wife created a story or an affront seemingly every time she showed her face anywhere or opened her opinionated mouth. She took no prisoners. She was right, and everyone else was wrong. She wanted control, like a prison guard over inmates. Her passive-aggressive communication style lured one into candor and entrapment that allowed her to achieve her goal of verbal and mental superiority. No one was spared – family members, neighbors, even friends. Mother, brother, mother-in-law, me, made no difference. She was so quick with the tongue, the barbs, accusations, reversing the role as the victim, producing brain-numbing arguments, her own brand of stultifying logic.

The universe revolved around this cute, brunette, shapely screamer and her frequent myopic tirades. Somewhere along the way she developed a fighter instinct. God help anyone that countered or argued a point with her and received a verbal lashing. There was no such thing as a different perspective. Everything was fair game to her. Within one or two drumbeats of dialogue she was on the offensive like a John Elway touchdown drive.

So, how did I come to be married to this Cheeta in pussycat clothing, this attractive, seemingly gentle lady? Just that, taken by appearances that I learned too late were only skin deep.

The year was 1978. I remember it well. How does one forget events that evolved into a life canvas splattered with lunacy, torment and misery? I had been working my way back to my office in southern Maryland after some assignments at Naval Station Charleston, South Carolina and Naval Station Mayport, Jacksonville, Florida. I stopped along the way to spend a night with a lady friend on Kiawah Island in South Carolina, and after a night in Wilmington, North Carolina, I arrived in the Norfolk, Virginia, area where I made a quick stop to see a colleague that was a department head at Naval Air Station Oceana, the Navy's East Coast Master Jet Base. We had a nice visit and I drove to my motel.

After checking in I called another Navy buddy, a guy with whom I had attended a Navy four-week course of instruction and who had just returned from a three-year stint in the Philippines at our huge Subic Bay installation.

"Bob, this is Dave. How you doing?"

"Dave! Good to hear from you. We're just getting re-settled in the area after a great experience in the Philippines."

"I know, and I'm anxious to hear all about it. Are you and Susan going to be around if I can stop by tonight?"

"Yes, and how about we invite Susan's friend, Carla, to join us? Kind of a blind date, but it will be a casual evening. She's attractive, and can be a bit quirky. What do you say?"

"Sounds great, Bob. I'll risk the quirky. How about I come your way about six o'clock?"

"See you then." He gave me his home address and directions, so I relaxed at the motel for a couple of hours before heading out.

Carla was a pleasant surprise. Cute, short brunette hair, and dark eyes that suggested mysteries. She was about my height and had a slender figure. She looked like she stayed in shape and had great looking legs.

She had never been married and appeared to be in her mid-twenties to this thirty-one year old guy that had managed to remain single. Not that I was always trying to remain unattached. I had been engaged to be married twice, but both times had been broken off. And there had been other "serious" relationships with women that for one reason or another ended up in the burn pile. Aside from those, there were numerous "girlfriends" and dates that kept me warm at night and fueled my incurable romantic tendencies, some of which of course led to the engagements.

The four of us had a very nice evening at a bar on Hampton Boulevard near the Old Dominion University campus, where Bob had attended college. During the evening Bob filled me in on their Philippines experience, and I learned from Carla that she was a bookkeeper at a large regional medical company headquarters in Virginia Beach, that she lived with her parents in Norfolk, that her father was a lawyer, and that her mother was a secretary at Regent University, a Christian education center that occupied a large parcel of land next to Carla's employer.

I enjoyed meeting Carla and asked her if she was interested in joining me for breakfast the following morning before I left town. She said, "Yes", so we made plans.

We went to a popular restaurant the next morning that specialized in serving breakfast only, where we had an opportunity to get better acquainted. I had told her I was a Navy instructor working out of a Navy base in southern Maryland, from which I travelled to Navy Fleet Concentration areas overseas and in the states to deliver my course. I did tell her that there was a good chance that I would be relocating to Washington, D.C., in the near future.

After a tasty breakfast of eggs and pancakes, my favorite, and pleasant conversation, we started to exit the restaurant, but not before she told me about a rather unpleasant matter involving a friend of hers. With some bitterness she told me about her long-time neighborhood friend, Billy, who had been arrested for marijuana possession about a year prior, but more recently had been apprehended, arrested and charged with breaking in and entering with use of a firearm. Neat.

I took Carla home and made the two-hour drive to my place in Maryland.

So, there you go. That is how the craziness started. We had a nice time together, and before I knew it, I was calling her to get a date. Along the way, I was recruited for a headquarters position in Washington and accepted it.

I was smitten by this young lady, enjoying her company, and to my utter disappointment and regret probably ignored a signal or sign that might have raised a red flag in our developing relationship. After all the girls I had dated, destiny lead me to marry Carla. They say fate and timing in life is everything, and I truly believe that. Things happen at a good time or a bad time, like when you're jogging down a narrow two-lane country road, with virtually no traffic, when suddenly two cars are driving on that road in opposite directions and, in an example of bad timing, fate has them passing one another at precisely your location on the road and you have no choice but to step off the road and onto the "rough".

You see, I didn't have to make that call to Bob. I could have relaxed at my motel after a busy week on the road. But, I didn't. I called him, and as they say, the rest is history.

It is now twenty-two years later and I sit on the dock near my Lake Gaston, Virginia, cabin, reflecting on the destruction, demolition derby-style that was my marriage to Carla and the later post-divorce decree years that continued to inflict unabated pain and suffering akin to being bitten by the chopped off head of a dead venomous snake. Her childhood friend Billy of the criminal mindset became part of the problem, but also surprisingly the solution. Because of the nostalgia freak that I am, I subscribe to the value of nostalgic thinking and that it increases life's meaning, thus I reflected also on those pre-marriage, wonderful single-life years that I obviously too casually and quickly relinquished. What in the hell was I thinking? Why did I leave that wonderful period of my life, a time of no social or relationship boundaries, a peaceful time void of marriage chaos, and in my particular case, with those words, "I do", plunged me into a life of unpredictable volcanic eruptions by that "cute little brunette", a cauldron of evil. She was a viper, a monster, that did not stray off course or auto-correct even after our divorce.

I felt like the actor Richard Carlson in the 1950's TV series, "I Lead Three Lives", so let me tell you about the good (incontrovertibly the wonderful single life), the bad (lunatic wife), and the ugly (the head of the snake, post-divorce).

Didn't swerve to avoid my fate.

1973

CHAPTER ONE

Life was treating me pretty darn good, a roller-coaster ride of delights.

I had completed four years at Happy Valley College in northern California, arguably the best four years of my life – I think most college graduates would admit to that qualitative assessment of their college years – and my active duty time in the Army was behind me.

Having returned to the San Francisco Bay Area, I was restless. A young lady I cared deeply about named Debbie was no longer a part of my life. She returned an engagement ring after I completed Army boot camp, so it was probably best that I try to put her behind me and put some distance between us as well. I still missed her, and we had talked so much about having a family, but I had moved on after the break-up. I had written some verse about her. In fact, my poetry later became a standard and frequent means of communicating with girls I was dating. They loved it!

Sausilito

I didn't know you
until
the second time
   i loved.
She and i strolled often
   along the Bridgeway
pushing our way up
   little Lombard
     in the village fair
and stepping inside every shop
that begged entry.
We never tired
   Of your graciousness
     And pleasures.

I've brought someone new
   That is special to me.
We marveled at the jewelry
In eaton's
And sat on the wharf
With the city
The bay
Angel island
   And twisting sailboats
Set out before us.
If only I had a bankroll
   I'd buy something more
Than
Lunch at the kettle
   And flowers for my friend.

Sitting on a ramp
At the boat harbor
Gazing at the symmetry
  Of masts
    And gleaming wood,
And being mesmerized
By the sound
  Of lapping water
    Against the hulls.
Arm in arm
It was easy
  To drift
    Into incalculable depths
Of tranquility.
I told her so,
And she responded
  With a touch
That spoke of her thoughtfulness
And appreciation.
I was drawing
  Tri-masters
On the jeans of her thigh,
When I returned
  From Tahiti
Met her gaze
  And touched her warm lips.
Home again, and safe.
Sausilito
You will never be the same
To me.

Attending graduate school, especially out of state, became

my focus. I ended up at Indiana University after a long, lonely drive from California during which I had second thoughts on my decision to leave family and college friends for an unknown destination and endeavor. It turned out to be the best decision I could have possibly made. Grad school at IU had provided so many memorable, cherished opportunities, countless new friends from different parts of the country, particularly the Midwest, and new experiences. My close friends, all MBA students, lived in the Graduate Residence Center like me. Thursday night meant Village Inn Pizza for beers and the occasional bladder bursting contest, Friday's we met at a bar downtown to play the pinball machines, and during football season, we found a pre-tailgate party at an apartment complex within a short walk of the football stadium parking lot. That was where and when we unwound from a week of academics, found some girls with whom to chat it up, and just have a hell of a lot of fun mingling with everyone. A flask was brought into the stadium, and we continued on rum and cokes during the game. Finding a post-game party became a worthwhile pursuit. Basketball season meant watching Bobby Knight-coached teams in action.

While I was fully occupied with studies, I did make time for extracurricular activity, namely playing on the Rugby Club side. Good guys, the usual "rugger huggers", great parties, and fun playing rugby. We were not varsity athletes. My more memorable weekend was playing in the Big Ten Rugby Championships at Purdue University, where we lost our games to Illinois and Ohio State but won the parties! Back at IU, we didn't let weather affect our outdoor party plans, sometimes holding our outdoor post game keggers during a snowfall. Our scrum half had a morning shift driving a courtesy student commuter bus, so we frequently crossed paths as he drove east on 10th Street as I was walking down the sidewalk toward the campus center and, seeing me, would open the bus door at a bus stop, yell out, "Hey, Dave!", and I would react with a hearty, "Hey, Gabe, good morning!"

School let out my first semester right before Kentucky Derby weekend, so our grad dorm group, one of which was from Bardstown, Kentucky, headed out of town for the weekend. The Kentuckian, Jerry, was also an Honorary Colonel. We drove to Bardstown to party at Jerry's parent's house, where there was no shortage of alcohol since Jerry's father owned a liquor store next door to the house. Wow. Convenient or what? Very simply, the Derby was a unique experience – when we arrived in Louisville, we hoofed it to Churchill Downs from a distant parking lot where we had emptied 7-up bottles, filled them with bourbon, recapped them, and placed them carefully and readily distinguishable in a cooler. The center field lived up to its reputation – thousands of college students gathered around flags and pennants proclaiming their college affiliation, and under a warm sun, shirtless, we were merry with our bourbon and sevens.

I had met and dated a number of girls at IU, including "Chico", an undergrad in the dorm at which I was a Resident Assistant, Karen, a fellow grad student, Ginger, a "rugger hugger", and Suzy, a sorority girl – they had not met too many California guys, so there may have been some innate curiosity, and one girl in particular I will never forget. It was my last night on campus on a lovely May evening with the spring colors exploding and I had taken a final exam study break at the Regulator, a college bar right off campus. I met a girl named "Cricket". We had a couple drinks, danced, and got to know one another. I spent the night at her place, overslept some, and had to make a beeline for the academic building to take my last final exam. After the exam, I drove to Cricket's apartment for nostalgic reasons, hoping to see her again, but she had already departed for home in Syracuse. I then drove to the undergraduate dorm where I had been a Resident

Assistant my second and third semesters, packed up my limited belongings, threw them in the "bug", and drove east to start the next chapter of my life.

That next chapter had started in early April with a flight from Indianapolis to Washington, D.C., for a job interview at a Navy headquarters building near the Pentagon. The Personnel Director, Harry, had met me at what was then National Airport. It was a short drive to our destination, but Harry used the time to begin the interview process.

"I noted from your resume that you attended college in California. What was the location and what did you study?" he asked. Harry had a bit of a jowl, had a rather stern look, and didn't smile much. I later learned he was a retired Air Force officer. He was probably in his 60's, walked slow, and was a bit overweight. Friendly, though.

"Happy Valley College is in northern California, sir, where I studied Business Administration. Great school. Small campus in a typical California valley agriculture town."

"Did you do any extracurricular activities?" I know he read about all this in my resume, but was being pleasant and talkative, so I was cool with it and enjoyed the opportunity for discourse, which also helped calm my nerves for the interview.

"I did. Played football my first year, but decided I was too small to make a future of it, but made the gymnastics team, where I earned a varsity letter my freshman year. My senior year the student body president appointed me to the Student Judiciary. We didn't have many cases as I recall. I was also active in our Block HV letterman's society."

Like I said, it was a short drive. By the time we had some conversation, we arrived at our destination.

"This is the Navy Annex, Dave, a World War Two Navy complex that is now shared by various Navy and Marine Corps headquarters elements or commands. She's a tired, old structure, but quite useful."

I could see what he meant by his assessment. It was drab, painted a pale standard government color beige, and was lacking in landscaping that might have given it some added "curb appeal", not that the Navy would be particularly interested in that. With its many wings it may have been a former hospital building at one time, probably during the war. It reminded me of Oak Knoll Naval Hospital in Oakland, California, where my twin brother, Dan, and I had visited a grade school buddy who had been shot up pretty bad in Vietnam.

Harry parked around back, and we entered the building after Harry showed some form of identification to a Marine guard. The interview board was headed up by a Navy Commander, the head of the unit within which I was applying for work, and the interview went well. The Commander, at the conclusion of the interview, gave me some hope when he said, "I think you have the tools we are looking for, Dave. Harry will be in touch with you." Harry drove me to the airport and I flew back to Indianapolis, where I retrieved my bug and drove back down to the Bloomington campus, full of hope.

Five days later, on a day I will never, ever forget, on Friday the 13th, I was studying in my dorm room when Harry called and offered me the job. I was ecstatic and told him so, and he offered that they felt I would fit in perfectly with my academics and military background. To this day, I am not superstitious about Friday the 13th! In fact, while still at school I received in the mail my first set of official Navy travel orders. Wow, that was fantastic, and made good conversation material with my friends and classmates. While eventually my orders were changed, as I learned would and could often be the case, my first set had me scheduled for Key West, Jacksonville, FL, Charleston, SC, and

Norfolk, VA. I was stoked. They weren't kidding when during the job interview I was told that my mission was to travel, to keep my bags packed, and that I would most likely be on the road about ninety percent of the year.

That first day leaving Bloomington I drove as far as Washington, D.C., where I stayed at the home of a San Jose, CA, lady named Nancy that my brother and I had met when our aunt and uncle took us on a camping trip to Lake Shasta in northern California when Nancy and a girlfriend were young San Jose State College co-eds and Dan and I were younger high-school guys. They "tolerated" us, and we got along great, becoming close friends. When I visited Nancy in Washington, she was married to a Secret Service agent, and the day after my arrival he invited me to the White House for a personal tour. That was incredible. I saw President Nixon sitting in the Oval Office as we walked by, and I lifted a small notepad from the Cabinet meeting room as a souvenir. It was blank!

The next day I said goodbye and thanked them profusely for such wonderful hospitality, and continued on to Lexington Park, Maryland, my home base for a good part of the next five years. With no accommodations pre-arranged beforehand, I took a motel room "downtown" for a few nights while I did the requisite apartment hunting in this typical military town with bars, retail and other services fanned out from the main gate of the base. I found a small studio apartment on the second floor of a house close to the base, on Route 235, and affordable considering I would be out of the area much of the time. With that, I settled into this new life with so much opportunity. One of the first things I did was to write and send a poem to Cricket in Syracuse. She later flew down to visit me.

Hang on for a great ride.

1979
CHAPTER TWO

My twin brother, Dan, lived in northern California. We grew up in the San Francisco Bay Area, in a town called Danville on the east side of the hills from Oakland, and he now lived in a small college town called Happy Valley, where we both attended college, and where he had remained after college graduation. Dan had flown out to Washington, where I picked him up at Dulles Airport on a typically cold day in January, 1979. My small apartment in Georgetown, near the intersection of 34th Street, NW, and N Street, was a short walk from the university campus and a ton of great watering holes. One of the nice things about living close to the Georgetown University campus was that very occasionally I lucked out and got my hands on a basketball game ticket that enabled me to watch the likes of Syracuse, Villanova, Providence, and other Big East teams. We hit the bars in Georgetown that first night, and I was able to introduce him to a really cool bar named Nathan's on M Street. We talked about old times at Happy Valley College, the many great friends we had made, and all the crazy, typical college stunts we pulled. The next day I took him out to one of my favorite laid-back places in the area, a restaurant in the Potomac Village area called Old Anglers Inn. Nestled in a wooded area off a narrow, winding two-lane road heading out to the canal, cozy, and with great charm offered by the stone exterior, it was a wonderful venue to take dates to. An Indiana University classmate of mine who worked in hospital administration in the city had introduced me to the place, for which I remain most grateful.

We did the tourist thing, snapping a photo of Dan standing in front of the Inn, in his Kansas City Chiefs tee-shirt given him by a mutual Happy Valley College friend, Doug, who played in the National Football League.

The next day we headed south down I-95, making the very long drive to Kiawah Island to spend the night. The island held special memories for me of a lady friend that lived there. The next day we hopped back in my Porsche 914 to Miami to hook up with Happy Valley buddies to attend the Super Bowl. Had a great time poolside at the hotel, hit a local beach south of Miami, and saw a great football game between the Cowboys and Steelers. We all lucked out by finding some very reasonably priced scalped game tickets. Dan and I stayed that night with one of the guys who then lived and worked in Fort Lauderdale, and the next day I headed back toward Washington.

No sooner was I back in Washington after my Super Bowl trip, that my girlfriend Carla called me one night to inform me of her devastation at receiving the very unpleasant news that her friend from childhood that she had previously told me about, the guy that was playing Russian roulette with the law with his marijuana possession misdemeanor charges, and the more serious excursion into the criminal and legal system after being arrested for breaking in and entering and use of a firearm, had his day in court.

Carla was in tears. "Dave, you remember my neighbor, Billy?

He was arrested a short while back and faced burglary and firearm charges. It's a felony, you know." Warning flags.

"I did not know, but okay." I did not want to tell her I was already losing interest in this matter involving someone I did not know facing felony charges, regardless of the fact he was a "dear friend" that she had grown up with, played hide and seek, spin the bottle, who knows? I didn't hang around with felons so emotionally I was a blank slate that I intended to remain as such. Fortunately, I had been spared the unpleasantness of attending a party with Carla's friends and being introduced to this slime ball.

"Well, I went to his hearing today and watched with horror as the Judge took no pity on poor Billy and found him guilty of a felony and sent him to prison. I can't believe this is happening."

"How long a jail term?" I'm just going through the motions. No emotion at my end, no real empathy or sympathy. You make your bed, you sleep in it, yes? This guy had a bunk bed of charges going against him, along with the prior marijuana conviction. But I learned you don't play cool hand Luke with Carla and get away with it.

"Two years! My God, that's an eternity. That poor guy." She was getting warmed up.

"Well, he's unfortunately learning the hard way that you don't play with the law and come out ahead, Carla. There's a price to pay when you commit felonious acts. I know he's a friend of yours and that you feel distraught about his conviction, but there's regrettably not much you can do at this point."

"Distraught?! You think I just feel distraught? I'm devastated and ready to explode. I can't get it off my mind. I feel like a zombie. I talked to my mom and dad about it because they know Billy very well, but all they can say is they're sorry it happened. You sound like them. That doesn't help me deal with it." She's wound up tighter than the line on my fishing reel.

"I'm sorry, too, Carla, but there's nothing I can say or do to help you feel better." I've lost interest. Let's move on.

"Yes, there is. You can come down here tomorrow and help me deal with this. I need you here, Dave." That blind side came out of left field and certainly got my attention. Demanding.

"I can't do that. I'm expected at work and there's a lot going on in the office. I have a couple of assignments due by the end of the week and when the Navy Secretariat sets a due date, that's it. No wiggle room, and I'm the sole action officer on the taskers. I didn't want to go into the strong work ethic I learned from my father, coupled with an inherent fear of losing my job if performance and productivity suddenly went south.

"Bullshit!" she screamed. "I want you to come down here tomorrow. Your boss will understand. It's just a job. I'm a wreck." That goes without saying. I also did not want to suggest to her that she was expending a bit more emotional capital than would seem normal under the circumstances, and that I had no obligation to screw my employer and be in Norfolk the next day.

"I'll be down there this weekend. That's just a few days from now, and we can talk about it then." Can't wait.

Click. Phone line dead. Okay, that was fun. This cute little brunette number has a temper and clearly wants things her way. I didn't catch the warning flag, for I was a bit shook up and certainly not accustomed to dealing with this outward display of angst in someone I was dating. She was self-centered, for sure.

I did not call her back. Let her cool down. Right.

She called me the next night. "Dave, I'm still upset that you would not come down here. I don't want to see you this weekend."

"Well, that doesn't sound good. I was looking forward to seeing you and trying to help."

"Not this weekend. Bye." Another click.

The following week she called, apologized, and almost sounded like she failed to recall the temper and anger she unloaded through the phone at me the previous week. She said she would drive up to my place, which she did that Friday, arriving in a mild snowstorm. We had a nice weekend. I didn't bring up the dreaded topic of her jailbird friend, and interestingly enough, nor did she. Jekyll and Hyde? Display of anger, thereupon forgotten? Mini-Mount Vesuvius volcanic eruption, swept under the ash?

Things continued to go well and were obviously serious, notwithstanding the Billy episode. We enjoyed one another's company, in Norfolk and Washington, and I honestly thought I loved her. She accepted my marriage proposal, followed by the proverbial question I posed to her father, "Do I have your permission to marry your daughter?" He and her mother were thrilled, and thus followed all the multitudinous wedding planning.

We got married in May of that year in a large Methodist church in Virginia Beach, a wedding ceremony attended by my family that had flown out from California, and a number of my close friends and work colleagues.

The bachelor party was modest. We were all staying at a reasonably priced hotel on Shore Drive in Virginia Beach, and there was no one local that could have made party arrangements at a different venue and hired ladies to perform lap dances as well as other typical farewell to singlehood shenanigans.

Instead, we bought a couple cases of beer and got down and dirty right there on a grassy patch of the hotel common area between buildings. What a group! Brother Dan had flown out from California, four of my best friends from Indiana University, Jerry, Lenny, Ray, and Wally, flew in from parts remote, and my good Navy field Rep traveling buddy, Pete, constituting a hell-raising group if there ever was one. We drank and told stories on a beautiful afternoon under a blue sky, and everyone became good drinking buddies. There were no strangers.

We were having such a great time we almost blew off the wedding rehearsal at the church.

"Guys," I exclaimed, "we need to pull chocks and get our butts to the church for the rehearsal."

"Ah, screw it, Dave, you don't need to rehearse. They'll tell you what to do when you get to the church tomorrow. Basic stuff," bellowed Jerry. Jerry was one hell of a partier at IU, whether in the grad dorm, at Thursday night Village Inn, Friday afternoon pinballs, and especially at football tailgate parties and inside the Derby infield. Outragious. I remember the trip we all made to Lexington, Kentucky, for an IU-Kentucky football game. Being an Honorary Kentucky Colonel, Jerry was deeply disturbed at the final whistle of the game and an IU victory, and once out of the stadium, simply took off running like a fox escaping hounds, running through the parking lot and disappearing from sight. He found his way back after a near-empty parking lot cleared his line of sight to see us.

"No, no," I yelled, doing all I could to hold back laughter. "We need to go, seriously."

Ray helped me out. "Guys, this has been great fun, and I know we would all rather continue the party, but Dave's right. We gotta get ready to go to the church."

A chorus of resignation ensued. We weren't thrilled with the end of the party, but going to the rehearsal was the right thing to do.

"Okay," said Wally. "We'll follow you, Dave."

And with that, off we went, still clad in our party clothes of shorts and tee-shirts. Oh, my goodness, what a beautiful motley crew. If we couldn't continue our party, we'll be damned if we're going to dress up.

Mistake.

We descended on the church, noisily entering the chapel, and

I know everyone present heard us before we got through the front door.

Up to Carla I sauntered, smiling, asking what I needed to do. "You'll pay for this. How disgraceful and inappropriate," she whispered, although I'm sure others nearby heard the venomous dress-down.

"Hey, we were having a great time at a bachelor event at the hotel. No harm done. We're ready to rehearse," which was accompanied by a hellacious beer-belch from one of the guys. I couldn't help laughing, but of course it only made matters worse in the eyes of my fiery dragon bride-to-be.

"Enough," she exclaimed. "Let's get this done and get you guys out of here."

"Works for us, Carla," I replied, knowing damn well that my enchanting life of singlehood was going bye-bye.

The rehearsal completed, I lead the way back to the hotel so we could clean up for the rehearsal dinner.

The wedding ceremony was simple and blessedly short, and everyone found their way to the reception at a nearby catering venue. I couldn't drink because I was driving us away that night to a hotel down I-95 in North Carolina where we would spend the evening before continuing on to Kiawah Island, South Carolina, for our honeymoon. I remember extremely well the look of outright pleasure and true delight, and maybe even a large sense of relief, on the face of her father, whose arm was around his wife's waist, her smiling face resting on his shoulder, as we left the reception. He didn't have to say a friggin word, but I know he was giving me one big "Thank you, Dave."

Kiss the enchanting single life goodbye.

1973

CHAPTER THREE

Having secured an apartment on the main drag into town, my first week in the office on Naval Air Station Patuxent River, Maryland, was uneventful and rather boring, for my new boss had me wading through Navy policy manuals. But things picked up the second week as I was shuttled by the office duty driver to National Airport for a flight to Memphis, where I was met by a Naval Air Station Memphis base rep and taken to my base lodging, the Bachelor Officers Quarters, or BOQ as they were known. I was not impressed, but not really knowing what to expect I accepted the accommodations. I was not going to be picky, which was my nature anyway. Laid back, don't get too excited about things, let things roll off your back like water off a duck's back, even-keeled. That was me. This particular BOQ was in an old, unimpressive two-level WWII-era building with exterior white-washed walls and green trim around doors and windows. My room had a double-size bed, an attached bathroom, a simple, wood chest of drawers, and a similar style table on which stood a small TV and a "Welcome to NAS Memphis" book. That was it. Spartan. No dignitaries stayed in this room! But did I really care? Hell, no, for I was on my first Navy business trip.

Late in the afternoon while studying some work materials there was a knock on the door. I opened the door to a black gentleman I did not know, but who had a broad smile on this face that I would come to learn was almost a ready laughter. He had a full face with noticeable cheeks, very short hair that was almost a buzz cut, and his size and shape, or girth, suggested that he had not missed very many meals. He came across as a happy guy. I invited him in.

"You Dave Pedersen?" he asked.

"Yes, sir, I am."

"Hi, I'm Ralph Churchwell, one of the Mess Field Reps from our office at Pax," as he extended his hand to shake. "Pax" was the much shortened term we used instead of Patuxent River.

"It's a pleasure to meet you, Ralph. I had been told I would be working with you this week and that one of two things would happen, either we would find some time to go fishing or that you would take me to a restaurant serving the best catfish in the area."

He got a big kick out of that. "Who told you that?" he replied with a chuckle from down deep. "Must have been 'ol Dale, the only Field Rep home in the office at the moment, or maybe Furney, the auditor."

"Yep, it was Dale." Dale was a Recreation Field Rep, had just returned from an assignment in the Philippines, and was mentoring me while in the office for a few days before heading back out on the road. Great guy, and definitely one of the world travelers. I wanted to get to that point, but it would take a while, training under people like Ralph and others before I got my "solo Field Rep wings" and assignments overseas.

"Did you just check in today, Dave?" Ralph asked.

"Yes, sir, I did about a few hours ago."

And then he surprised me with, "Well, you're not staying in this fleabag BOQ. I don't care what they say about BOQ's, but this one is old and unsat and I'm not going to let you stay here. I'm at the Navy Lodge down the street near the runways and Air Operations, and that's where you're going, so go right on ahead and pack up your stuff and meet me down in the lobby. Oh, and by the way, you can knock off the "sir" stuff and call me Ralph."

"Will do, Ralph. I can do that, and thank you so much." What was readily apparent to this novice traveler was that Ralph was a veteran, knew his way around the Navy, and cared about his teammates. I entered the lobby in time to hear the tail end of the brief conversation Ralph had with the front desk clerk.

"I can put Mr. Pedersen in a different room," she told Ralph.

"No, you are not. He is checking out and you will arrange the appropriate credit or refund for tonight. He is not staying here, and frankly, I would not let anyone else I knew stay in your BOQ." Ralph was harsh, and could get away with it.

"Well, I'll take care of the refund, and you can talk to the manager about your concerns."

"Thank you, and I will when I have more time to do so."

It was a great week working with and learning from Ralph, and the Navy Lodge digs were definitely superior to the BOQ. The highlight of the week was our invitation to dinner at the home of the base Special Services Director, Joe Duggar, a retired Navy Lieutenant Commander that had a gruff, no nonsense demeanor that took some getting used to. That aside, we had a wonderful catfish dinner after a couple of cold beers. In later years, I would learn to expect a bus load of Joe's employees attending Navy meetings.

Earlier in the week, Ralph and I went to a local restaurant where we dined on, yes, catfish. There, I learned a lot more about Ralph. He called the Memphis area home, was a retired Navy

Master Chief, had been a Navy Steward his entire active duty career, and knew many Navy Flag Officers from his years of work in Flag Messes and Commissioned Officers Messes Closed, or officer dining facilities. He also told me that he currently lived in Rhode Island with his wife and daughter, and that he had two sons, both of which were military commissioned officers.

I didn't meet any women in Memphis, but I did at my next duty assignment location, Norfolk, Virginia. I also had my first assignment reviewing Recreation operations on one of the many bases in the Norfolk Fleet Concentration area under the expert tutelage of a veteran Field Rep named Ray who I eventually referred to as "Dad". He loved it, and we got along great. We often went to a restaurant on Ocean View Avenue, just down the street from our motel, and one night I finally struck up a conversation with one of the waitresses we got to know, a cute young lady named Karen.

On one of her trips to the table, Ray and I asked her a few questions.

"You're very good at this, Karen. Have you been doing it very long?" Ray asked.

"Oh, it's just a summer job, but I also worked here last summer. I'll be returning to college in August."

That got my attention, so I asked, "Where do you go to college, Karen?"

"Indiana University. It's a great school, and I live in the state," she proudly replied.

"I know," I said, adding, "I just finished up grad school there last month. Maybe we can get together and share IU stories, Karen."

"I'd like that," she said, and with that she gave me her phone number before she dashed off to another table.

"Not bad, Dave," Ray exclaimed with a twinkle in his eye. I

knew Ray had an eye for good looking women. "Cute girl, and very nice. I'm sure you'll have a good time when you get together."

Within the week, Karen and I spent time together at "Grandma McKay's", sitting out back of her house on the Chesapeake Bay beach, drinking a beer and chatting up a storm about IU experiences.

Ray moved on to his next assignment and I remained in Norfolk for a four-week course of instruction. I dated a girl that worked at the motel, and saw Karen a few more times before returning to the office in southern Maryland, where Ray and I hooked up for our next assignment in Beaufort, South Carolina, where I ran into a fellow classmate from Norfolk, followed by assignments at the Navy complex in Charleston, South Carolina. The director at one of the Charleston installations invited us to a crab cookout at his home attended by a large number of his friends and local dignitaries. Along with our host's wonderful southern hospitality, a lady I met there and had a nice time with took me to her house for a very pleasant evening of romance, which highlighted my Charleston stay.

From there, my boss sent me to a professional conference in Washington, D.C., where I was fortunate to run into Laura, an IU grad school classmate currently working in New York City. We struck up a bit of a relationship, and she invited me to her parent's house in Northern Virginia for Thanksgiving. The following week I was in Key West performing my first solo management review. "Dad" had told our supervisor I was ready. While I frequently relaxed poolside after my afternoon jogs, I did all the typical Key West stuff, including hanging out at Sloppy Joe's, Hemingway's hangout on Duval, and met a girl named Joyce at the base Officers Club. Great looking lady, with a dynamite body, but what a tease. Got her out onto the club's private beach out the back door a couple times, but nothing doing. Oh, well. Move on.

Dad and I worked together on follow-on assignments in Pensacola and Corpus Christi, and in between we worked in New Orleans, where Ray had family. They gave me a tour of the French Quarter, and Ray and I were treated to outstanding homemade seafood gumbo at his in-laws. More fantastic southern hospitality, a treat this California boy was experiencing for the first time and certainly never tired of.

Ray and I left the mild southern climes and headed to the Navy base north of Chicago. Winter had arrived early. During my first weekend there, Ray drove me down to O'Hare Airport for a flight and weekend in Bloomington, Indiana to see my wonderful IU friends and attend a football game. They were still finishing up their MBA degree work. Only problem was that the full bladder from a few beers in my excited state at O'Hare prior to boarding could not be relieved because my plane was a small prop job sans toilet. Oh, my, was I in pain, and upon arrival in Bloomington I had to run past my welcoming friends and get to the head, fast! Had a great Saturday with a pre-game party, a half-pint in the stadium, and a post-game party at Lenny and Annie's apartment complex. Took Nancy, a fellow former dorm Resident Assistant, out to dinner and dancing. It sure was nice to roll back into town with a few dollars in my pocket in decent threads vice being a poor student.

From Chicago I had solos in Philadelphia and Earle, New Jersey. In Philly, I dated a sweet young lady at the base that I was convinced would be a super wife for someone, just not for me, since I was definitely not ready for marriage. While in New Jersey, visited Mike, another fellow IU grad school classmate, who showed me where the local Mafia lived, and I spent a couple of weekends with my dear IU friend, Laura, who had a very small two-bedroom place on East 89th Street near First Avenue in New York City. I took in as much of the city as I could – Christmas shopping on Fifth Avenue for my mother, dinner with Laura at Mama Leone's, followed by a stroll through the Village, and while Laura was at work, jogs on the city streets and afternoon visits to local bars. And Laura and I had special times together romantically before I flew to California to be with family for Christmas. My poem to Laura:

Laura

Seeing you again
Was like feeling the sun
   After stormy days.
Being with you
   In America's rival
   To the "city of lights"
Created a parade
   of happy thoughts
   and much-awaited
   Togetherness.
You
And 89th street
Reached out
   And offered
   Another world.
Stars light years away
   Almost meaningless,
   With no promise,
So you showed me
   A new feeling
   A reality
That I often
   Disregard.

28

What would 86th be
  Without you at "Wednesdays"?
And new york's touch
  Would have been incomplete.
Your hand on my arm
  Forbade my disappearance
  In the subways.
Your presence at 89th
  Kept me warm
  And prosperous.

On the Friday after Christmas I took a girlfriend from the summer of 1972 up to Lake Tahoe to look at a condominium timeshare I was interested in buying. It was situated on the north shore, was beautiful, and I bought it. We had a nice evening at the casinos and the lodge where we stayed before heading back to Danville. My poem to Carol:

Carol

I'm a weak person
  When it comes to
  Your touch.
It can quiet
  A raging storm
  Within,
And make commands.
Every fiber in my body
  Responds,
As I go limp
  With tranquility.
Your fingertips

Hold the reins
Of my moods,
And I am
Uncontrollably
Yours.
My mind is moved
To the threshold
Of dreamland,
And my body
Is tantalized
By your softness.
I am yours,
But
Please
Be gentle.

New Year's Eve I had joined a bunch of Happy Valley College guys and their wives and dates at a ski cabin. I do remember the embarrassment I experienced when we were all playing charade, and it was my turn to help my team generate an answer. Unbelievably, the movie title I was provided was "Cincinnati Kid", but in my somewhat inebriated state, but we were all were, I failed to take advantage of the tee shirt I was wearing that said Cincinnati Bengals! Are you kidding me?! But on the plus side, I had an unexpected nice New Year's Eve with an unattached girl that had come up with the host couple.

To say the year was special would be gross understatement. It was a single man's dream. The travel, the new Navy friends, and certainly the young ladies I met that helped make my stays in new, strange places very special.

Didn't savor enough the single years.

1979

CHAPTER FOUR

The honeymoon with my new bride, Carla, went fine. Like other resorts on barrier islands such as Hilton Head and Edisto, Kiawah was awash in splendor with beautiful resort hotels, golf courses, golf and tennis complexes, and those wide, marvelous South Carolina beaches excellent for biking and jogging.

Well, not truly fine. Somewhere and somehow along the way, Carla figured out that I had been to Kiawah, which from a practical standpoint made it easier and more comfortable for me to plan the honeymoon, and also that I had dated a girl on that very island. Oh, heavens, did I step in it!

"You mean you brought me to a place where you dated someone?" she exclaimed with deep down incredulity and resentment. Like a cold engine cranking up, low tach reading, she was slowly building revolutions and horsepower.

"I think I dated her twice, no big deal, okay, Carla?" I countered, struck with the absolute absurdity of her questioning my date life prior to our marriage. I had travelled extensively all over the world, and dated girls from many places. My friends from California, from grad school, early travels and my Navy travels, gave me a bounty of friends that was a pleasure in life. I'm thinking, she doesn't need to find out about my girlfriends in Taiwan, Japan and Iceland, not to mention here in the good 'ol U.S.A.

"But here! While we're on our honeymoon. You dirt bag." In full throttle. Tach hitting red.

"Hey, don't let it ruin the honeymoon. It's been a long time since I last saw her, and it really isn't important." What I didn't tell her was that yes, I had dated her a number of times in Kiawah and Washington, and the former was over a few visits or stopovers on the island as I travelled up and down the east coast on Navy business. I also didn't tell her that I had actually seen her that January when Dan and I stayed on the island en route to Miami for the Super Bowl. We ran into her quite unexpectedly at a bar we hit that night and she happened to be working there. Small world, you know?

"Is she still living here?"

What the hell difference does that make, damn it, I'm not going to go out searching for her. But little did I know that a few years later they would be face to face in a most unexpected way. So, I lied. "I don't know, and what difference would it make, Carla? Damn. Get over it. I don't care if she's living here, plus it's been a long time since I last saw her." Oh, boy, lovely honeymoon.

She eventually calmed down, but as I was to learn about her, she stayed in the "cocked" position, ready to pounce like a cougar on a food source. It didn't take long. The second night in the hotel, after a nice day on the beach and poolside bagging rays in the warm South Carolina sun, we had made love and were sitting up in bed, backs against the head board. Out of nowhere, with no warning, the cougar pounces.

"You know, we should have postponed the wedding." Calm as a cucumber, matter of fact.

"What?" I gasped. Not a real serious, big gasp. It was a reaction to something out of left field. Of course, after the past few days, I'm beginning to think we should have kanked the wedding and gone separate ways, admittedly a horrible state of mind, and definitely not a very healthy revelation on a honeymoon.

"I haven't forgiven you for not coming down to be with me when I learned of Billy's conviction. What happened to him really hit me hard."

"Really? You're still hung up on that? That was a long time ago. I couldn't get away from work on such short notice. Plus, I was coming your way in a few days. I'm sorry, Carla, but this is ridiculous." What I wanted to say, similar to what I was thinking at the time of the incident, was that he was a common criminal, belonged in the "gray bar hotel" where they sent him, and that she shouldn't be obsessing over it. But I didn't, for obvious reasons. Then again, her anger engine was adequately stoked, so it would not have made any difference.

"Damn right. He was a special friend and you should have felt my pain enough to come help me." Once cranked up, she's like a heat-seeking Tomahawk Missile that has only one objective, to destroy the target. In this case, me.

"Well, I didn't, and it's a bit late to make an issue of it, Carla. Anyway, he'll have an opportunity to think about his actions and hopefully get his life straight."

"Suddenly, I don't like you, and I don't want to be in bed with you right now. I wish you could get out of here for a while."

"Wrong. I'm not getting dressed and paying a late night visit to wander around the hotel lobby like I'm looking for some action." With that, I got out of bed, turned on the TV, and sat in one of the armchairs. A few minutes later she had fallen off to sleep. I would learn this was the pattern. Volcanic eruption, although this was mild, followed by withdrawal and sleep, and ignorance of what had occurred when she awakened the following morning.

At the conclusion of our wonderful honeymoon we drove back to Norfolk, spent the night with her parents, and the following day I drove my car and she followed in hers as we drove to Georgetown to take up residence in my apartment as Mr. and Mrs. Pedersen.

My apartment wasn't luxurious, but it was the best I could do on a mid-level government employee salary, and it worked. Couldn't beat the location. A couple blocks to the east was Wisconsin Avenue, with all its stores and restaurants, and a block south put one on M Street, with even more night life. The apartment itself was rather small. My IU friend had lived in it while he was doing some additional grad work at George Washington University, and he let me know it was available when he moved out of the area. It had a master bedroom, a second bedroom for guests, a full bath with tub and shower, and actually a decent size kitchen with modern appliances. The common area was large enough for a combination living room and small dining area. For now, it was all we needed. It would allow us to explore the wonderful, picturesque, historical city from close in.

Carla had parlayed her bookkeeping experience to a decent job up Wisconsin Avenue, not far from the apartment and where I worked. She didn't have to job search for very long as we learned that Washington, D.C., had plenty of job openings in clerical, administrative and bookkeeping positions. Piece of cake to find work.

Two weekends after settling in, we drove Carla's car to her parents on a Saturday morning, where I rented a U-Haul truck within which her father and I loaded her rather limited personal belongings, along with a couple pieces of bedroom furniture her parents were kind enough to give us and headed back to Georgetown on Sunday.

The following month, her parents came to visit for a weekend, which got Carla excited as she could show her parents where we were calling home. I felt good about the visit as well, since I liked her parents and we got along great. We set up a table, covered it with a bunch of newspapers, and got into the crabs her father had brought with them to accompany a few beers. It was a nice evening, and they had a place to sleep for the night without needing a motel. Having just the one bathroom created some minor challenges, but we managed.

As the year drew to a close, Carla was comfortable in her new job, and I was doing well in my Navy job in Rosslyn. We were doing okay, and taking advantage of some neat bars and restaurants in the city, not to mention the multitude of other Nations Capitol sites and venues. We were consciously trying to have a baby, and in the fall Carla had greeted me upon arrival from the office one day with those proverbial, universal words, "I'm pregnant. We're going to have a baby!"

The fun was about to start.

1974

CHAPTER FIVE

What a remarkable year it was to be, traveling to the west coast, back to the east coast, across the Atlantic, across the Pacific, then a stopover in Hawaii and California before returning to the office in southern Maryland. Met a lot of ladies along the way, and some of them were kind enough to let me share their bed.

After an organization semi-annual meeting in early January, I spent the remainder of the month and early February at the office attending a four-week course that would help prepare me to review our Navy clubs and package beverage store operations.

At the conclusion of the training I had a short three-day assignment at a Navy base in Washington, D.C., then headed north to Boston to review some operations at Naval Air Station, South Weymouth. My first order of business was a phone call to an old friend.

After three rings the phone was answered by Dick Sverluga, a fellow undergraduate dorm resident assistant at Indiana. "Hello," he said.

"Dick, this is Dave Pedersen. How you doing?"

"Dave!" he exclaimed. "I'm doing great. Where are you?" It was great that he expressed genuine pleasure in hearing from me.

"I'm just down the road, in Weymouth, near the Navy base there."

"Wonderful. You're not too far away, only about fifteen minutes from my place in Boston. How is your schedule? Will we be able to get together for a cold one?"

"Schedule is clear until Monday morning, Dick. Tomorrow is Saturday, so how about I come your way mid to late afternoon if that does not interfere with your plans?"

"Perfect. Here's my address and some directions. Give me a call when you're on your way so I can keep an eye out for you." With that, he gave me directions and I told him I was looking forward to seeing him. Before we hung up the phones, we talked about a mutual resident assistant buddy, Tom Clancy, who was a lawyer practicing in Chicago. Dick was quite a character. At IU he was the editor of a staff newsletter called the "Croatian Bugle", and went by the editor name of Justin Tyme.

Dick was working on the residence halls staff at Boston University. The next day I found my way to his place, where we had a few beers, had dinner at a Chinese restaurant nearby, and attended a BU-Boston College ice hockey game. We then drove to the Harvard campus for an SAE frat party that had plenty of young, snotty broads from Harvard.

Having completed my Navy assignment at Weymouth, a Navy helicopter flew me to a two-day assignment on Nantucket Island. What a blast! The pilot flew our twin-jet SH Tre-Alpha chopper right over Chappaquiddick Bridge, pointing out for me the site where Mary Jo Kopechne lost her life and Teddy Kennedy did damage to his political career. I lodged in a converted Georgian mansion built by a whaler years back, and enjoyed meeting some people in the basement bar. The island was truly an intriguing, idyllic setting. The return chopper flight was not so pleasant, as they neglected to bring along an extra set of headsets. Ouch on the ears.

The following month I was fortunate to receive travel orders sending me back home to San Francisco. Saw the family, did some work at our bases on Treasure Island and at Alameda, and hooked up with a good San Jose State buddy, Rich, who had joined his father's insurance agency. We hit the Treasure Island Officers Club, and had a good visit, but I wanted to meet some women.

From the Bay Area I travelled to Stockton for a review. I called the mother of a Happy Valley College girl I dated, learning she was just up the road in Sacramento. I called Phyllis and she was kind enough to drive down, whereupon my fellow Field Rep buddy, Pete, who was also in the area, and I took her out to dinner. It was exciting seeing her for the first time in about six years, not counting the time we saw one another in 1971 for a fleeting moment when I was three sheets to the wind during the Happy Valley College Western Week parade and I was a passenger in the sawed off Rugby Club pace car. Pete and I had a fun time with Phyllis. We teased her a bit about our government work, so that for a while we had her thinking we were CIA. She looked great, having shed some weight from her college days, and was divorced. The next weekend I drove to Sacramento and we double-dated with friends of hers. She is still the ever-virtuous woman I came to know in college, and I'm not being critical, but I did have my hopes up. Stayed at her place that night, in a separate room, damn it, and said goodbye to her at the airport for my flight to Reno.

Along with a few other Field Reps, Pete and I attended a slot machine school to prepare us to inspect those operations at overseas Navy bases. While there, I contacted another Happy Valley, and Danville, girlfriend, who drove up from north shore

Lake Tahoe so we could spend some time together. Went out for dinner, dancing, and drinks, and caught a few hugs in her car before she had to drive back to Tahoe. As with Phyllis, I later stayed in touch with Linda. We Field Reps had a good time in the casinos when not in school. Pete, a possessed gambler, taught me how to play craps, at which I did very well, and a colleague won $1300 at a "21" table.

Pete and I caught a flight to Chicago, where we stayed with his family en route back to our Maryland base. I called a lady named Shelley, who I had met through mutual Indiana University friends who had known her at the University of Illinois, and she drove to Pete's so we could go out for drinks and talk about old times. She was a Pre-Med student in Chicago. Had a nice evening, and we promised to stay in touch. Pete thereafter gave me a hard time about my coming to Chicago, his home, and having a date.

"I can't believe this. We come into my town, and you pick up the phone and get a date. It's not supposed to be this way, Dave, but then I'm not surprised. Didn't take you long to have a date in Reno, either."

"It's because I stay in contact with many of the girls I have met. Just a simple postcard."

When Pete and I returned to Maryland, I took off for Alexandria where I shared an apartment with a couple of IU friends. It was a reasonable commute to southern Maryland, and of course the commutes were always temporary. While "home", I took out a lady named Nancy, who I had met one night at the Fort Myers Officers Club, and it was our last date. I did not understand her. She was a real strange one when it came to romancing. Our date took us to Georgetown, where I was having a lousy evening until we met a couple of other ladies at Nathan's on M Street, and we had some good laughs to rescue the night.

For most of April I was working at Navy bases in Maine,

from Brunswick up to Down East Maine, and a base adjacent to Acadia National Park, travelling with a Field Rep named Henry. Henry was older than me, was a veteran Field Rep, and dressed to the nines. He was a bit controlling in terms of our schedule, and talked a little weird. He appeared effeminate, but that made no difference to me. I wasn't bothered by it. Hit some snow, but a small problem, and the countryside was beautiful. The folks at our base in Winter Harbor invited me up for some recreation, and I hoped to take them up on it. In Brunswick I made the mistake of trying to pick up Janie, the divorcee of a cop. Her ex-hubbie's friends were buzzing around me like flies, ready to "escort" the fair maiden safely home. Rotten luck. One of them sauntered up to me when Janie went to powder her nose, or whatever she was going to do after leaving the table.

"Hey buddy, Janie's a nice lady. I hope you don't have any plans to try and take advantage of her."

"Me? No way. Such a nice lady. We're just chatting up a storm and trying to solve the world's problems."

"You trying to be a smart ass?"

"Nah. Just playing with you. But don't you think that as an adult she is capable of making the decision whether or not she wants to get to know me better?"

That sort of slowed him down, because I think he was lacking in some brain matter, if you know what I mean. "Well, don't mess around, okay?"

"I'll keep that in mind, but you know what? I think you're safe and all this threatening business is moot." With that, he left, and Janie returned. He probably went out into the parking lot to stand vigil.

"What did Joey want?"

"Ah, he was just reminding me in his own way to be awfully sweet with you."

"That fool. I'll talk to him later. I've told him before to stay out of my personal business, and that I can take care of myself. Damn him."

"That's exactly what I told him. Let's dance."

To add to the dysfunction, she had informed me I could follow her home and come in for a beer, but don't expect anything else. Oh, super. My fun meter is ticking to have that beer with you at your abode. I told her I had consumed enough beer that night, and suggested she drive home alone. I added, just to stir the pot with Joey, that I was fearful of my well-being if I followed her home. As I left the joint, I was thinking, "What was I doing with Janie? Hell, her butt was just shy of two and a half ax handles wide."

Before leaving Brunswick, I spent a Saturday on the Bowdoin College athletic fields to observe lacrosse, baseball, and rugby competition events, and got invited to a post-game rugby party. I also got in a round of golf on the base course.

I put Brunswick in the rearview mirror and Henry and I drove the short distance south to the Navy base in Kittery, Maine. I used the weekend to explore, checking out the nearby University of New Hampshire athletic facilities, of which I took advantage, using their fitness center, and had some good jogs on the roads around the old, one-level motel that sat above town sports fields. At the Ramada Inn in nearby Portsmouth, New Hampshire, I crashed a Greek Orthodox function one evening, getting some free drinks before they realized I was not one of them. I was surprised it took them that long.

Henry dropped me off at Logan Airport in Boston and he continued on to another assignment. It was Derby weekend and I was intent on joining my IU friends for all the fun and festivities. I was already well-oiled from a couple beers on the flight and a couple more drinks in the Detroit airport. Ray and Doyne met me in Indy and from there we drove to Louisville. The whole gang was there, and Lenny and Annie had gotten Shelley away from her med studies in Chicago. In Louisville that first night we attended a frat party, but those knuckleheads ran out of beer, so we hit a local bar where I met and got friendly with Merriam, a friend of my buddy Jerry and who lived in Cincinnati. Told her I wanted to visit her if I was ever in that fair city. Had a great time in the infield on a Churchill Downs beautiful, sunny day, got blown away on bourbon and sevens, broke two ice chests, did some "dead gophers" that drove people nuts, and passed out on the drive back to Indy. That single life was great, but was going to kill me! And I paid the price on Monday when I had to fly from Indy to Detroit to Boston to Halifax, Nova Scotia, and to St. John's, Newfoundland. Oh, my goodness. I could barely drag my butt off that last flight. What a milk run!

Newfoundland was beautiful, thick with pine trees that gave off that wonderful smell that so reminded me of the California mountains, and the highlight of the assignment was trout fishing on a secluded lake with a base staff member, catching the limit and bringing it back to the base so my old travel buddy Ralph could supervise cooking the fish in the Officers Club. An evening in a local bar called the "Latin Quarter" (don't ask me how the heck a bar in Newfoundland could have that name) was a waste of time – too crowded and smoky.

On to New York City, where my dear IU friend, Laura, met me at the East Side Terminal. Not a bad flight, except on the Boston to NYC leg the guy in front of me enjoyed hearing himself talk and apparently wanted everyone else to know his business.

As I entered the terminal I spotted Laura and headed in her direction. "Hi, Laura! You're looking great as always." And she did, really.

"Thank you, Dave. Did you have a good flight?"

"Well, considering I was up at five-thirty this morning to catch a flight out of St. John's, Newfoundland, and that on the Boston flight to New York the guy in front of me enjoyed hearing himself talk and wanted everyone else to hear him, I had a good flight."

"Oh, no, don't you just hate it when people talk too loud?"

"Hey, will you hang with me so I can get some baggage to JFK Airport for my flight next week to Iceland?" We had to take a bus to the Icelandic Terminal. Geez.

"Sure. No problem."

That done, we took a shuttle bus to Manhattan. We passed by a graveyard that appeared awfully crowded because the head stones were so close together, like it was for small people. "Laura, what's with the graveyard?" I asked.

"Oh, they bury the dead on top of one another there." She replied. Strange. I had seen the graveyards in New Orleans where they did not bury anyone due to the high water table, but this one was weird.

We finally got to Laura's on East 89th Street. It was a beautiful, sunny day as we strolled on the sidewalk near her apartment building, her arm in mine, and I'm thinking, "This is nice. The affection." But not so fast, cowboy.

"You know, it's nice being back in civilization, but after more than a month in Maine and Newfoundland, immersed in rugged, open country that begged for fishing and camping adventures, and getting pretty laid back along the way, it's an adjustment arriving in the City with its relentless activity, pace, and all the crushing sounds of people and cars. But I enjoy them both, and I am so very lucky for that."

"I know what you mean. I've taken some vacation time up north with friends, and it is so peaceful and wonderful, but it gets much colder than New York. I think you'll adjust just fine," as she gives me a comforting smile and leans in closer.

I took Laura to Alda's on East 86th Street for dinner and

drinks. Upon returning to her place, she surprised me with, "My roommate is out of town for the weekend. You can have her room."

I did a double-take, scrunched my eyes and curled my mouth, giving her the "Huh?" look.

"I don't feel the same as when you were here last Christmas and when you were at my parents for Thanksgiving. I don't know what it is, Dave, but let's sleep in separate rooms."

"Okay, Laura. I understand." Like hell I did! I had never forced myself on a woman in a romantic way, and was not going to start now. If that was what she wanted, so be it. In hindsight, I think it had something to do with an incident that night before I was to leave New York last December. I had made special plans to take Laura to dinner at "Broadway Joe's", Joe Namath's place, and was excited about what would be a memorable evening, when a girlfriend dropped in unexpectedly and obliterated those plans of dinner and sex. I had let her know I was upset, and had a bit of a chip on my shoulder all night, in other words, acting like a jerk as the three of us went to another, lower cost restaurant. She took issue with my attitude, and the rest of the night was like that major east coast power outage, lights out. I wasn't going to say anything more that night after being relegated to another room. Here's my guess – she can swing both ways, but now leaned more to another female. That's just me. That's what I think, and I am probably correct because I can read people pretty good.

Hey, I had a good night's sleep after that long day in the air from Newfoundland, and the next day had a good jog around the neighborhood, running by Gracie Mansion, the Mayor's residence, viewing Queens across the river, and jogging under high-rise apartment buildings towering over me. It was idyllic, not Maine mind you, but pretty cool, and I was reminded of how fortunate I was and thanked the Lord for my good health, great job, peace of mind, good friends, and a great family back home in California.

Truly, the single life was wonderful, and I was in no hurry to settle down and stop enjoying and seeing the wondrous world around me from this current perspective. I'm kind of pragmatic, not questioning a lot of things in this travel routine, seeing the world as it is, making friends from strangers. I go with the flow. I know there is a reaction to every action, and bide my behavior accordingly. While on occasion I have a couple too many drinks, I take good care of myself, exercising every day. I learn about my surroundings by going for a long jog when in a new place. I spare myself the mental gymnastics of life, accepting things as they are. Some might say I live a boring life, but it was Einstein that spoke of the value of a calm, modest life and the happiness it can bring.

That afternoon I treat myself to a couple of beers in the middle of the afternoon, something that is rare. For that, I wander down Second Avenue, take a right on 85th, and enter Martin's Pub, where I join a few other guys watching a Stanley Cup ice hockey game. This is too cool, and I'm like a kid in a New York City candy store, soaking up the city vibes and environs, mingling with the locals. All the different faces, the activity, the feel of the city. Wow. Only problem is, this California guy doesn't have the New York accent, you know? Martin's strikes me as a neighborhood hangout. Most of the patrons are probably retired and frequent this place often. It's been a good day so far -- a good jog, completed some government work, and enjoying an afternoon here in Martin's. It's okay that I am a stranger, for I am a private person, keeping parts of myself inviolate, and some people at a distance. Look at certain things and pass, as the expression goes. It has been said that freedom is an untroubled mind. I prefer to remain somewhat a mystery, holding things close. Some people talk too much, for nothing is private to them, be it of themselves or someone else. Hey, like that knucklehead on my Boston flight. Same deal.

I think of my good fortunes to travel, see other peoples, other cultures, and see how they live. Should I be saddened by friends who are locked into a routine of families, homes to maintain, kids to look after? Maybe they feel saddened toward a tumbleweed like me!

There's some guy sitting next to me wearing a cowboy hat and talking about selling a horse for $20,000. A non-existent horse. He's a recording engineer for some TV station.

I spent the evening wandering on 86th. At John Murphy's Pub I had the distinct pleasure of trying to talk to a Jimmy Murphy (no relation), former valet for numerous New York celebrities, all five feet, two inches, two-hundred pounds of him, who blurted away with stories and anecdotes of movie stars and claims that certain male stars are queer. I asked him how he was so well-informed of all this, but I imagine my impetuosity might have caused him to clam up and not talk to me further.

My long weekend sojourn in this sophisticated, fashionable city, especially what I observed strolling along 5th Avenue and Madison Avenue comes to an end with a shuttle out to JFK Airport.

The good life is stroking me.

CHAPTER SIX

Other than the bullshit with which I dealt the prior year when Carla decided she had to continue to drill me for not coming to her aid when her worthless long-time neighbor friend was convicted of a felony and sent off to the gray bar hotel, including the not so subtle reminder while on our honeymoon in Kiawah Island, the year 1980 was "normal". We had a nice routine of work in the Washington area Monday to Friday, and often ventured into the city center on a Saturday night to bar-hop or have dinner in the Financial District, Georgetown, or in Old Town Alexandria. We were taking advantage of our pre-child freedom, sans the need to find a babysitter, not to mention all the other responsibilities that come with child rearing. Carla was also working hard with her employer and becoming ever more proficient as a bookkeeper. She was very comfortable working with numbers, and, according to her, had become a key component of the company's financial and accounting operations. Apparently, she had found her niche and was enjoying success and much satisfaction.

We awakened one Saturday on a bone-chilling winter morning that suggested we hunker down indoors for the day. I was obviously amazed and startled by her comment out of the blue and without any sort of warning that she wanted to make a day trip.

"Dave, I'm going to drive to Augusta Correctional Center so I can visit Billy."

"You're going to what?"

"I need to see Billy. He is my friend, you know, and I'm sure he needs a visitor."

"And it's you. It sounds like this was pre-planned, that you have been communicating with him. Am I right?" I ask as calmly as I can. She knows I am not empathetic towards this slime ball, so I'm trying to not go off the rails here.

"Well, yes, we've exchanged a few letters and had a few phone conversations," she replies in a manner inferring it is all justified and is nothing with which I should be concerned.

"It was nice of you to cut me in. You know how I feel about his situation." I'm avoiding direct reference to him.

"I don't care how you feel. He's my friend and I'm going to see him." Her emotional 340 horsepower engine is increasing in RPM's, and as I have learned, it won't be long before her tachometer is in the red, danger zone and all hell will break loose.

I know where his prison is located, and that it is a not a real long drive to it from where we live, but I ask anyway. "Do you plan to drive over and back today?"

"That's my plan, but just so you know, I may get a motel room overnight, and see him again tomorrow before I return home. I'm sure you're okay with that, Dave. You are, aren't you?" She proclaims in a revved up response to me that suggests I say, "Yes."

"Sure. Go for it." I don't feel like fighting her.

While she is away, I'm starting to wonder what sort of woman I married. Who is she? What is this temper that seems to simmer right on the surface, ready to boil over and erupt like a volcano? I wish I had seen this part of her earlier. And what's with Billy?

I am greeted with another reminder of this, another variation on the Carla theme, when she returns to the house one day a couple of weeks later after visiting one of our neighbors, Jan.

She blows into the house like a category three hurricane. No, make that a tornado, since hurricanes provide ample warnings of their arrival, whereas tornadoes are more sudden, unpredictable, with similar disastrous results.

"That damn Jan. What a bitch," she cries.

"What? What happened?"

"We were having a nice chat and visit, when I mentioned that I still smoke while I am pregnant. She was aghast, and told me I shouldn't do it. I told her I had already stopped drinking and doing the occasional pot, and that a cigarette now and then was not that harmful."

"Well, she's entitled to her opinion, and I would think the two of you could have a civil discussion about it. She may be right, you know." Wrong.

"She said she was against it and very disappointed in me. What is she, my mother? My doctor? I told her not to worry about it, that I knew what I was doing. She said it was stupid. Stupid! I hate that word. My father used to say that to me when I was in school. The only thing I could think to say was, "Goodbye," and I stormed out her door, letting it slam after me. I'm pissed, and don't you even think about taking her side, Dave!" She was fired up, and that was not the only time that she returned to the house after a blowout with a neighbor.

Oh, boy, the super-charged engine got another lap around the track to keep it primed. Just what I needed.

And it seems that conflicts follow her around like mosquitoes drawn to a bug tower. She came home from work one day to inform me that she had gotten into an argument with her boss. Apparently, she was a little late getting to work, and he discussed her tardiness with her. Nothing unusual there, just being a typical supervisor. Well, she took umbrage and there were a few words. Lucky she was not fired for insubordination.

Aside from the occasional spats and her temper episodes, our married life was okay. I was having a bit of a struggle adjusting to a new life with someone constantly in it, particularly someone six years younger than me. She was trying hard, I could tell. She had done very little cooking when living with her parents, so she was working on developing that skill and was actually doing pretty well. I helped out some, and we stuck to basics, some of which I had learned to cook over the years in my somewhat lengthy single life.

She had made a couple more day trips to see Billy, but I didn't intervene. If she was such close friends with that loser, I was not going to be successful in preventing her from making occasional visits.

The big change for me came late in her pregnancy.

"Dave, you know that we're going to need a bigger car once the baby arrives," she casually said over dinner one night.

"Yeah, I know. I've been putting it off as long as I can, dreading that day," I replied somewhat hesitantly, and certainly without enthusiasm. This was my first dip in the marriage pool, if you ignore the big dip that got her pregnant. My first sacrifice and forfeiture of a pleasure from my single days, although there were certainly others.

"Well, I'm sorry, but we can't put if off much longer. We need something for a family, and it needs to be newer than my Toyota Corolla and more reliable. Stating the obvious, we can't get three people in your car." No argument there, and she was absolutely right. It was time for the big switch.

There goes my Porsche 914. Don't get too excited. It had a charged up Volkswagen engine, so it wasn't anything souped up. It sure as hell wasn't my dream car, a Porsche 911, but even as a single guy I couldn't afford a 911, or put another way, I wasn't going in deep debt with a big car loan payment. Nope, I was putting my extra funds into real estate.

"Okay. No argument. I agree. We'll go out and do the car search thing this weekend. Get it over with. I think I know what we need." I wanted a full size car, but something that looked okay.

"Oh, yeah? And what would that be?" she asked coyly.

"A Dodge van," I responded, smiling, knowing it was a far cry from a Porsche.

"Yep, that's what I want, too. Can we look at those this weekend, Dave?"

"Sure. There's a Chrysler-Dodge dealership out Route 50. There is also one in Rosslyn, but the one out route 50 is larger. We'll take a drive out there and see what they have. Boy, am I going to miss my Porsche." I'm crying over spilled milk, because I know how it's going to feel. Carla had no ideas about the pleasure the Porsche had provided me since I bought it in my home town in California when I left my job in Hawaii four years prior. She also didn't know how many women had sat shotgun as I cruised up and down the east coast on Navy business, stopping in this town and that to get reacquainted. Not to mention a few ladies I had dated in Washington. Yes, this was going to hurt, like pulling a bandage off a scab. Goodbye sweet car memories from the single days.

And with that, the next weekend we became proud owners of a new van, and it even included a CB radio the dealer threw in. I accepted the CB, but I didn't see myself rolling down the road yakking with truckers about doing the double nickel because a state trooper had been sighted further down the freeway. Plus, double nickel speed was about as fast as I would drive in that glorified box, and it sure didn't compare with opening up the Porsche on a curving roadway, feeling the excitement and adrenaline from pushing the envelope, hoping to hell I wasn't going to come around some bend in the road and be eyeball to eyeball with a cop and a radar gun.

Well, we did have a little fun with the van before the baby was born, driving up to the mountains west of the city to spend a couple nights "camping" in a public, state campground. All we really needed was a small tent, Coleman stove, some cookware, and an ice chest for some perishable food items, all of which fit conveniently in the back of the van. Even made room for a six-pack of my favorite Midwest beer, Strohs. Oh, how cute. The newlyweds, for we hadn't been married a year, and yes, we did get right down to business having that baby. Later, I would be vociferously reminded that we had the baby because I was getting older at 33 and didn't want to be an old guy with a new baby, whereas she was still so young and, damn it, we should have waited. She was too young to have a child. So there you go. Problem.

Our baby boy, who we named Kyle, was born in April. I was in the delivery room, and paid about as much attention as I could handle. I didn't touch anything. Let the professionals take care of things.

And so, the new routine began. No different than any other couple with a newborn. Feedings through the night, getting sleep when we could, and trying to make things comfortable for the little guy. A few weeks after his birth, my parents flew out from California, and mom was a big help. I had stayed home from work the first two weeks after mother and baby were released from the hospital, but had now returned to the office, doing the best I could to perform some of the midnight feedings to give Carla a break, and trying to avoid feeling like a zombie at the office. To say it was a bit crowded in our Georgetown apartment would be understatement, but we managed okay. Things got back to normal after my parents departed a week after their arrival.

When the baby was old enough, we got a babysitter a few doors down, Jan's teenage daughter, so that we could rejoin the living. Drinks and dinner at either a nearby restaurant or someplace else in the city was the norm, and making a point not to be gone too long. There were also occasional trips down I-95 to spend a weekend at Carla's parents. Her mom was great with the baby, and we took full advantage and got out to some local restaurants while in Norfolk.

So, you're thinking everything was copasetic, that Dave and Carla were skipping through the tulips of marriage and parenthood. And you would be wrong. A couple things happened a few months after Kyle was born that kind of rocked my world.

Hello Billy boy and goodbye Porsche

1974
CHAPTER SEVEN

The shuttle to JFK Airport serves as a transition from the great few days in New York City, mitigated somewhat, well, a lot, by Laura regrettably relegating me to a different bed from hers. Kind of took the 'ol starch out of a few things. At the airport the shit hits the fan and I am cannon fodder for the impersonal flight schedules and delays. My 9:30 pm flight to Keflavik, Iceland, has been changed to 3:00 am, and I learned my lesson with excess baggage. My 3:00 am flight was changed to 8:00 am, then 11:45 am, with actual take-off at 3:30 pm. We had been taken to Manhattan for a nice steak meal and lodging off Broadway. Met some neat folks, especially Diana, who was going to be a senior at Hood College in Maryland. Really a sharp person with a good sense of humor and a lot of weird ideas. We spent some time around Times Square, and she invited me to her home in Westport, Connecticut, for the July 4th weekend. I'm in, I told her.

Iceland really freaked me out. I mean, experiencing the very long periods of daylight is weird. It was still daylight at 11:00 pm.

The sun took a quick dip in the ocean at midnight and showed itself again at 3:00 am.

I have a long government holiday weekend to kill, so I fly to Dublin, Ireland, with a few hours layover in Glasgow, Scotland, where I have a few beers and idle conversation with other patrons in the Sanderling Bar. My Navy Field Rep "dad" was right – the Scots are certainly friendly people.

Dublin was a unique pleasure. That first night I did not stray too far from the hotel, checking out the bar Pirates Den (how do you get a name like that for a bar in Ireland, for God's sake? Pirates in Ireland?), where I met and engaged in friendly conversation with a lively group of young local civil servants. Not college educated, but bright, aware. The chatter was non-stop and a real trip. One guy, Donel, wanted to be an Irish Army officer. Sheila surprised me, until Kieron informed me that the Irish are not possessive. I still couldn't accept this nice looking young lady allowing Nick, a scruffy, unkempt, ex-Army career private who loved forevermore to sing, particularly Elvis renditions, to kiss her and handle her. And fifty years old at that! Sport coats were donned by all the men, whether they're complementing jeans or good slacks. I was told that the volume of people in the city had slacked off that weekend due to the bombings the previous weekend. Bombs? But then, I was in Ireland! Heads up, Dave. It was fascinating to hear from my Dublin friends that the Catholics in Northern Ireland, even though a majority, have been discriminated against by the Protestants over the past 300 years, and that they demand an equal representation. Most people I talked to in Dublin feel that all will come to mass bloodshed. I am transfixed with hearing all this straight from the young mouths of Irish locals. Fascinating.

The next day I walk from the hotel, crossing over the River Liffey Bridge, strolling around a most picturesque and historic Trinity University, where I observe a Cricket match on campus, receiving a quick lesson from a pretty young lady on the aspects of the game. I wander up O'Connell Street, easing into a pub for a Guinness Stout. After all, when in Ireland, drink Stout, yes? The bartender was not my friend.

"Good afternoon, good sir," I exclaim with a hearty appreciation of this moment in time. It's close to 2:30 pm, by the way.

"And a good afternoon to you, my fine American friend. What will it be?"

"How about a pint of your local favorite, a Guinness Stout?" I am eager for this moment.

"You got it, mate."

I get my pint, I've taken maybe two or three mouthfuls of this unique suds, when I hear the clanging of a bell inside the bar.

"What's that?" I ask.

"Ah, mate, the bars here must close every day at two-thirty pm and canna re-open until three-thirty pm."

"Swell. It's great to find out the hard way."

"I'm fookin' sorry, lad, but it's city code. I probably shoulda warned ya." I try to keep my cool, but I'm pissed. Thanks a lot, buddy. I'm out the door, continuing to wander. Art galleries. A marketplace that had outstanding French bread. I eventually walk back to the hotel, but I stop on that bridge overlooking the River Liffey. It could be London or Paris, but I'm so content and happy to be in fair Dublin. I am a truly lucky guy, blessed with living a great life, and certainly so very grateful for it.

The next afternoon I walk up O'Connell. I'm among a huge throng of locals and visitors, wearing their colors, for we are all heading toward Croke Park and the league finals Gaelic Football match between Kerry and Roscommon. What an unexpected treat. It was obviously the first time I had attended such a match, and it was fascinating to see the resemblance to other sports. The match has ended, and I'm back on the bridge. It is dusk in Dublin.

It feels on this May day more like a Fall dusk in Indiana, a low-hanging, hazy sky that really has no lines, no differentiation in the clouds, and a steady color gray clothes me like a shroud. I will never forget the melancholy I felt at that very moment, so much at peace, with all of life's treasures sitting comfortably in my soul and psyche.

And there is so much I learned about Dubliners. As in many city centers, the people here, a majority anyway, appear basically lower to middle class, or upper lower class. They have spunk, and enjoy life to its fullest. Their attire is interesting – very little attention to color schemes, and almost always for the men, with a sport coat on. I doubt there is an Irishman that doesn't smoke, albeit some exaggeration, but honestly, a lot of people smoked in Dublin.

But back to Saturday night. I'm getting around. I started on Eden Quay at Mooney's, then went to the Waldorf-Astoria lounge a few doors down. A TV comical series was playing – the Irish, I am learning first-hand on their turf, have a strange sense of humor. I left, going up to Nineteen O'Connell. Got into a nice conversation with a student married couple, Shawn and Gerry. Good people. Joined some young men later to go across the street to a disco – "Good Time Charley's". I was having a nice time with a good looking woman named Kathleen, and we danced a bit. She informed me that it was obvious I was a foreigner, either American or German, by my attire. I left the disco and went to Luke Brady's party at the Medical Residence of St. James Hospital. I had met Luke in the Pirates Den the previous evening. A bad decision to attend, but they had some food. I tried to pick up a nurse that was really blown away, but my California charm didn't cut it.

Sunday night after dinner I took a walk with May Flaherty, who worked at the hotel. Couldn't figure out how old she was. I probably could have tried to get her to her place but decided against that. I got her address, so I'll stay in touch in the event I ever return to Dublin.

I flew back to Iceland the next day, with a long stopover in Glasgow that I used to tour the city.

I had a typical busy week on the Navy base, then a ride into nearby Reykjavik early Saturday afternoon from the Navy Commander with whom I was working. I checked into the Hotel Loftleider, rested up a bit, then took a taxi to the Saga Hotel, which was supposed to be the place to meet women. Problem. Even with a tie, my leather coat did not pass muster as the required "coat", so I was politely barred entry. No problem. A stranger, Aeid, with wife and sister-in-law, was also barred entry for the same reason, correctly gauged my dilemma, and invited me to join them for a drive to the Klubberin. What a totally wild place! Young people packed, jammed into every square foot of the place, all three floors of it. It was like being in a human pinball machine, moving this direction and that to avoid bumping into someone, especially since we were all drinking doubles. I met Esther, a young Icelandic lady slightly taller than me, slim, not beautiful, blond hair, fair complexion, but a pretty face highlighted by expressive eyes. She had a typical female Icelandic last name ending in "Dottir". After some dancing and a couple drinks, we decided to leave.

"I'll call for a taxi, Esther."

"No, I am not lazy. We can walk," she advised me.

So, we walked back to my hotel. There was a bit of a chill in the air, and my leather coat was having a tough time keeping me warm. And it wasn't like a block or two. It was a pretty good hoof to the hotel. But all was good, for Esther warmed my body and kept me close all night, showing me her sensuous side. I told her the next morning I wanted to see her again, possibly in November, and she caught a taxi home. I offered to pay for her taxi ride, but she declined. Very independent.

Upon returning to Norfolk for a short assignment I was able to see both Karen McKay and Carolyn from the hotel at which I now stay when in town. Then, it was off to Guantanamo Bay, Cuba, with my "dad", where we spent the entire month of June. Our evening routine was to walk to the nearby Officers Club from our Officers Quarters to sit in their outside lyceum to watch a movie. No women available, but the time on the beach looking up at a nearby ridge to see Cuban soldiers in their guard post was memorable. I made use of the tennis courts and officers pool, and we were invited to the home of a Jamaican group that fed us outstanding local food as we drank excellent Haitian coconut rum liqueur. The single, traveling life continues to bless and overwhelm me. Add in my first snorkeling experience in clear, turquoise waters.

As hoped, July 4th weekend was at Diana's in Westport, Connecticut, where I jogged by newsman Harry Reasoner's house. Diana's father was a retired Navy Captain, so we had some great chats.

I spent the following week at a semi-annual staff meeting at my office in Maryland, then it was off to the Far East for assignments at Navy installations in Japan and Taiwan. While in Japan, my travel partner, Henry, and I took the train from Yokosuka, the site of the large Navy base, to Tokyo to do the tourist thing, staying at the Navy's Sanno Hotel. A fabulous city, for sure. Saw a lot of the more well-known sites, spending time in the Asakusa entertainment district, as well as walking around the Ginza with its glorious bright lights. At a typical Japanese restaurant at the conclusion of an all-day tour, I had more than my fill of sake. Not good. I took advantage of the lovely Sanno gardens and deck the next day to recover. Back in Yokosuka, I jogged the local streets, fascinated by the so very close proximity of houses and the narrow streets. My host, Gary, invited me to join him and his Japanese wife, and a lady friend named Yasuko who worked on the base, for a day at a local beach. It was not the most beautiful beach at which I had been, for the sand was almost a black color, very dark, but on our way back we stopped at the lovely, large home of a friend of his. Bill was an airline pilot, lived a single life, and had a house full of beautiful Japanese artifacts. Absolutely stunning. We had a drink, then pushed off toward the base. We stopped to drop off Yasuko, who lived close to the base, and actually just around the corner from my hotel, and she invited me in to see her first floor apartment. Having jogged the area's streets, I was expecting a small unit, but was shocked when I actually saw how small her place was. I mean, it had to be no larger than maybe two-hundred square feet. Exaggerating, I felt like I could almost spread my arms and touch two opposite walls. Everything about the place was tiny. As I left she gave me her phone number, smiling, and asked me to call her.

At my request, Gary dropped me off at a nearby bar. I plopped myself down on a stool at this small bar, and practiced my wee bit of Japanese to order a beer. The female bartender smiled, and I got my beer. Later, when I asked her about the men's room, she chuckled, pointed toward the door, and said in halting English, "Outside". I kid you not. So, I go outside, and sure enough, there is an open-air trough for doing the number one thing. What a screamer. My Japanese was insufficiently polished to ask her what people did for a number two.

The next night I called Yasuko and asked if I could visit her. She said, yes, and I made the short walk from my hotel to her apartment, where we talked and got to know one another quite nicely. A pleasant, unexpected surprise. Working on the base, her English was good, so we had no problem communicating. I spent a couple of nights with her before my assignment regrettably came to a conclusion.

The assignment had a regrettable ending. I had decided to

rate the operation I was reviewing as, "UNSAT", for there were numerous issues. When I out-briefed the commanding officer he came unglued when I advised him of the rating. They do not like UNSAT ratings associated with their command, so he was obviously quite upset. The only thing good that came out of it was that he personally arranged our chauffeured drive to the airport for our flight to Taipei, Taiwan.

Taipei was made special by my wonderful hosts that had everything in order for my review and by my meeting a local Taiwanese young lady named Nancy Chen. She was petite, very pretty and personable, and we were able to spend many evenings together at my Taipei hotel. The location of the hotel afforded me jogs up Woolloomooloo lined by military with arms at the ready to the Madame Chiang Kai-shek Hotel, a most beautiful venue with an enormous lobby and wide, grand stairs to the second level. Nancy and I spent a few afternoons at the nearby Officers Pool, where I attempted to give her swimming lessons. Seriously. The poor girl had trouble mastering a basic stroke. I would dutifully hold her up from under her stomach as she tried to paddle with her arms. It was almost comical. I mean, it was like me trying to teach a pig how to fly. She did appreciate the inexpensive cosmetics I bought her at the Navy Exchange. I also took advantage of excellent jewelry prices and had an opal ring made for myself. With my assignment in Taipei completed, I then flew to an assignment in Kaohsiung, an industrial city that was not very picturesque, then was fortunate enough to take the train through flat, lovely, agricultural areas to Taichung, a more typical small Taiwanese city with tree-lined narrow streets occupied with retail establishments. The Navy compound was in the center of town and very small, and I was only there for a couple of days. While there, I took advantage of dining at a few different local restaurants near the hotel, and sampling their beer. Overall, my stay in lovely Taiwan, that even included a day at a Navy beach for body-surfing, was an unexpected delight. I had flown back to Taipei to complete our assignment, and on Saturday was driven to the beach by a summer employee of the operation I was reviewing. Bill was a Taiwanese-American, with family in Taipei, and was a student at Eastern Michigan University. Bill and his wife also took me to dinner at the home of his family one night, and oh, what a spread of local cuisine his mother laid out for us. Very memorable, indeed.

My return trip to the U.S. went via Honolulu, where I debriefed Navy staff, and I was able to enjoy that city and Waikiki Beach during the two-day layover. I flew to southern California for my next assignment, and while there took advantage of being back home to take a three-day weekend up at Happy Valley to attend a football game. I didn't have a date at the pre and post-game parties, but a friend told me one of the ladies, who was with a date, wanted me to come by her apartment after she shed her date. Twist my arm! Jan was a lovely blond with a great figure that I did not know that well while we were at Happy Valley College. I borrowed my brother's car and drove to her apartment late that night and we got to know one another, but she was understandably burdened by the untimely death of her husband from an auto accident the year prior.

It was while I was in the Far East that my father was in an auto accident and for a long time was confined to a bed set up for him in the den of our house. My boss in Maryland was kind enough to place me on an indefinite assignment in San Francisco so that I could spend some time with him and help my mother take care of him. However, by the time I arrived in the area he was no longer fully bed-ridden, so I got an apartment in town near the house. My new friend, Jan, visited me one weekend. My poem to Jan:

October Weekend

Cast before strangers
So much
It seems, not able to feel
The real warmth
Of friendship.
How wonderful again
To give
And
To share
To hold you
    In my arms
Knowing I might be
    Lucky enough
To do the same tomorrow.
I need someone to give to,
To hold tightly
Under stars,
With hints of gentle sighs
Competing with
    Whispering breezes
    In nearby treetops.
I need walks with you
    On beaches
Where we can be mesmerized
    By crashing waves
And frolic in frothy foam
Whilst seagulls glide overhead
Speaking to the wind
    Or to us?
What might they be saying –

Two young lovers
    Searching for one another,
Building a friendship
As important in love
    As a free flow
    To a mountain stream.
October weekend
    Left me
    With reflections of all these.
I felt the significance to you
    Of inverness
Hoping someday to add of myself.
It was good to show you
    A part of me from marin
And to share thoughts
    Over hot-buttered rum
    At sausilito's "no name".
Los Gatos I am sure
Will never be the same,
And I thank you
For keeping me close
    In San Francisco
To prevent my disappearance
    Among strange faces.
All these things I need,
    But really,
    I just need you
And more October weekends.

Did I tell you that one of the nice things about that October weekend Jan visited was that we used her wheels to travel to San Francisco and the Pacific Coast? A real Porsche.

The year 1974 ended with my assignment in the Bay Area, and oh, what a year it was. Travel and new lady friends and companionship highlighted a remarkable year in my life.

Don't ever relinquish a good thing.

1981

CHAPTER EIGHT

My marriage world was rocked by a couple of incidents. The first was yet another visit by Carla to see jailbird Billy. It could and should have been just another visit, but this one took a different turn.

Upon her return from a latest visit, I became somewhat curious about the nature and substance of the visits. "So," I began, "what are your visits like? What do you do?"

"We mainly talk. That's about it," she offered. Not much there, but it was a start.

"Are you in the same room, or is there like a wall separating you like you see on TV?"

"There's a small room and we're able to sit at a table and talk, you know."

"Are the staff nearby, watching in case anything crazy happens?"

"Yes. On the other side of a glass partition on one side of the room."

"Oh. I always thought there was a wall separating inmates

from visitors, to prevent exchange of any contraband, and each used a phone to talk."

"Nope. We're in a room. Is there anything else you want to know with your sixty-four questions?" she bristled.

"Actually, there is, and I think under the circumstances of those visits that I tolerate you can take it easy."

"Screw you. These are just visits to see my old neighborhood friend. I don't think anyone else visits him." I am shocked.

"Oh, cute. Let me ask you, are you allowed to bring items into the prison to give to your friend?"

"Yes, I am."

"And these would be?"

"Candy, snack bars, things like that."

"That's it, nothing else, Carla?"

"No." A rather quick, possibly rehearsed reaction.

"Are you sure?" Maybe she's thinking I know something, or at least suspect something, but honestly, I have no way of speculating what she is doing and what might change hands.

"Well, okay, there is something else I give him, and from what he has told me it's alright."

"What is that, Carla? I sure as hell hope you're not slipping him some pot. That would be rather dangerous, yes?"

"No fucking way." I've got her engines revving. Generally, it's the other way around. She controls the throttle, so she is quick to me, "Money. I give him a few bucks so he can buy some stuff in the prison store."

"Geez, Carla. Money? God, how much of your hard-earned money, or our money, are you slipping him?" I'm in disbelief. This is a whole different situation. I'm a mid-level government employee, and she is no longer working since she has decided she is going to be a stay at home mom. She probably has a few bucks in her personal savings account, but still, I'm now the lone breadwinner and we have a baby to feed and clothe.

"If you really want to know," she exclaims rather defensively, "It's normally ten or twenty dollars. That's all. His parents don't send him any money. And I'm probably going to stop doing it. He probably will not be too happy about that, but I'll just tell him no more."

"Shit. He won't be too happy about it? What's going on? Is he in charge? Does he have some leverage over you? This is bullshit, and I suggest it stop, probably including your little soirees at the prison," I add with some emphasis.

"Damn you! Okay, okay! I'll stop giving him money, but I may still want to visit him occasionally."

That was too easy, but I don't press it. Drop it for now and see what happens in the future. I'm totally beside myself. My wife is driving to a state prison to see a slime ball ex-neighbor, and she's passing him money. What the shit? What other surprises does she have in store for me?

It didn't take long for shoe number two to fall, and it was a gut-wrencher, a hit to the belly that would ultimately become part of a pattern of an emotionally troubled person. It was a wake-up call and I saw a different side of Carla's kaleidoscope of emotions. I couldn't help but reflect on the smile on her father's face when we left the reception for our honeymoon. He knew something I didn't, and he was thrilled to see her go. The thing of it is, you don't and you can't really fully know a person before you tie the knot. It can be a roll of the dice. Of course, we didn't know one another that long before we committed to a marriage. Our courting period was relatively short. Duh. There's a problem, for sure, of my own doing. I thought I knew Carla. In hindsight, did I miss some signals, some possible red flags before we got married?

I was charging ahead to marry this cute brunette and didn't notice a downside.

We had a nice dinner and a quiet evening of TV and reading. We went to bed. Everything normal. Kyle was in his crib a few feet away in the other room and asleep.

"Dave, I think you're screwing one of the ladies in your office," she almost yelled, coming out of nowhere. No build-up. No warning. It certainly wasn't a casual statement said almost under the breath, or in the more preferred context of a premonition she had for whatever reasons that we needed to discuss. No. This little anger-laden speed demon with her emotional engine already revving at high RPM's was cranked up and did a 0-60 in less than six seconds number on me.

"What? What are you talking about? I have no intention of doing anything like that," I stammered, for she really caught me off guard. I'm aghast.

"You are. I can feel it, and don't tell me different," she screamed. She was getting louder and I was concerned that she would awaken Kyle.

"When? How? If I'm not at the office, I'm either commuting or I'm home. If I'm not actually in my office, I am out for a noontime jog or at the gym."

"You're taking someone to a motel room during your lunch break!" She's jumped out of bed, standing next to it.

"Oh, my God. That's absolutely absurd and ridiculous, Carla, and you know it. What in the hell makes you think of this stuff?" I'm getting pissed, too, for she is so over the top and her accusations are baseless. "Get back in bed and let's go to sleep."

"I don't trust you, you bastard, and I don't feel like getting back in bed."

"Well, that's your problem. I've never given you a reason not to trust me. They're nice professional ladies. I'm professional around the office. I don't flirt. It's all business, and we all stay very busy. A hotel? I couldn't afford a D.C. hotel for a fling. This whole thing is crazy. Please get back into bed so we can get some much needed sleep. Stop this foolishness."

With that, and nary a word, she's into Kyle's room and turns on his bedroom light. Holy shit, I'm thinking. What an idiot, a monster.

She and I pass as she returns to the bed and I am going to Kyle's room to turn off the light before it awakens him. I come back to bed.

She's up again, doing the same thing, turning on his bedroom light.

This bullshit goes on for about ten or fifteen minutes. I'm telling her she's lost it and she has to stop messing with Kyle, an infant. She says nothing. It's too late. Kyle wakes up, crying. "Nice going, Carla. You idiot." She has caused me to lose it. I get Kyle out of the crib, hold him, and take him into the living room to help calm him down. He eventually stops crying and I return him to his bed. The light is off.

Carla's in bed. Silent. Good. Stay that way, you bitch, I am saying to myself. What the fuck was that all about? Why the accusations? What kind of mental issues is she possessed with? What decent mother intentionally abuses her child in that manner? Why subject him to the emotional tantrum she has laid on me? Leave the poor baby out of it.

The night is again quiet as I slowly, silently slip back into bed. She's still not stirring, her back to me. Good. Sleep comes hard to me as I cannot help but lay awake to digest this and ponder on what just transpired. Her volcanic eruption is troubling.

Morning arrives. I'm up, doing my normal routine. Kyle is still sleeping. Carla's in bed, which is routine for our house. I quietly get ready for work. I'm almost out the door when she walks into the living room.

"Good morning, honey," she says in a sleepy voice.

"Hi." I'm not feeling any tenderness toward her this morning, for what to me are obvious reasons.

"Are you okay?" she asks.

"Sure. Just had a rough night of sleep," I tell her, purposely not bringing up the topic of her evening tantrum that blew the lid off the household like an unexpected July fourth backyard cherry bomb. "I need to get to the bus stop so I don't miss my bus," I add. As if I need an excuse to get the hell out of there.

"Okay. Well, you have a good day at the office, and I'll see you this afternoon. I'm going to make spaghetti and meat balls for dinner since you run tomorrow for your workout."

"Sounds good, Carla. I'll look forward to it." And with that, I'm out the door and walking briskly up the sidewalk to the bus stop. But I'm also thinking. Thinking really hard. She was acting like absolutely nothing happened last night, and that the wheels didn't come off her emotional wagon to cause mayhem in the house when we all should have been asleep. What is going on? What's her problem? Is this the new norm, that we act like a somewhat normal couple for weeks at a time and then a switch is turned on in her screwy head and she turns into a cougar and lashes out at me for no damn, earthly reason? I answer myself, I guess so, and I'm asking myself, why me? Why is this happening? I never, ever saw this sort of behavior in my parents. I don't think they ever fought! No spats. No harsh words. The Cleavers of "Leave it to Beaver" fame. Or Ozzie and Harriet. None of those couples experienced the sort of venom that Carla was spewing. They did not behave that way. So, I'm thinking, what's wrong, why are we different? And because I never saw this sort of thing, and how spouses might respond or resolve differences, I was clueless on what to do. Do I bring it up to discuss it with her, knowing to do so would require resurrecting the how and the why, her angry accusations about me and my office mates? Oh, yeah, right. Let me do that so I can experience an instant replay of her delirious behavior. I really want to go through that again. Doctor, please pull another tooth, just for grins. My fun meter's ticking!

I'm on my bus, and I don't want to think about it anymore. The next thing I know, I'm coming awake instinctively because the bus has arrived at my stop for the office, and I know damn well that during the time of my respite on the bus my head was bobbing up and down like a bobble head doll.

I arrive in my office and say good morning to the wonderful ladies, well, most of them, for there is one woman in the office I can do without, because maybe it's her incessant gum chewing, and I honestly chuckle to myself as I ponder, what if I said to them, "Hi ladies. Guess what my wife accused me of last night?" Nah. Not good. I pass on it.

Life in the Pedersen household goes on. Kyle is a cute little guy and brings us so much pleasure. He seems a bit "chunky" for me and I am hoping that he sheds the baby fat. I know he will, but I worry about a fat child anyway. Some normalcy exists and there is lovemaking, particularly on weekends when we have caught up on some sleep and have spent a nice afternoon either in the city doing the tourist thing or driving out to lovely Potomac or Seneca Falls to walk the canal towpaths or visit village shops.

We get down to her parents when we can. Free babysitting, a pleasure we are denied in the city, far from family. On one particular fall weekend we attend a party at the apartment of one of Carla's best friends, Amy, who lived in Norfolk. Amy and Carla attended high-school together, and if I'm not mistaken, Amy is an occasional source of pot for Carla. The party was actually a lot of fun, for a while. Carla was reminiscing with friends inside the apartment, talking about the baby, and I was wandering around and engaged in occasional conversation with some of the guys, none of which I knew beforehand.

The next thing I know, as I stand outside enjoying a nice cool evening with a cold one, there are shouts. Fists are flying. One guy goes over the keg, knocking it over. He jumps up, yells, "You mother fucker!" and charges head on to his opponent. More fists flying. It's like the Gillette Friday Night Fights from the fifties, Carmen Basillio and Gene Fullmer. I don't know these guys, so I'm not jumping in to try and separate them. Uh, uh. No way, Jose. Let them fight. But there are some buddies of theirs that do step in and get them separated. There's more words between the two, but no more fisticuffs. They're in their respective corners cooling off.

Carla has come out of the apartment, as have many other partyers, to see what the commotion is all about.

"Carla, let's get out of here before the police arrive." Probably a damn good idea, since Carla has probably partaken of some MJ, and we don't need the police talking to her.

"Okay, Dave, let's go. Damn, that's ridiculous."

We get in the car and are heading away from the apartment when I see the flashing lights of a police car driving down the road from the opposite direction.

"Those guys are crazy. I've been to other parties where they've done the same thing. They get drunk and fight. Would you believe they're brothers?"

"Brothers? You're kidding me." I'm incredulous, but I'm learning not to be surprised by anything that now happens in my new life with the cute brunette girl or her friends.

"Yes. Let's go home."

"Got it." And home we go, slowly.

As the expression goes, the hits keep coming. Billy. The

accusations. Child abuse. Brothers that turn to fisticuffs after a few drinks. Hell, I went through four years of high school and four years at Happy Valley College, throw in grad school, and never saw a fist fight. This woman and her friends are different.

Know your dance partner, real well.

1975
CHAPTER NINE

Being assigned in the San Francisco Bay Area, back home, permitted me a re-familiarization with the city in which I grew up. I enjoyed being re-united with San Francisco and all its splendor, and my assignment went well. An IT contractor on the staff, Jim, and I spent many a Friday night after work bar-hopping in the city at places like Henry Africka's, and I dated a couple ladies during my short tenure there, Bonnie, a cute girl on the IT contractor staff, and Leslie, a friend of Jim's that occasionally joined our bar-hopping escapades. This time, however, I did not have the luxury of a Chevy Monte Carlo rental car, for before the year ended I had been contacted by the Navy Commander I de-briefed in Honolulu after my Far East swing and been offered a job on the Pacific Fleet Commander staff there. I drove my VW to Danville from Maryland after our home office semi-annual meeting in early January, and used it for business transportation until I relocated to Hawaii in the spring. I had family in Hawaii, which eased the transition. They lived near Waimea, not far from Presley's place, up Pupukea Ridge, and I was frequently invited to spend a night at their lovely home and enjoy a home-cooked meal. I had purchased a condo in Waikiki, so I wasn't suffering. The world famous beach was a short walk from the condo. There was a large school property adjacent to our condo building at the corner of Kapahulu and Ala Wai Boulevard, and when doing wind sprints on the school lawn I would occasionally pace myself with cars making the turn off Kapahulu onto Ala Wai as they built speed. Nuts. I had also rekindled the enjoyment I had with my Honda 250 Scrambler at Happy Valley College by purchasing another 250 in Honolulu. I rarely used my car, using the cycle for trips to Hanauma Bay to snorkel or over the Pali to Kailua to visit a different beach, and often to commute to the office at Pearl Harbor, sometimes jumping on the freeway and other times travelling the more leisurely route up Kam Highway. I also took the bike high into the surrounding hills above the city to get fantastic views of the area. I occasionally accompanied Ron, my office workmate and a Korean American, to a Korean bar he frequented. He would not let me pay for anything, saying, "Dave, this is my place. Put away your wallet."

So, single life continued to give me pleasure, this time on "the rock". I wasn't traveling as much, but for a while that was okay. It was good to have some roots and be in one place for more than a week. I did have one very unique assignment, and it was on Oahu. I was part of an inspection team going to the Fleet Commander emergency relocation site. You know, if all hell breaks loose, he and his key staff relocate somewhere else. Anyway, we drive to the site, and to my surprise, we pull up to the entrance, park the car, and enter into a tunnel to board a shuttle bus to take us into this installation that is totally underground, under a pineapple field! Upon entering the operational areas I felt like I was in any other "normal" business office. On a different note, and in the category of "what could have been", I had my bags packed to join the Admiral and other staff for an inspection visit down under, on the ice as they say, to travel to Antarctica, followed by some diplomatic stops in Australia and New Zealand, but some planes crashed on the ice just prior to our planned departure so the trip was cancelled.

My trips to San Diego were made more pleasant by a couple ladies I dated there, Sue and Karen. Sue was athletic, a great date and we had fun together. I took her one night to the Hotel Del Coronado for drinks and dinner. What a fabulous hotel and resort. Wow. Played tennis and racquetball, and water-skied behind her brother's boat in San Diego Bay. Sue was "the girl next door" type. Karen was the more romantic of the two, and I usually ended up spending the night with her after a date. There was some awkwardness one time with Sue. I was in my Waikiki condo when the phone rang.

"Hello."

"Hi, Dave. This is Sue."

"Hi Sue! What a pleasant surprise hearing from you. How are you? And where are you?"

"I'm doing well, and I'm at home in San Diego."

I breathe a sigh of relief. "Oh. Okay."

"I'm calling because I'm going to be in Hawaii later this week on vacation and hope I can see you."

Oh, shit. "Sue, I'd love to see you, but a dear friend of mine is visiting from Australia and she'll be here into next week." This was a lady I had met while bar-hopping a few years prior in Sausilito, California, who happened to be vacationing in Hawaii and had called ahead to see if she could stay with me, and I was not going to give her the heave-ho.

"Oh, I see. Okay. Well, goodbye, Dave."

And that took care of that. It just meant that I would be

spending more time in San Diego with Karen, the romantic one, and would not be seeing Sue. Hurt me.

For some varied experience, I guest-lectured at the University of Hawaii, enjoying talking to the students about my occupation and inter-acting with them and their professor. I also gave serious thought to playing on a local rugby team, but I decided against that when I saw the play of some local Hawaiians. I wanted to keep my fair looks and good health, along with my teeth.

I met a Happy Valley College couple that lived in my condo building, and through them attended a number of parties and beach excursions. At one of their parties I met Diane, who pleased me by jumping in the shower with me after a romantic night. She lived out by the university and I saw her a few times, but the relationship eventually fizzled.

My brother Dan flew out to visit for a couple weeks in the fall of that year. We did a fair amount of partying, and I was dragging my tired butt to the office every day, but it was worth it. A couple of weeks before he was to visit I was sitting poolside at the condo and chatting with a fellow resident I had met. Dianne was a former model that still plied her trade on occasion in Honolulu, and was dating the coach of the then professional football team in Hawaii.

"Oh, Dianne," I stated, "I don't think I've told you that my twin brother is coming out to visit and will be here a couple of weeks."

"No you had not told me. Does he look very much like you?"

"Well, not really. He played football in college, and I did more gymnastics, so our builds are a bit different, plus the fact we're fraternal and his face is broader than mine. When we were growing up, our friends referred to him as "walnut head" and me as "peanut head". Dianne cracked up at that. "Really."

"That's too funny. Well, I'll tell you, I have a girlfriend that might be available for a date if you're interested in double-dating one night when he is here. I'll call her to see if she's interested and let you know."

"Hey, that sounds great. I'm sure we'll have a nice time."

With that, we changed subject and also took in the warm afternoon sun and cooling trade wind breezes. We also talked about my poems and verse I had let her read. She absolutely loved it.

A couple days later, Dianne called me to say we were a go to double-date. I told her I would call her when Dan arrived and we would make some plans.

I picked up Dan at the airport and we headed to my condo. Dan was taken by the location, which was inside the Waikiki area, a short walk from the popular beach, and with a view of the mountains off the lanai and overlooking the Ala Wai Golf Course and canal. That first night in town I took him to my favorite bar and dance place, Bobby McGee's, on the Waikiki oceanfront somewhat across from beautiful Kapiolani Park. We went there a few other times, and he fell in love with the place. It was my Thursday and Saturday night hang-out and the door staff got to know me pretty well. We also spent as much time as possible on the beach, out at Waimea with family, and I took him with me one day when I was lecturing at the university. On one particular Saturday, we met up with a couple of my San Jose State buddies that were attending the Hawaii-San Jose State football game. We set up a small keg under the bleachers before the game and had a great time. One day on the beach Dan and I had the pleasure of seeing a Hollywood celebrity up close and personal. We were laying on the beach when I happened to look up, and none other than Farrah Fawcett and her boyfriend at the time, Lee Majors, walked right by us. Great looking legs on Farrah! Her blond, wavy hair looked pretty good, too.

So, the double-date night arrived and Dan and I were pretty

excited. We had a beer at my place and drove to the meeting place where we were to pick up the ladies, a condo complex right on the oceanfront down from Waikiki Beach. Gorgeous area. High rent district, for sure.

We enter the building and take the elevator up to the top floor, found the unit and knocked on the door. We're still a bit giddy, looking forward to a fun night. I had told Dan that Dianne asked to be his date, and that she was a looker. Short blond hair, full-figured in a good way, about his height, and a killer smile along with sexy eyes. I guess that's why she was a cover girl model. A sweet lady.

The door is opened by Dianne. "Hey, guys. Welcome. And you must be Dave's twin, Dan. I'm Dianne, and it's a pleasure to meet you. Come on in."

"Thank you, and it's certainly my pleasure to meet you, Dianne," my brother responds. This is a gorgeous lady he is meeting and I can tell he is impressed.

"Melody will be out in a minute. In the meantime, here's the bar and make yourself a drink."

Dan finds the rum and some coke, and he makes a couple of drinks. We look around. The place is large, gorgeous, has expensive looking prints and other art work adorning the walls, and has a million dollar view of the Pacific Ocean. Oh, my, we say to ourselves, then Dan says, "Well, now we know how the poor folks live." Laughter. We're having a great time, enjoying drink number two for the night, and simply feeling like a million bucks in this luxurious Waikiki condo, about to take two ladies out for dinner, drinks and dancing. It just does not get any better than this for two single guys.

And then it gets even better when Dianne and my date enter the living room and I am staring at this shapely knock-out blond with big, expressive eyes, and a fantastic smile and a kick-ass attitude. Another model? If I thought to myself that I was looking at a movie star, I would have been right. I didn't watch much late night TV, so upon being introduced I did not know the full history.

"Dave and Dan, this is Melody. You may have seen her in the 'F Troop' TV series." Dianne tells us with this big grin on her face, for she knew we would be surprised and impressed. I am somewhat stunned, as I am going to have a date with a movie star. I tell myself to be calm and cool, and not to blow it.

"Hi guys. It's a pleasure to meet you. I see you found the bar," Melody jokes, adding, "how about we have a drink here before we head out?" It quite dawned on me that Melody saw this as a lark and was doing her girlfriend a favor as a double date. She knows that Dianne and I were good friends, and probably thought, why not, I'll go out with a non-Hollywood type. What the hell.

"Sounds good to us, Melody." The ladies put in their drink order and it's done. We're sitting around, goofing off, yakking away about stuff, and taking photos, Dan with the two of them on each side of him, then me for the same. Along the way, Melody shares some stories from her TV series. I'm thinking maybe it was just as well that I did not recognize her when we were introduced.

We all agree we're hungry and need dinner, so we leave the condo, talking about all of us hopping in my VW. Wrong. What self-serving actress would be caught dead in a Bug? Melody has a Porsche 911, oh, my God, and says we'll find a way to fit everyone in her car. I don't know how we did it, but we're all in, and it's off to the restaurant with Melody driving pedal to the metal after a LeMans Race start. We scream through Waikiki, past Kapiolani Park, then head up Kapahulu. Dinner was fun, Cornish Hens all the way around, and Melody shared more stories of her TV work. At this point in time, I have no idea if Melody is a single lady or is divorced, or separated, or whatever. After dinner we pile back in her car and head to Bobby McGee's. The door guys recognize me, or maybe tonight it is Melody they recognized, but regardless, we're in with no problem. We luck out by finding a table, order drinks, and head to the dance floor. We do a few fast dances, then a slow number comes up. She's in my arms, sort of you know. I mean, this is a real celebrity and this government employee is probably chopped liver in her blind date eyes, but I'm having a super time and feeling good. And everything truly is good until I feel a tap on my shoulder from obviously someone that wants to dance with my date. I'm thinking no way. Who the hell is brazen enough to break into my dance? I'm ready to call the person out as I turn toward them. I don't say a word, for I know precisely who this person is and he undoubtedly, indisputably knows more important people in this city than me. For the person I am looking at is none other than the man that must be Melody's husband, James, a more well-known actor from the nationally popular TV series filmed on the island. So, what do I say?

"Oh, Hi Dano. She's all yours. Don't book me," I add with a smile as I look at this guy shorter than me. A big night, for sure. Met two Hollywood celebrities. One was my blind date, and the other was her estranged husband, at the moment.

He gives me a smile as if to say thanks, and I find my way back to the table, knowing I will not see Melody at that table nor anywhere else for that matter.

So, with Melody and our three-hour "relationship" or friendship in the rearview mirror, hey, it was a fun few hours knowing her, and brother Dan back home in California after a memorable visit to the islands, life is back to normal until I meet Carol, an Air Force officer stationed at Hickam Air Force Base.

That damn incurable romantic strikes again.

1982

CHAPTER TEN

These days I get out of bed each morning and wonder if Carla will again cause me to step on a third rail, or if, for analogy purposes, figuratively castrated by Carla, similar to the Greek mythology Titan chief, Cronus, who obtained his power by castrating his father, Uranus. I'm becoming more a believer in the notion that in life, timing is everything. Like a "jog fart". That's when you've been out for a long run in the early morning hours before the sun even starts to rise, seeing no one, and you get back in your neighborhood, and damned if when you're about even with a neighbor walking their dog and you're saying "Good morning", hoping not to spook her, your body decides it can hold it back no longer and you lay a big fart. That's bad timing, not to mention embarrassing.

It's not like every day or even any given week is like fraternity hell week. We have our good days, like getting a babysitter and going out for dinner, or even staying in with a pizza and I'll have a couple beers. I'm still working out every day, which is my equalizer.

It really helps. I would be a basket case, stroke victim, were it not for my exercise program. Nowadays, I've largely shifted my fitness regimen to jogging in the morning vice after work when the energy level sucks. I still run from the office now and then, but mostly now, it's a morning thing. My jogs from the office take me over Arlington Boulevard, circling the Marine Corps War Memorial, toward the Arlington National Cemetery, looping up and around onto Memorial Avenue with the Custis-Lee Mansion above and behind me, then over the George Washington Memorial Parkway and jogging around the Lincoln Memorial and along the Tidal Basin before heading back from where I came. If I do not want to deal with traffic and exhaust, I hop over the Key Bridge and curl around onto the canal towpath that goes west for miles. I lift weights in a corner of the guest bedroom. Yes, we have occasionally talked about getting a bigger place. Kyle is getting older and it's been a long time since midnight feedings and his colic.

But make no mistake, living with Carla reminds me of a golf joke my father told me so many years ago when he, Dan and I would go out on a Saturday morning for a round of golf. It went like this – So, two golf buddies are standing at the first tee and they are discussing how many mulligans they would allow for that day, when one of them says, "Two gooses." "Two gooses?" the other replies, totally perplexed, having no earthly clue what his buddy means. "Two gooses. You'll see." The confused partner agrees and they start their round. The "two gooses" clueless partner is set to tee off first. He's at the tee, ball setting on a golf tee, driver in hand, addressing the ball, totally focused on his grip, stance, really focused. His golf buddy is standing behind him. The guy teeing off is now in his back swing when all of a sudden his partner takes his driver and sticks the wood end into his partner's ass. Oh, my God, the other guy jumps halfway to the second tee, absolutely incredulous, steaming mad. "What the hell was that all about?"

he fumes. "That was goose number one, his partner replies quite calmly, and knowing there is a second goose coming at some time during the next seventeen holes, the "accosted" golfer's posture at each tee box is a sight to behold, butt cheeks tight, snapping his head around to check his buddy, and obviously unable to focus on his golf game. He's all over the course. I was that guy who got goosed, not knowing when Carla was going to hit me with another "goose", or worse.

Like a fool, one day on my bus ride home from work I allow a seat partner to tell me about the Herbalife business and its potential for earnings and success. Tony is a good guy, athletic, Italian, and very friendly. No, he was not Mob. We've chatted on the bus before, when I have not fallen asleep, and have become "bus buddies". So, this time he goes for it, and I agree to Carla and I going to his house to let him and his upper chain person give me the spiel. I'm interested, as is Carla, and it goes from there. Tony and his wife take us on a drive in the country to show us the Mcmansion of someone very successful in the business, and we make our weekly runs to buy products, and although it is hard for me since there is a shy, reticent side of me, I'm calling friends and work colleagues left and right, asking them to come to the apartment so I can get them excited about being a part of this pyramid scheme. A few take us up on it, and most politely decline. Reflecting back, I can't believe I called them and put them through that knothole. The good thing, we all remained friends and collegial co-workers. I've got one or two very interested people, and I think things are going well, but it is agonizingly slow and tortuous, and I'm out of names to call and am not into the bus ride cold calls. The point of all this is that Carla thinks we have a gravy train working and that we're going to be rich. She's nagging me, kicking this mule in the hind quarters at every opportunity to get out there and do it. She is constantly saying, have you done this, have you done that, pushing me relentlessly to make the cold calls, build the business, but I'm now slowing down, and this provides but one more opportunity with which to explode and curse me. I've intentionally given her yet another arrow in her emotional arsenal quiver.

This goes on for months.

And about that time, something else happened that she never, ever forgot. In view of my position at work, I was asked to be the Officer-in-Charge of the Navy Women's Softball team for their upcoming Inter-service competition at Fort Bragg, North Carolina. It was a great assignment and I agreed to it. Carla, as usual, wasn't too thrilled, but we got through that, somehow. We had the one child, and she was pregnant with number two, so her parents said okay to she and Kyle staying there and I drove to the Army base. I performed my duties and did nothing socially with the team. But when they won the championship, I went to the hotel to celebrate with them over a few drinks, dinner, and I even danced with a few of the ladies in celebration mode. When I got back to Norfolk, Carla, using her passive-aggressive posture, persuasively drilled me with questions, and I actually casually and innocently told her, "Yes, I had a few dances. We were celebrating a championship, for goodness sakes. That's all. I left their hotel early to return to where I was staying." Of course, the result of my honesty and candor was a royal lashing, an in your face event. Had she been Queen for a Day, she probably would have ordered cutting off of one of my appendages, down low. So, the proverbial shit hit the fan, and it escalated from me being a total scumbag for dancing with a few women, to the eventual accusations that I also screwed at least one of them. My explanation and defense failed to resonate with her, and thus you may as well have put a scarlet "D" on my forehead, for again, she constantly brought it up in future tirades. What Carla failed to realize or accept was that messing around on my wife was not in my DNA. I would never think of doing something like that to my wife. And I would be a liar if I said a certain phone call in 1973 didn't have a bearing on my decision never to play around on my wife. I was in my dorm room at grad school when the phone rang. I picked it up, said hello, and bam, the caller laid into me, yelling that if he ever caught me with his wife he would kill me. I tried to tell him he had the wrong guy and number. Didn't work. I was not playing around with someone else's wife while in grad school, and would never do such a thing. Anyway, the call scared the crap out of me and I never forgot it.

Along the way, baby number two arrives. I'd had enough fun in the delivery room with Kyle's birth, so I tell her I'm going to pass on doing that again. She's not too happy about that, but I was with her pre-delivery and after the baby is wrapped and in her arms. She's somewhat out of it when I enter the post-delivery room, and she's thrilled with Katie's birth, but I know she'll remind me from time to time that I wasn't present with her for the big event. Her "quiver" is getting fuller by the week.

Not long after Katie's birth, I bring up the subject of a vasectomy for me.

"Carla, I don't know how you feel about this, but I'm not getting any younger, and for a host of reasons I very much want to get a vasectomy. Two children is enough. I am not one to want a large family. No way. What do you think?" I did not want another child with this fruitcake.

"Actually, I'm okay with it, Dave. I feel the same as you about two children being our limit.

"Great. I was hoping you would agree. We were fortunate to have both a boy and a girl."

"All-American family," she adds.

So there you have it. No more kids for me. Decision made,

and the wife agrees. I made the needed appointment with the Urologist, got the pros and cons from a doctor, and made an appointment for the procedure. A snip here, a snip there, a wince from some pain, and it is done. Here again, I unintentionally provided her yet another arrow for her emotion-charged quiver. Like Artemis of Greek Mythology, she kept her bow and quiver at the ready. Years later, she would venomously throw it in my face that my vasectomy "selfish act" denied her the ability to have more children. Don't get ahead of me on this.

All was not wine and roses. I was occasionally asked to conduct official travel by my boss. In my previous single years I was all in. More travel? Sign me up! Nowadays, it made me shutter, for I knew what Carla's reaction would be when I brought up a topic that should have been unemotional, understanding that my job required me to be away for a few days, maybe a week at most. No big deal, right? Wrong.

"Carla, Greg has asked me to travel down to our bases in Charleston."

"Hmmm. How long will you be gone?"

"A few days. I'll leave on a Monday morning and should be back by Thursday."

"Isn't there someone else that can go?"

"No. It's in my specialty area, so I'm logically it." I don't know why I used the word logically, because Carla did not understand or value "logic".

"Damn. Here you go again. Another damn business trip." The emotional RPM's were rising, and I'm getting a little pissed that my wife has to take this attitude about my limited business travel, a requirement of my job, which also allowed us to live comfortably. But that does not resonate with her. I was ready for her.

"Carla, my last business trip was three months ago. It's not like I'm gone every other week. This is nothing compared to men that travel extensively in their jobs, especially in corporate America. I need you to understand this." I wasn't racking up frequent flyer miles.

"Bullshit! You're going to leave me with two kids."

"It's a short assignment. You'll be okay. I'll be back before you know it." What I really wanted to say was, "You're not working. That was your call, and I was okay with us living on my salary alone. You can do this." Oh, no, but her 340 horsepower mill was already cranked up, so what difference would it have made? How I hated these discussions with her, and she put me through the meat grinder every damn time.

"Who else is going?" she screamed. "One of those ladies in your office that you're fucking at lunchtime?" And then, suddenly, she struck me on the side of my head. It didn't hurt physically, but I was stunned and it sent emotional shock waves through me at seeing yet another side of this woman I married.

"What the hell? What are you doing, Carla?" I yelled. God help the kids who were taking a late afternoon nap in their room. "This is crazy, and you know it. Don't ever do that again."

"I will if I want to. Go on your damn business trip. I don't care. When is it?"

"Two weeks from now. I'll keep you posted on my plans."

"Don't bother, asshole."

And with that, another walk on the third rail. It was like, borrowing again from Greek Mythology, Carla was Rhea, the wife of Cronus, who, vexed at having him swallow their children, hid Zeus from him and gave him a stone to swallow instead. Carla was Rhea, saying, here, take a walk on this rail.

A lot of things were bothering me about my marriage. I didn't have any close friends that I could talk to face to face or over a beer to seek advice or if nothing else, listen. I did seek out an older guy in the office, Al, who I knew was single, or divorced, and asked him one day if I could talk to him about some personal issues I had. He was cool about it, and when I laid it all out, he was sympathetic and felt I might benefit from talking to a lawyer. The next day I did that, walking from my office to an attorney's office a few blocks away. He was also sympathetic, agreed there were some major issues, and interestingly did not suggest outright that we draft separation papers but instead suggested Carla and I first seek counseling.

I went home that day and walked into the proverbial buzz saw with Carla when I told her about the legal counsel I sought earlier that day.

"Carla, I think you would agree we're having some marital issues. I didn't know who else to turn to, so I visited an attorney today."

"You what?" she yelled. No halfway emotion here. Straight to full power, pedal to the metal, she's on fire like burning rubber from a dragster tires.

"You heard me. I needed to talk to someone about our marriage issues. I found an attorney near my office and made an appointment to see him."

"I don't believe you. Why would you do that? What did you tell him?" she roared.

"I told him what you would expect. The mental trauma you put me through. Your lack of trust and understanding of my infrequent business travel. That too often you make me feel very uncomfortable. Billy." I didn't mention the physical abuse.

"You're sick. This kind of stuff is normal in a marriage, you dickhead. Poor Dave never saw this sort of stuff in his parent's marriage. You can't handle it."

"Frankly, I don't want to have to handle it. And don't tell me your behavior toward me is normal."

"Does that mean you want to divorce?" I have to think the next door neighbors could hear her.

"No. I don't know what I want right now. I do know I've had enough of your emotional outbursts and verbal and physical abuse toward me."

"Well, that's not going to change any time soon. I'm sure I'm suffering from post-partum issues. Plus, I'm very young and now have two children that at times drive me nuts. What else did he say?"

"That we should get some counseling. I'll contact our church Pastor and see if he can help."

"Okay. Maybe that will help. No more attorneys."

That was the end of that episode. I did not have a lot of confidence in counseling, but I knew we had to give it a try. I spoke to our Pastor, and we had a first joint counseling session with him. I did my best, in Carla's presence, to tell him, and of course her, how she was making me feel, what was troubling me. It was awkward, to say the least. It was difficult to be totally truthful and forthcoming in front of Carla, a person with an emotional hotwire, the type of person that would unleash her vengeance on me like an attack dog the moment we were away from the Pastor, and heading home, and to absolutely no surprise, that's what she did. Kept to the script.

"Damn you! I can't believe you told him all that stuff." She was hot. Molten lava spewing.

"That was the purpose of the session, I thought, Carla. A chance to let you know through a professional counselor how you make me feel. And now you're condemning and beating me up me over it. That's just wonderful. How am I supposed to react for a follow-on session, knowing you'll rip into me again?" We had agreed with the Pastor's suggestion to have individual sessions. Worked for me. When Carla returned from her individual session, I made no comment or queries about how it went. That was between her and the Pastor. Oh, contraire, however, when I returned home from an individual session. She was on me like a starving cougar on fresh meat. There obviously was to be no "I've got a secret" between me and the Pastor.

"Well, what did you tell him this time?"

"I think it's appropriate that I not tell you, Carla. What we discussed is between him and me. That's the way it's supposed to be."

"Bullshit. You tell me what you said, you prick, or you can go find somewhere else to sleep tonight, asshole." She was again fired up. Same old shit. Her way or the highway, or in this case, a hotel room. This was getting old and tiresome.

Like an idiot, knowing what and who I was dealing with, I shared a few comments I made to the Pastor.

"You didn't!" she screamed. "How could you tell him that?" Oh, the venom, the fury, the mental torment. The agonizing presence of her, stripping me emotionally like she was skinning a dead animal. But that was how she was. She was right, everyone else was wrong. You didn't disagree with her unless you were ready for a frontal, in your face, verbal assault. She was dominating, domineering and her brain worked on overdrive to take the initiative and keep you on the defensive. It was actually quite useless to argue with her, or try to take a different perspective in what should not have turned into an argument.

"I needed to be honest with him. You have a problem with that?"

"Yes, I do. I'm not going to anymore sessions, and I suggest you not go either. And furthermore, you can get the hell out of here tonight. I've had it."

"No, you can't kick me out of my own home."

"Oh, yeah?" And with that she struck out at me again, slugging me on my upper body, yelling profanities. The shock was more damaging than the blow, and the screaming continued unabated.

She was gone, totally out of it. I'd had enough. I grabbed some clothes and headed to a nearby hotel. I wasn't going to stick around to see how much worse things could get. As I walked out the door, Carla yelled, "Oh, and guess what? Billy has been released from prison. Isn't that great news? I know you're happy to hear it."

"Wonderful," I shout without turning around.

As I drove to the hotel I had thoughts of suicide. End the craziness and the torment. I knew I wouldn't do it, and it's not like I started planning to commit suicide. No, it was a passing thought, scary, and told me the depths of despair I was feeling with Carla.

Hell hath no fury like Carla's.

1975/1976

CHAPTER ELEVEN

I met Carol, an Air Force officer, at Bobby McGee's in Honolulu. Yes, I returned to the scene of that devastating "break-up" with my three-hour friend and blind date, Melody, the TV actress. Oh, how that tore me up. Just kidding. I hoped she and James got back together and all was well in their marriage. Carol is short, about five feet, two inches, cute as a button, with an alluring smile, slender, with long black hair that she of course wears short when in uniform, and has this pixie look. She graduated from the University of Massachusetts. We date, and I end up spending some evenings in her bachelor officer's quarters, particularly after Thursday prime rib night in the attached officer's mess. We really hit it off, and before you know it, we're engaged. Well, it's not like it happened in a week, for we were dating for a while. I know I've got to find a cure to this incurable romantic side of me! We often hit a favorite Irish pub and a wonderful disco place in Honolulu, two of our favorite things to do on a weekend night, and we even went to see the movie "Peter Pan" at a local drive-in theater. We frequently went to nearby Bobby McGee's for dancing. My senior enlisted Air Force cousin who also works at Hickam helps me out by pulling some strings to get us into a cabin at Bellows Air Force Base on the island for a weekend, where we mostly relaxed on the beach. We also motorcycle around the island, going to Hanauma Bay to snorkel, or to Kailua to enjoy a different beach. And of course, there's Waikiki Beach a short walk from my condo. My poem to Carol:

Bobby McGee's

Bobby mcgee's
To me
Is many things.
Some good,
Some sad.
Bobby mcgee's
With you
Conjures
A heartfelt toast
A birthday wish
A dance to "If"
Holding you close.
It is
Touching your lips
Telling you
    You're pretty
And never wanting
To pull a hand from yours.
It is all these things
But mostly
A dream come true

On a wonderful night
With you.

Carol moves into my condo, and everything's going great. Well, until a few months after our engagement, with invitations ordered and weekly visits to a Catholic priest to get this heathen Protestant singing from that hymnal if you know what I mean. I wake up one morning, tell her I'm going for a walk, head across Ala Wai Canal to the public library where I can have some privacy on a pay phone, and I call a good Happy Valley College buddy that was in California during the off-season from his National Football League playing days.

I made the proper arrangements with the operator to have the call billed to my condo phone and she dialed me to California. I lucked out, as my buddy picked up the receiver after a few rings.

"Doug, how you doing? This is Dave, calling from Honolulu."

"Hey, Dave, what's up? This is a pleasant surprise hearing from you."

"I need your advice, big time, Doug."

"Okay. I'll try to help, Dave."

"Well, as you may or may not know, I'm engaged to an Air Force officer. Super lady. We get along great, and we're planning the wedding. Everything is going smooth and we're looking at a possible fall wedding date here in Honolulu."

"Okay. Sounds good."

"I'm getting cold feet, Doug. I woke up this morning and I swear the thought of getting married just scared the crap out of me. I don't think I can go through with it."

"Well, here's the way I look at it. There's three parts to this. One, do you love her, two, do you want to marry and spend possibly the rest of your life with her, and three, are you prepared to marry her now?"

"I love her, yes, but that feeling is now being trumped by the fear of making a mistake in marrying her. It's all me. I'm just not ready. I'm twenty-nine, but I think I need to give the marriage thing more time. And just recently, we were driving out to the north shore for a weekend getaway at a resort there, and as we drove out there I had the strangest feeling, that I did not want to be around her at that time. I needed space."

"There's your answer. If you cannot commit, now, then you shouldn't marry her. If you feel that way, it's probably best for her, too, and it wouldn't be fair to either of you to go through with the wedding if one of you has serious doubts. Not a good way to start, Dave."

"Okay, Doug. I think I know what I have to do. Thanks. I really appreciate your thoughts on this."

"Good luck," he said, and then asked, "So, how is life in paradise, the other notwithstanding?"

"It's wonderful. Beautiful place, as you know. I live in Waikiki, so you can't beat that, and the local girls are absolutely gorgeous. The only tough part is living on a small island."

"Well, I'm sure things will get better for you," he opined, and with that we ended the call.

Carol was up when I returned to the condo. She gave me a good morning hug and kiss, looking pretty through the sleepiness. This wasn't going to be easy, I thought to myself, but it had to be the right thing to do.

"Carol, I need to tell you something."

"Yes? Is it about our orientation at the Catholic Church? I know you really enjoy that," she said with a smile.

"I can't go through with it."

"With what, Dave?"

"Carol, I can't go through with the wedding. It hit me this morning and I've been struggling with it all morning, trying to figure out why and how I got cold feet." I didn't tell her that a couple of weeks prior when we were driving out to the North Shore to spend a weekend at the Del Webb resort hotel, that during the drive I knew there were issues for me. I felt emotionally empty about her and could not get a strong feeling for her all weekend. It was the strangest feeling, a void in my heart for her. I wanted to be away from her.

"Oh, great, Dave. I can't believe this. I don't know what to say. I don't think saying I love you will make any difference. Wow. What a shock. I hope you're happy."

"I'm sorry, Carol. I really am. I don't know what else to say. There's nothing I can say that would make you feel any better, other than the obvious, as stupid as that sounds."

"I need to call my parents to stop the wedding plans. Maybe the invitations haven't been sent out yet. I'm not going to say anything else. If that's how you feel, it's over. We can't force this. I need to find a place of my own." I wonder if she, too, had doubts.

"I'm heading to Happy Valley in a few days. I need to get away." I had been thinking about attending the college's Western Week events and seeing Dan, and this made it convenient and more compelling. It would give Carol some time by herself and time to find new lodging.

"I'll be moved out by the time you return. I'm going to visit some friends for the day."

When I returned from Happy Valley, Carol wasn't fully moved out. I helped her with one or two carloads of personal belongings, and remember the sigh of relief as I walked from her apartment to the parking lot to return to my condo, emptier in many ways, but knowing it was for the best.

There was still one more test. We agreed to have lunch together at the Naval Station Pearl Harbor Marina across Kam Highway from my office. The conversation was pleasant and we discussed how our respective lives were proceeding since we were no longer living together. At the end of lunch, Carol said, "I thought I would give you one more chance to renew our engagement. If you feel you want us back together, now is the time to put the ring back on my finger. If not, it's over and we walk out of here and go our separate ways."

Crunch time, for certain. A lot of thoughts are banging through my head at warp speed like a meteor shower. I know it cannot happen. "Carol, I'm sorry, but I cannot change course and go through with the plans we had. It's not going to happen. I really am sorry."

"Me, too, Dave. Goodbye." And she up and left the restaurant. That was the last time I saw her. I paid the tab and returned to my office.

I wasted no time in resurrecting my Bobby McGee's routine, where I met a few ladies. Erika, who was big into full body massages with oil as well as skinny-dipping together in her apartment pool, and Jeannie, a cute, wholesome, straight-laced girl from Minnesota that was looking for a husband. Wrong guy. We did have a few dates, and I often hopped on the motorcycle to run up Ala Wai to spend a few hours visiting her in the evenings. Same deal with Erika, who lived across Kapahulu near the park, close to my condo.

I wasn't getting as much official travel in my job as I had hoped, and the island of Oahu started feeling small. I was suffering from "rock fever" in paradise, believe it or not. How could I possibly pull myself away from all those beautiful beaches, the gorgeous local girls, cruising around the island on my motorcycle, and on and on? But the extent of my official travel was a few trips to San Diego, and a meeting in Seattle followed by an admittedly interesting trip to our Navy base far out the Aleutian chain. It had been a fascinating trip. I flew out of Anchorage in a small prop job and headed toward Adak Island with a fuel stop at Dutch

Harbor. The Navy base was quite desolate, although I was told it was a hunter's and fisherman's paradise. On the return flight to Anchorage I met a very nice lady. That night, she and her husband were kind enough to pick me up at my hotel and take me out to a fantastic bar well outside of the city that must have had thousands of business cards plastered on the walls. There were no Navy business trips to the Far East bases, which troubled me. They needed some attention from headquarters, but it was not to happen. I sent a letter to my previous office in Maryland, asking if they could take me back, and shortly thereafter received a letter in the affirmative from Harry, the Personnel Director. With that, I put in my resignation papers, even though the Admiral called me into his office and tried to change my mind. I politely told him it was too late. I also contacted the Porsche dealership near my hometown and over the phone put in an order for a Porsche 914 that I would pick up upon departing Hawaii. I said goodbye to Erika and Jeannie. When I arrived back home I wrote a poem to Jeannie and sent it to her.

Missing You

I miss you
More than a song
    Might miss its lyrics,
More than a rainbow
    Would miss its color.
A palm tree
    Without a gentle breeze,
A sailor
    Without the seas,
Would not be more
Pronounced

Than days without you.
I miss you
More than San Francisco
    Without its golden gate,
More than a realist
    Without fate.
But
After all is said,
After all the foot-twisting,
I can say
In no other way
I miss you.

I picked up my new car on the first business day after returning to California. I then drove to Happy Valley to see Dan and attend a party he was having at his place. He set me up with a neat young lady. The next day Dan and I hopped in my car and drove to Lake Tahoe, where we partied and stayed at friends of ours from our college days. After a couple days there, he got a ride back home and I pushed on east to Salt Lake City, where my new car got a 1,500 mile check-up and I killed some time by visiting some Mormon venues.

On my cross country drive I stopped to spend a couple days with Doug at his Kansas City Chiefs training camp at William Jewell College, and spend a few days visiting IU friends now living in Illinois and Indianapolis. A whole new vista now opened up for me as I envisioned using my Porsche for as much of my official travel as possible. And that's exactly what happened after my "awakening" with Carol. Most of my new Navy assignments had me on the east coast, so I was able to use my car. My friend Pete and I were teamed up for a two-month special assignment in our Washington headquarters, where I dated Paula, who worked in our office, Dottie, a Virginia DMV employee, and Kathy, a lady I met sitting poolside at my motel in Norfolk while in a training status before my Washington assignment. Paula and Dottie were simply dates that provided a little bit of romance, not much, but Kathy was quite romantic, and had such smooth skin. Coinciding schedules with Pete meant lots of physical activity. We lifted weights on the small back patio off our hotel room, jogged through Georgetown, and played tennis. Doing the latter meant finding a tennis court very early in the morning prior to going to work since tennis was at its most popular at that time and it was tough finding a vacant court in the afternoon. Pete and I had a great time smashing the ball back and forth, and it was great exercise. Pete was a Jimmy Conner fan, and I liked Borg.

October always meant attending a national professional conference, this time in Boston, where I met another Kathy, this one from Charlotte. Pete and I found time to go on jogs and throw around a football in Boston Common, which was near our Copley Plaza hotel, and also spend some time with Kathy and her hotel roommate. From Boston I travelled to bases in New England, retracing earlier assignment paths in Maine. I then travelled to San Diego for the months of November and December where I stayed with my childhood friend, Frank, who lived on Mission Boulevard, two blocks from the beach of San Diego Bay. Good times were had in San Diego with Frank and his beach friends, along with the always great weather. Also spent a weekend in Vegas with Pete and another Navy colleague, John. I controlled my gambling and did not lose any money, but John took a beating playing what he thought was "21", but was really Baccarat! The fool. Saw my friend Karen a few times, then headed north for Christmas with family, and to Happy Valley for a party at brother Dan's and a blind date. New Year's Eve found me back in Washington at a party with Navy friends and colleagues.

So, my single life was alive and well and still intact and preserved as 1976 came to a close. I had avoided a wedding with Carol, and had lived life fully without killing myself. Speaking of which, I damn near bought the farm in Hawaii. Not from Melody's TV celebrity husband, but from body surfing. I thought I would try a body-surfing hotspot on Oahu called Makapuu. Armed with swim fins to give me some extra leg strength and leverage, I entered the busy surf to challenge a wave or two. It didn't work as planned, for my timing was off on trying to catch a big wave and it took me down and under. The strength of the wave was tremendous, and rather than popping up to the surface, my body was kept underwater for an agonizingly long time. I tried to no avail to get to the surface, and I honestly thought that I would never breathe precious, fresh air again. Remarkably, luckily, maybe owe it to divine intervention, the wave finally spit me out on the shore, where I dragged my tired, beaten body up the sandy beach until I could stand, walk to my towel, pick it and my belongings up, and departed that beach, never to return, leaving it to the pros.

As I entered 1977, little did I suspect that things would get serious with my new friend Kathy in Charlotte.

I really missed Erika's oil massages.

1982
CHAPTER TWELVE

I had spent yet another night at a motel in flight from my rabid dog wife. Like other times, I returned from work the next day and you would think nothing happened. And that's how things were for a few weeks. The night before my business trip to Charleston, a topic of ferocious backlash from Carla when I announced the trip, she got a little testy, but I did my best to ignore it. The next morning I was packed and ready for my taxi ride to the airport and she continued to be a little bitchy about my trip. The taxi arrived, I got in, and he made his way slowly up the street. I don't know why I did, but I looked out the rear window of the cab, and what did I see? My nutcase of a wife was running down the street following the cab in robe and slippers, with arms flailing and yelling something I couldn't hear.

"Get out of here, quickly," I told the taxi driver in no uncertain terms. I did not need her catching up to the cab at a stop sign and creating a scene.

Over the next few months, with no business trips or meetings with the Pastor, there was an even ebb and flow to life. We did our normal social things, using the neighbor babysitter, and I dabbled with the Herbalife business, just enough to hold Carla and her visions of millions of dollars, at bay. We also went house-hunting. Yep, you read that correctly. Divorce wasn't in my lexicon. Were my feelings for that cute little brunette the same as when I married her? Hell, no. Was there as much love-making? Another hell, no. Some sex, but no "Love-making". I was going with the flow. Work was going well and I had received a promotion. My workouts were good, some sleepless nights notwithstanding, so getting a decent night sleep in that apartment was the goal. The children occupied a special part of our lives. We saw Carla's parents from time to time. But here's the thing – Carla went through life on a very short fuse, with me, with neighbors, with even her own family, and she was always a volcano that could erupt at any time. I thought of it as her "volcanic personality", and convinced myself it was something I was resigned to live with.

We found a lovely house in Burke, just outside the Capital Beltway and near a bus stop, thus a bit less expensive than homes located inside the Beltway, and some Navy friends of mine helped us move. The house had plenty of room for us. It was an older two-story house, exactly what we had been looking for. Vinyl-clad exterior, painted a light beige, with burgundy shudders. An attached two-car garage with a paved driveway. The lot was not super large, which would make yard care a bit more manageable, and had a nice, enclosed back yard with plenty of room for the kids to play. The deck would be great for the barbecue grill on weekends. It had one bedroom downstairs, and three upstairs with a second bathroom, with ample size kitchen, living room, den and dining room. It was plenty of house for us.

Carla's parents came to visit and really liked our new house. I wish I could say "home", if you know what I mean. It was a lovely house, period, and certainly larger than our Georgetown apartment. But make no mistake, we would miss the excitement of Georgetown. My Sunday routine during the fall was to do yardwork, followed by watching the Redskins game on TV. That was a great time to be a Redskins fan – Joe Gibbs, Joe Theismann, John Riggins, The Hogs. Super team and exciting.

One of the first things to happen after we "moved up" was that, further geographically from our business up line friends, and busy working on the new house, like interior painting, making the full basement useable, doing some new landscaping, and so on, I stopped doing Herbalife. When Carla demanded to know why I was not working hard to build the business, I cited the many reasons why not, and she grudgingly accepted it, or so I thought.

So, things were somewhat quiet in the Pedersen household, but that was not to last. Carla was like the Sirens, the three Greek Mythology sisters who sat on rocks by the sea and lured sailors to their doom by singing to them. She sure as hell wasn't Hestia, the mild virgin goddess of the hearth, family and peace. No way. I was convinced that Carla had a deal with Hades, lord of the underworld, a stern, dark, inexorable god, and his kingdom was dark and lifeless.

We found a babysitter in our new neighborhood, and continued with routine dinners out, purposely selecting some of the more popular, but more expensive, restaurants in Old Town Alexandria, downtown Washington, and even Middleburg in horse country. We occasionally went skiing, to places like Seven Springs in Pennsylvania and a ski resort in western Maryland that had a day care operation.

Carla knew I was working hard and could use a break. She knew how much I treasured my IU friends and that I had not seen them for quite some time. I'm sure she also had not forgotten the scene we made for the wedding rehearsal. But regardless, when

I mentioned that in talking to my buddy Wally that the "Brew Crew", as we called ourselves, planned to get together and have a reunion at the Kentucky Derby that May, she totally blindsided me by suggesting that I attend!

"I think you need a break and I know you want to see your friends, so why don't you go?" she asked. Changeable Carla, who so loathed my business trips. This was a most surprising and unexpected side of her I was seeing.

"I'd love to. You know that. You sure you're okay with it?" I replied, still stunned. And maybe she had an ulterior motive.

"Sure. Do it. Call Wally and tell him you want to attend."

"Okay. I'll do that. Thanks. I'll probably be gone about five days, Carla. Maybe Wally will be driving and I can get a ride from him to keep the cost down."

"Sounds good. I know you'll have a good time." Huh? Who is this?

With that, I hooked up with Wally for a ride, and we met up with the rest of the Brew Crew in Bardstown, Kentucky, Jerry's home, just like so many years before.

Needless to say, we had a great time, played a round of golf, got drunk in the Churchill Downs infield, and somehow found our way back to the motel. I didn't feel up to partying more that night, so I asked Wally to run me to the bus depot so I could take a Greyhound bus back to Washington. It was the longest bus ride of my life, a real milk run. Matters were made incrementally worse when my bus pulled into the bus depot nearest our house and Carla met me.

"You sonofabitch. I hope you had a great time leaving us to fend for ourselves and me with two kids while you were out having a great time at the Derby!" she exclaimed. She was revving her engine pretty good. This was reverse behavior. In this case, she obviously forgot her encouragement that I attend the Derby and see old friends, and was now crushing me with venomous criticism.

"Carla. What is this? You suggested I go! You encouraged me, and now you want to berate me for taking you up on your offer. Shit. Thanks a lot. I'm also tired because I came back early and to do so and save money I took a damn bus all the way from Louisville."

"Oh, poor boy. He's tired. Tough shit." And she continued to lay into me all the way home. Fortunately, she wore herself out and I didn't have to resort to spending that Sunday night in a motel. Geez. I don't get it. Decent one minute, an attacking cougar the next. She's definitely full of surprises. And that wasn't the first time she had pulled that. A year earlier, again under the legitimate guise of needing a few hours break and doing something on my own, she was cool with me driving to nearby Annapolis to attend a Navy football game. I wasn't a golfer and I didn't have a stable of male friends with which I had bonded and had occasional evenings with for a few drinks, laughs, camaraderie, or to watch a game on TV. I didn't have that, so I was normally around but for work. So, a few hours out of the house seemed reasonable. Right. I headed to Annapolis, with her blessing, encountered extremely heavy traffic just outside the Beltway on Route 50, so said screw it and turned around. The mistake I made, if one would call it that, was in getting back to our area and going to a local sports bar to have a beer and watch some college football on the tube. I got back home at a very decent time mid to late afternoon, and upon sharing with her what I had done, she became totally unglued and could not believe I would or could do such a thing. This was fairly early in our marriage, with only the one child, so I was starting to see the handwriting on the wall as to my mistake in marrying this evil bitch.

The next weekend Carla was spending the afternoon with a

neighbor friend so I took the kids over to a nearby park that had a neat children's playground. I liked those moments, sans Carla. I was perfectly comfortable with taking care of them on my own and not losing it, and it was always better without her around. It was evident to me that the kids playing in the house and being a bit rambunctious caused a bit of stress when Carla and I were also in the house. But get Carla out of the house, and me alone with the children, and all was fine. Interesting, but then Carla had a way of keeping tension in the air, certainly with me, which had a regrettable spin-off affect toward the children.

We were having a great time on the playground, on the swing set, the little merry-go-round, and the bars. Little Katie is laughing and shouting and beside herself, and slips out with, "Daddy, we met mommy's friend, Billy."

"Oh? When was that, Katie?" I'm stunned, but nothing really surprises me anymore with Carla.

Kyle chips in with, "When you were gone last week. He's kind of a weird guy, and I didn't like him. There was a strange smell in the house."

"Okay," I tell them. I didn't want nor need to extract more information from them. Save it for Carla.

When Carla returned and the kids were playing in the basement, I confronted her. I was not happy at all that Billy had been in my house, unbeknownst to me.

"The kids shared with me that Billy visited while I was away." The ulterior motive?

Caught off-guard, she automatically let fly with, "Damn them! I told them ...," and she caught herself and abruptly stopped.

"Yes. I'm sure you told them not to say anything about the visit, but they're just kids, Carla, and don't know better. So, tell me all about it." I remained calm for obvious reasons.

Put on the defensive, which is certainly rare, she stammered,

"I don't think I need to tell you any more than Billy was in the house for a couple of days."

"No? That's all you feel you need to say? No explanation as to how or why a convicted felon was in my house and with my children and I was not made aware of it? Really, Carla?" I was getting a little hot.

"What's there to explain? I was talking to him on the phone after you went off to get drunk with your IU buddies and invited him to stay here. What's wrong with that?"

"There's plenty wrong with it, don't you see? He's the last person I want to have in my house. I don't even know him. Two convictions. Prison time. He's a loser, and should not have been around Kyle and Katie. We were upfront with one another about my getting up with my friends for the Derby. I find out about your little maneuver done behind my back from Katie. Don't you think there is something wrong with that?"

"Bullshit. If I want to invite him to my house I can and will do so. He's a new person and is okay around the kids. They're safe." Engine revving big time.

"Wrong. I'll say when it's okay for him to be in my house. So until then, he's not welcome back."

"You sonofabitch. You can't do that," she screams.

"Try me. I'll call the police. I'm sure they'll understand my complaint."

She knew she was wrong, and stopped putting up a fight. But she had a long memory.

"Oh, by the way, Carla, where did he sleep when he was here? I hope to God not my bed, if you know what I mean." It felt good to suggest infidelity to her after all her false accusations to me and to put the proverbial shoe on the other foot.

"In the guest bedroom," was all she said. Of course, I would never know if she was lying.

"Wonderful. I hope you had a nice visit. Gee, if I didn't know better, I'd swear I detect a bit of a pot residue odor in the air. Does he have a job these days?"

"No. No one will hire a convicted felon. He's living with his parents and hoping he can get work with his father."

"Oh, so he came up here to sponge off you. I can see it now. Next time I have a business trip, he'll probably get his butt up here. I don't want that to happen, Carla. He's not invited back."

She looked at me with dagger eyes. In a different scenario, her attacking me, I have no doubt I would have "pulled an adios" and headed to a hotel for the night. "I'm going to visit Janice. Bye." And she was out the front door before I could respond or wish her a pleasant visit.

I couldn't believe it. That worthless shithead was in my house. Damn. With all the bullshit she's thrown at me, she pulls a stunt like that. Idiot.

Carla had made new friends with a few of the ladies in the neighborhood, and spent many an hour visiting with them. Surprisingly, no arguments or flare-ups to that time.

That summer, when we were pretty much settled, my parents visited. Everything went fine until Carla made a derogatory comment and my mother, now more sensitized to the type of person Carla could be, gave it right back to her. Well, that was most unpleasant, as they exchanged words and Carla was over the top with her usual anger and vitriol. Carla headed to the bedroom, and my parents headed out to a nearby motel. Fortunately, Carla had made plans to leave the following day with a neighbor lady who was a sales rep and was attending a product show. So, Carla was gone for a few days, mom and dad returned to the house to spend time with the children, but all was not totally relaxed. Mom felt terrible about the emotional confrontation with Carla, and decided it best that she and dad depart early. Even with Carla the cougar gone from the house, the stench from her behavior remained ever-present. Once "bitten" by her, a victim does not easily recover or deal with it.

As you can imagine, Carla's return only refueled a fire that should have been extinguished.

The first words out of her mouth upon entering the house early that evening after the business tip were stinging. "So, did you defend me and tell your mother she was wrong?" she asked icily.

"No, I didn't, Carla, because I felt you were wrong in what you said to my mother."

"Oh, shit, you're not serious? You're sticking up for your mother? She deserved it."

"No, she did not. She was responding to your unkind remark, and you lost control. She's an older woman, Carla, and should not have been spoken to that way."

"You're full of crap, and you'll pay for this." She was screaming and throwing things in the kitchen, fortunately towels and unbreakable items.

It was ugly, and things got worse. I went to the bedroom to hit the rack and get away from her. I got into bed, and she lit into me again, yelling profanities, telling me to get out of bed and to sleep on the couch, while at the same time she was pulling one of her routine tricks by throwing all my clothes on the closet floor. To myself, I said, screw it, and made a bed on the sofa. That didn't work, as I was the victim of a new form of vengeance from this bitch. I was trying to go to sleep when from down the hall she came storming, lights up a cigarette, proceeds to yell at me, and to make things even more uncomfortable for me, decides she's going to punctuate the anger by blowing smoke in my face. My exhortations for her to knock off the cigarette smoke and yelling were to no avail. Since she did not have to go to work the next day, she could keep this up all night, so I told her I was getting a motel room for the night and was gone. By now, my monthly household budget included at least one motel night.

Over the next few months I spent a night or two with an IU buddy, Frank, who was now married but kind enough to let me sleep in a spare bedroom, which also saved me some money. I was always very apologetic to him, but he understood. Good guy.

I'm still opposed to seeing a lawyer to file for divorce. I don't want to go through that knothole, nor put the children through it. We need to remain together as a family even though their mother took pleasure in crashing me into the rocks of emotional upheaval and verbal, sometimes physical, domestic abuse. This was not a fun time in my life. Gone, in a different lifetime, were the single, carefree years when no one was beating up on me or tormenting me. Like an idiot, I hung in there. Again, divorce didn't happen in my family, aunts and uncles, grandparents, no one. I took each day a day at a time. Enjoyed the good days, and was battered on the bad days.

I got a break from her when my boss asked me to serve as the deputy officer-in-charge (OIC) of the United States Inter Service Cross Country team that was to compete against other international military teams in Khartoum, Sudan. The OIC was a really great guy, a Navy Captain assigned to the Naval Academy. Decked out in matching sports coats, the team flew from National Airport to New York, then on to Rome for a brief layover, proceeding to Athens, then on to Cairo. We stayed at a beautiful hotel by the airport where I joined the team for a jog around the area. The next day the OIC and I paid a diplomatic call on the United States Ambassador to Egypt, followed by a team excursion to the Giza pyramids and site of the Sphinx. Wow, what an exciting opportunity to see a different part of the world. But make no mistake, I saw an incredible amount of poverty as we traversed the Cairo streets. The next day we flew to Khartoum, staying at an old, elegant, turn of the century hotel, with large fans in the dining and lobby areas, like from "Casablanca". I went for a jog to the confluence of the White and Blue Nile rivers, and the OIC and I paid a call on the U.S. Ambassador. The OIC and I also joined the senior dignitaries from other countries for a visit to a Sudanese wedding and a get-together at the lovely home of a local businessman. Not surprisingly, alcohol was served.

On that trip, and like so many other business trips, I hated with a passion calling Carla back home to say Hi and to check on things. Always a total disaster. The kids were acting up, this neighbor did or said that, not so subtle reminders that I was on a business trip and she was left behind to manage things. Oh, goodness, get a grip, lady. It just got to be too much. Because of her rantings over the phone, I always felt immense relief to hang up and put her out of my mind for another day. I was good for a couple of days until the next call. Torture.

We did go on a trip together a few months later. A Navy east coast conference was being held in the Charleston, South Carolina, area. Carla was successful in getting her parents to take the kids for a few days, so we dropped them off in Norfolk and the next morning drove to Kiawah Island, where we had spent our wonderfully pleasurable honeymoon and had those unfortunate conversations about Billy, the wedding, and my friend Kathy who lived on the island. Our plan was to spend the night there, not in the same hotel we stayed in for our honeymoon, then drive back up to Charleston. Oh, the bad luck and timing! Here again, things in life happen at a good time or a bad time. This was bad timing of the first order. A hurricane was forming out in the Atlantic, and although it was still relatively far out to sea and not a major tropical storm, hotel guests were advised to vacate and head inland for safer lodging. So, we did it. We found a hotel off the island, and were comfortably in our hotel room when there was a lot of commotion, or noise, outside, like from people having a hurricane party. I opened the door to see what was going on and right there was face to face with my dear old friend, Kathy from Washington and Kiawah Island, and who was also eyeball to eyeball with, yes, Carla! Carla was stunned and speechless after I said to the young lady, "Hi, Kathy, what a surprise seeing you! Carla, this is Kathy, a friend of mine." Kathy responded with, "Hi, Dave. I was wondering why I had not heard from you in a long time." Ever the teaser, Kathy. Carla quickly connected the dots. I exchanged a few comments with Kathy, told her to enjoy their hurricane party, and the door was closed after a "goodbye". Holy shit. Can you believe it? I'll just leave it that Carla was not too thrilled with meeting my friend and let me know. A ruined night. The conference went great and I was desirous of more east coast director meetings. Good seeing many Navy colleagues, and my friends Pete, Jim and his wife, and Carla and I got a personal tour of one of the Navy destroyers homeported in Charleston by the ship's CO. Awesome.

It was a nice trip, with a mix of good and bad. We picked up the kids and returned home, but along the way Carla still gave me an earful about our Kiawah Island encounter with Kathy.

Deal me a new hand, please.

1977
CHAPTER THIRTEEN

My bedrock was my financial independence.

During this period in my life, the single life was still stroking me like Erika's warm oil massages in Honolulu. No relationships to hinder the good life, and the continued blessed official Navy travel required in my job. I was no longer living on "the rock", had a Porsche 914, and I could roam like very few. It was the rocker Alice Cooper that said, "No matter how old you get, you never lose the feeling that cars are freedom". I say that about no relationship, but I homed in on Kathy, the lovely southern belle I met in Boston that lived in Charlotte, which became an epicenter of my travels for the first half of the year.

After our staff semi-annual meeting in early January, I wasted no time in packing the Porsche with work materials and personal gear and driving to Charlotte to spend a night with Kathy en route to my assignments in Jacksonville, Florida, a hub of Navy presence. We had a fantastic weekend, which included a game of tennis and attending a double-A baseball game, but I had to wait until the conclusion of my six-week assignment before I had the pleasure of seeing her again. I completed my assignments in the Jacksonville area, at Naval Air Station Jacksonville, Naval Station Mayport, and Naval Air Station Cecil Field, including a late add-on assignment that took me on a one-day drive down and back south of Jacksonville to a small Navy installation called Pinecastle hidden away in the forests.

That second visit to Kathy was even better than the first visit. We went dancing Friday night, and drove to Southern Pines to see her family. Toured the Pinehurst golf course area, and had a fun, riotous dinner Saturday with her wonderful family. I wrote some verse to Kathy:

One Day Closer

Let us
Be patient
In separation
My love
For while the distance
In miles
Will be great
The distance in the heart
Will not.
Each day
Will be immersed
In thoughts of you
Each night entered
Knowing
The day completed
Brings us closer.

But, like all good things, it had to come to an end as I pushed off for my next assignment, which was absolutely incredible, for my work the next thirty days took me to Navy installations in the Caribbean located on Eleuthera, Grand Turk, Antigua, and Barbados. I missed Kathy, but oh, what a treat. A short walk from my lodging on the Eleuthera base was dynamite snorkeling in crystal clear waters revealing thousands of colorful fish. On Grand Turk, the base commanding officer and I went out snorkeling, letting the gentle waves work us toward shore in a coral head as we dove for conch shells to pile on a surfboard. The CO also arranged for me a chopper flight around the island where I got some great photos of the base. At the time, there were few motels and virtually no tourists. My Navy host on Antigua and his lovely wife took me bar-hopping and to a couple of the beach resorts, and I enjoyed my last night on Barbados by taking in all that my Bridgetown Hilton Hotel beach resort nearer the airport could offer. My lodging for the week had been a fabulous place on the beach near the base, called Cobblers Cove Hotel. The bungalow-style units were surrounded by palm trees and other lush vegetation. All through the assignment, I got plenty of Caribbean sun and my workouts in the humid, unfamiliar clime kept me perspiring for what seemed like hours. Jogging on all the islands on narrow two-lane roads was a bit challenging, however, but I managed to stay alive.

I flew out of Bridgetown, via San Juan, to Charlotte, where I was re-united with Kathy for a weekend and with my Porsche that she watched over for me. I drove to Orlando, where my Navy hostess invited me to a house party at her lakefront home for water-skiing and beer drinking with a group of wonderful strangers.

My next assignments were Pascagoula and Gulfport, Mississippi on the Gulf Coast, where my Pascagoula host took me out deep-sea fishing. We caught our dinner, and dropped anchor for a night on the water. Gulfport was a fun visit, for one of the younger staff members invited me for a day of beer drinking with his buddies and tubing behind a speed boat. A follow-on assignment in New Orleans was short, and I didn't get to Bourbon Street.

In May, I had driven back to Jacksonville and had made arrangements to pick Kathy up at the airport, whereupon we visited Disney World the next day en route to my two-week assignment in Key West. Nice. I was able to arrange lodging in VIP Quarters for the stay. Spending that much time with Kathy was something I wanted to replicate. We enjoyed a couple evenings with base staff for barbecues, and did the tourist thing on Duval Street. We also used the base swimming pool and hit the beaches. But I will say Key West proper did not have the greatest beaches.

My orders were modified for a return to the home base. A strange thing happened and caught me totally off guard as we drove to Charlotte. Kathy told me she no longer wanted to see me. There were tears, and I wasn't sure that was really what she wanted, that there was some other reason behind her decision. It may have been that she was giving serious thought to return to college, to attend graduate school in Michigan. Yikes. It was a melancholy, sorrowful, lonely drive for me back to Maryland. My Navy buddy, Pete, and his girlfriend, along with my IU friend in Washington, helped me get through the following week.

It became a short turnaround as I drove back to Mississippi via, yes, Charlotte. Kathy and I had talked, and I was welcomed back in her arms. I had another assignment in Gulfport, Mississippi, and New Orleans, where I had the pleasure of meeting and mentoring a new Field Rep, John, at both sites. Good guy, and we played some tennis together and occasionally had a few beers in the officer's quarters bar. Upon completing my work in New Orleans I drove all the way straight to Charlotte, arriving at Kathy's in the middle of the night. Wow, but it was worth the long drive.

The following three months were both good and bad from a

travel and assignment perspective. The good part was that I was traveling to Spain, Italy, Sicily, and London. The downside was the longest assignment was in Naples, Italy, which was definitely not my favorite place.

My first stop was at our Navy base in Spain. I flew Washington-Dulles to Madrid, caught the connecting flight to Seville, then a short flight to Herez. I had planned on taking a shuttle to the Navy base in Rota, but a couple of young officers asked me if I needed a ride. I quickly told them, "Yes", and they asked me to join them. With the gently rolling hills, I thought I was in the California foothills back home. Rota was a large installation with a nice Officer's Club where I spent a good deal of my free time in the evenings, and a decent golf course. Jogging was safe on the back roads of the base. My host had me out for dinner at his home on the beach near Puerto Santa Maria. The highlight of my non-work time was driving a rental car from the base down past Gibraltar, through the lovely resort town of the rich, Marbella, to a place called Fuengirola. But a funny thing happened at the base car rental agency when I was filling out the paperwork to rent the car. The local Spaniard working in the agency asked me for my international driver's license. Not thinking much about it, I pulled it out of my pocket and handed it to him. He gave me a concerned look, stating it was expired, but then grabbed his pen, changed the last year number on the document, and with a smile handed it back, saying, "You're okay." The drive through the countryside reminded me a lot of California, and I marveled at the beauty and quaintness of the villages built atop hills with their white-washed exteriors and red-tile roofs, all the villas looking so much alike. I stayed the night up the hill from Fuengirola at a lovely hotel in Mijas where I had the most spectacular view of the blue, sparkling Mediterranean far below me. Oh, what a sight. Thank you, Lord.

The cold beer on the bar terrace was extra special. That evening I drove down the hill and strolled the Fuengirola boardwalk.

Before I departed Rota, I drove over to nearby Cadiz, a lovely Spanish city, and wandered its streets and alleyways, eventually settling down at a local taverna with a cold beer and watching Spanish life carry on around me in the city center plaza.

And then, with a sorrowful wave goodbye to Spain, off to Naples on a Navy plane sitting with my back to the cockpit. Using Navy aircraft did help our office travel budget. Team player! Naples was a challenging assignment, so I stayed pretty close to the hotel and to the base, a reasonable walk away, during which I occasionally viewed "Humpty Dumpty", a well-known prostitute that yes, sat on a wall. I kid you not. Ran the streets of Naples, a bit polluted from diesel vehicle exhaust and with crazy Italian drivers. Did the tourist thing my final two weekends in "Napoli", taking a tour bus out to walk the Pompeii ruins, a fascinating and educational experience seeing very much what Roman life was like at that time of the volcanic eruption that buried the city, and taking a boat ride out into the Bay of Napoli to the lovely, enchanting Isle of Capri. It was quite obvious the island was a destination for the rich, with storefront windows citing retail locations in Paris, Beverly Hills, and New York. I walked the narrow streets and alleys, taking in sights of the surrounding Mediterranean when offered. While in Naples, my Italian host, who had driven us up the coast one day to Gaeta, the Sixth Fleet headquarters and homeport, to review that operation, invited me to a home-cooked Italian family-style meal with his wife, daughter, and her Navy officer husband. My American host took me to a local restaurant. And oddly enough, one night at the invitation of my hotel neighbor across the hall, I joined her and her children for a restaurant outing. It was a nice change, since most evenings I walked to the Navy base for dinner at one of the clubs. Six long weeks in Naples was enough, and I headed for Sicily.

The Navy base was in a somewhat rural area not far from Catania. In fact, there were two bases, a command and support headquarters at the air station, and a community support site with recreation and club facilities, shopping, schools and government housing. I stayed in the Bachelor Officers Quarters, made frequent use of the nearby Officer's Club, and jogged the safe streets off which the base housing was constructed in a large circle. The highlight of the two-week stay was the doubles tennis match I played against two junior officers on a clay court in Catania. My partner was the base clubs director, an American who had married a local Italian woman. We may have lost, but that was a disappointment short-lived, as we all attended a dinner party at the home of one of the junior officers where we dined on steaks and consumed a bit too much Amaretto. A quick excursion to the resort area of Taormina, sitting below Mount Etna, was a delight.

The other notable occurrence was my "Dear Jane" letter to Kathy sent from Sicily. I had accepted a different position in the Maryland office, one that required less travel, and I was anxious to settle down in a house of my own and enjoy the benefits of it. I didn't want a "relationship". So much for a long distance relationship, most of which do not work, anyway.

On my way home from Europe I had a two-day stopover to de-brief Navy staff in London. Oh, what a wonderful city. Didn't meet any women on this trip, but it reinforced my desire to remain single and continue traveling, albeit a little less. While in London, a fellow Field Rep also passing through to de-brief staff, Tom Jones, no, as he would say, "Not the singer", and I walked the city and took a tour bus excursion. I was also able to do some jogging in Hyde Park and environs. Tom and I thoroughly enjoyed the parks, Piccadilly Circus, Regent Street, and other interesting areas.

I returned to Maryland in time for the wedding of my Navy Field Rep buddy, Pete, and Karen, in the Naval Academy Chapel. Karen worked in the Naval Academy Officer's Club. Along with a couple other Navy friends, I was honored to be an usher. I had a great weekend in Annapolis, where I met Judy, a friend of Karen's who was a flight nurse in Miami. We had a fun evening dancing, and I did see her one other time when I visited Pete and Karen in Charleston, West Virginia, where Pete ran some bowling centers. He had flown Judy up for the weekend as a surprise to me, which it was!

My new job was in my current office building and took me to Jacksonville, Florida, Charleston, South Carolina, Seattle, Norfolk, Virginia (regrettably), San Diego, San Francisco, Pearl Harbor, and Japan, in other words, to Navy Fleet Concentration areas. My assignments in Charleston and Jacksonville afforded me the opportunity to take detours off I-95 and Highway 17 to run in to Kiawah Island to visit Kathy of the smooth skin and romantic ways. The other Kathy was a different matter – after leaving Kiawah Island on one particular stopover I mistakenly thought I could make a stop in Myrtle Beach to pay my respects to her family. They let me know in a phone call I was not welcome, so I pushed on to Wilmington, North Carolina for the night, where I had a great jog in that lovely city.

My travel was spread out enough that it gave me an opportunity to have at least a small measure of roots and enjoy southern Maryland and Washington, D.C. Even dated a couple young ladies that worked in the accounting office, both of which mitigated against lonely nights in rural Maryland.

Fortuitously, I had an assignment in San Francisco just prior to Christmas, so brother Dan drove down from Happy Valley in his 280Z, picked me up, and off we went to southern California. Spent a night with our great college buddy, Benny, in Santa Maria, where we picked up from where we left off in our college drinking days, then Dan and I drove to L.A. Saw our college friend, Jack, and his wife, and spent an afternoon walking around the Budweiser brewery and tropical grounds enjoying all the free beer samples. Earlier that day Dan and I got in a long line outside the studio that was filming "Laverne and Shirley" and were fortunate to gain entry. It was fascinating to watch how they filmed a live episode and the transformations on the stage. At the conclusion, rather than making the required exit left from the studio seating we made a quick right, found a passageway that lead to the backstage, and before we knew it we were elbow to elbow with the actors. What a hoot! We saw "Laverne" and "Shirley" on the far side of the area, and closer to us were "Lenny", "Squiggy" and "Carmine". I walked up to "Carmine", slapped him on the back, and said, "Good show, Carmine!" He was cool with it. We also spent a day at Disneyland, where we ran into a couple young ladies Dan knew in Happy Valley. It was a great way to finish off a super year of business travel and all the myriad accompanying delights of the single life.

Almost time to turn lights out.

1983

CHAPTER FOURTEEN

I got the hell out of the house as quickly and as quietly as I possibly could. Stealth. Little sound and certainly not lingering over anything. I was like a sandpiper scurrying on the beach to evade the onrushing water from a wave, legs moving fast. No extra cup of coffee. Not even going to the children's bedrooms to kiss them goodbye. And no way was I going to say, "Goodbye, dear, have a nice day, kiss my ass, love you," to the wife, that bitch, who was sleeping off another "eruption". It had been another one of those nights when she unleashed a torrent of her viciousness on me, making my life absolutely miserable, including throwing that evening's dinner out into the backyard, something she did more than once. Given a tall building, I think I would have jumped off. At least I wasn't relegated to a motel for the night. My wife, the instant, unpredictable volcano, Mount Vesuvius reincarnate, or Cyclops, the three storm demons representing thunder, lightning, thunderbolt, rolled into one human facsimile. Hot, molten lava spewing one moment and sweet, repentant, seemingly clueless of the monster unleashed by the cute little brunette the next, dormant until the next eruption.

I drove my car down to the bus stop at the shopping center near our house in Burke, parked it in the large parking lot that always offered empty spaces with no threat of being towed, and queued up with other half asleep commuters awaiting arrival of the Metro Bus for our sojourn into the city. I was not rested for another day at the office, hoping my productivity and attention to detail would not suffer unduly, and knew full well what lay ahead – falling asleep on the bus, lights out, hopefully not snoring or making some other innocuous sounds, dozing off despite the shake, rattle and roll, Elvis-style, lurching, swaying of the bus, head snapping up before it figuratively descended in my lap. And with my fellow riders of the morning witnessing the multiple, incessant head jerks. I guess it didn't bother me, because shortly out of a head jerk my chin again rested on my chest.

Into Arlington we arrived, actually a Metro hub in Ballston, marking the transfer point to another bus, queueing up again of course, or walking briskly to the giant escalator that took one down far into the bowels of the earth to catch a subway train that would ultimately put me at my destination, the office and retail complex of Rosslyn, just over the Potomac from quaint, forbidden Georgetown.

This morning I had transferred to another bus, and my stop was a couple of blocks up the street from my office building, an eight-story modern building that for the right people had views across the Potomac to the enchanting city. It also had underground parking for the same right people who had big bucks to spend on daily parking under cover, near an elevator exit. Nice. Anyway, I wasn't one of those. Mid-level government pukes took the Metro or, as I sometimes did, got an extremely early start to avoid the HOV tolls and search for a street parking space. The main problem

I had was that we had a lot of Marines in our building. Anyone knows that there is no such word as "early" in their lexicon or culture, and they snatched up a lot of the street parking, probably even before the sun rose out of the Eastern sky. Normally, I was lucky to find a spot less than a mile from the office. No kidding. City life. It was called a crapshoot and a long ass walk to the office.

The early morning was gray and cold, overcast, but it was that seamless, steady dull gray without any cloud definition, no cumulus stuff going on, and no wind. I liked that low-hung cloud cover. For some reason, it always pushed me gently into a nostalgic, melancholy state of mind. It was soothing and enveloped my torn psyche like a blanket. Maybe it was because it reminded me of similar weather during my many visits to Nathan's in Georgetown in my single days and that reflective moment on the bridge over the River Liffey in Dublin.

I longingly observed the many older apartment buildings lining Wilson Boulevard and other nearby streets. Nothing fancy. Stucco or brick exteriors, maybe three or four levels. At any other time, to a person enjoying all that life had to offer, they were simply apartment buildings. No big deal. But right now, after another night of Carla's highly charged, 340 HP myriad false accusations, they were much more. They spoke to me of a different time in the kaleidoscope of my life, of freedom lost, of a much-needed change of venue from the house, not a home, that I shared with my wife, Carla, and our two small children. The apartment buildings represented freedom, like viewing West Berlin from the East Berlin side of the Wall. I wanted to live in one of them, alone. Silence. No one to bother me. I so much needed that respite, a break from a woman that surely had to be bipolar, a woman that cared not for my emotional well-being, that viewed our marriage and life as an opportunity to taunt, create chaos, bring fear, and for me, to return to a carefree life sans lunatic wife. Further down the street, I saw the Key Bridge. It, too, was not unlike the Berlin Wall, preventing me from crossing over that bridge, as I had done countless times in the past, to that casual, eclectic tavern called Nathan's, at the corner of M Street and Wisconsin. There, I often hung out by myself, taking in the dull cacophony of people having a good time, and sometimes even having nice conversation with a young lady.

The bus trip home from the office that day was not unlike other bus trips – head jerks all the way to the parking lot where I miraculously realized I had arrived at my destination and alighted from the bus. And, of course, I was met by smiling, cheerful Carla, unrepentant, unaware of the damage she did the previous night.

That next weekend I walked into the family room and kitchen area after having completed some chores outside, when I caught Carla's side of a phone conversation she was obviously having with her older brother, Jim, a nice guy that I liked being around and always looked forward to seeing when and if he was at their parent's house when we visited or at Thanksgiving and Christmas events. A good person. Friendly demeanor and even keeled. Married, and had a couple small children of his own. Jim had attended William and Mary College and was an accountant at a large CPA firm in downtown Norfolk.

Carla was telling Jim, in somewhat raised voice, no surprise, which suggested the conversation had recently started and was building to the requisite crescendo, "I don't care what you or your wife think, I want that hutch in the living room." Silence while Jim was trying to respond. "And I want their bedroom suite. You can have the other furniture, Jim." More silence. It was telling and to his credit that, standing near Carla, I could not hear Jim. I'll bet that wasn't the case at his end if his wife was standing near him. "I don't care that they're still relatively young and that we don't need to have this conversation. I want you to know now what possessions of theirs I want when they do pass away. You got that? And I'm sure I'll think of some other things and will let you know." Holy shit, I'm thinking to myself, I'm now seeing a greedy, pushy side of my wife, ready to push around her own brother in her quest to claim possession of family property that will hopefully be in that house for years, decades to come. More crap I'm learning about her. "Goodbye!" she yelled, and hung up the phone almost tearing the phone receptacle from the wall.

"That didn't sound too pleasant," I quietly suggested to her.

"It's none of your business what I want of mom and dads' when they die," she replied, still wound up and now ready to launch into me.

I took the high road, as I suspect Jim had done, and dropped the conversation, heading back outside to the quiet of the backyard, finding anything I could do to keep from being in the house at the moment.

Life goes on in the Pedersen household, where it's often the calm before the storm, or volcanic eruption, or a "second goose". Some evenings dining out were enjoyable, while some evolved into a calm discussion of divorce. Oddly, no anger, rancor, eruptions, just polite talk about divorce but living together. Insane.

I walked into the kitchen one evening after work and got both barrels. I tried to explain that my bus ran late. They do that sometimes. Buses are funny things, where often a schedule means naught, especially in the winter with snow flying around. But she would hear none of it.

"You sonofabitch! Where have you been?" Already ramped up. Dale Earnhardt pedal to the metal.

"Commuting home from my job, Carla. The buses ran late, something I couldn't help or avoid, okay? Buses don't always run on schedule. " Crazy.

"I don't believe you. You probably took Sharon to a motel and fucked her." Sharon was an attractive woman that worked in my office. Carla had seen and met all of the ladies in my office at our annual office Christmas parties.

"Knock it off, Carla. Dammit, you know I wouldn't do that. Can you please stop these stupid, senseless accusations?"

Oh, I did it. She hated the word "stupid" and any suggestion of it toward her. And I knew why she went livid with that term. The next thing I know, she's taken the pot of cooked, drained spaghetti noodles and thrown it in my face. The children are sitting at the kitchen table watching all this. Lovely. I cannot believe they have to observe this kind of ranting. Shame on us for subjecting them to it. Well, more like shame on Carla for causing this mess and for failing to understand what she's doing to destroy this family.

"Shit!" I yelled, an automatic reflex action from the surprise face full of spaghetti from my wife. "Damn you, Carla. This is crazy."

This doesn't stop her. Over to the kitchen table she walks, looking at the children, and then has the audacity to say to these small, innocent kids, "Your daddy fucks other women. He fucked a Taiwanese woman!" She's lost it. Totally out of control. What she needs is a fist in her face to put her lights out and shut her up, for nothing else works. But of course, the last thing I would ever do is strike a woman. This one needs some form of straight jacket to slow her down.

I lose it. "You bitch", I tell her in a stern voice. "You are too much, Carla. Just leave us alone." Surprisingly, she turns on her heels and goes to the bedroom. There, she will most likely lay down on the bed, fall asleep, and wake up in the morning with no recollection of what she just did and said. She fortunately does not make matters worse by continuing her tantrum and ultimately telling me to leave the house for the night. She senses, somehow, that she's already done enough damage.

After I put the kids to bed I sat in the den and reflected on some stuff. When I wanted to torture myself, I reflected on some of the other women I dated, especially those to whom I was engaged. I thought of lovely, fun Debbie, but that was moot because it was her that broke off our engagement. Not much I could have done in that relationship. Then there was Carol in Hawaii. I think she would have been a good wife, with a good demeanor, but neither of us was ready for marriage and it was just as well that I broke things off. None of the three ladies I dated while on that long assignment in Washington, D.C., were marriage material. Not for me, anyway. And then there was Kathy in Charlotte. I wonder what could have been. She had been previously married, and if we let time take its course and allow the relationship to evolve, geography considerations notwithstanding, it might have worked out. She was sweet and truly a southern belle. I didn't know her or date her long enough to assess her true personality, but I really think that she would have been a great partner and was not a "screamer", or at least I don't think she had those tendencies. She had a quiet, calm demeanor that made it comfortable and relaxing to be around her. And, she had professional career aspirations. That was a plus.

Yes, that was torture of the first order, comparing some of my lady friends to Carla the cougar. What a stark contrast. And to think I was stuck with Carla. I went to bed.

I decided to go to the library that weekend to review some medical texts to learn about bipolar disorder, or by whatever other name from which she might suffer. Is there something that has more recently affected her? Has she always been like this, obviously a personality, or medical trait totally unbeknownst to me, that I did not see before we were married? I decide not to call her parents to discuss this matter and ask questions. First, it would probably get back to her somehow and I will be put through the danger zone of another tantrum. Second, my guess is they experienced this sort of behavior, dealt with it best they could, and opted out of saying anything to me. It also might upset them. Again, I reflect on her father's smile of relief when we left for our honeymoon and I physically removed this albatross from their lives.

From my research, I'm beginning to think she suffers from bipolar disorder. Her antics in the kitchen are akin to bouncing off walls, followed by the stupor. Her mood swings seem obvious. But then, I'm not a doctor. Hell, for all I know she is a sociopath, not knowing right from wrong. Will she agree to see a doctor? I need to ask. She rather displays the normal bipolar signs of feeling on top of the world one minute, and feeling in the pits the next, which she takes out on me. Although I could be wrong about that, for there could be variations. For all I know, maybe she felt on top of the world just prior to her eruptions. There could be something else triggering her behavior. I resign myself to continue studying bipolar symptoms. In my reading, I came across some interesting stuff about domestic violence. Not much had been written on it, and possibly because it either wasn't that prevalent or because it wasn't discussed in public, probably the latter. People did not like talking about it.

I learn that domestic violence is not just physical abuse, that it can be verbal and sexual abuse, threats, intimidation, property destruction, and so on. Women are not the only victims. More and more men are victims, some having suffered from severe physical violence. It is a learned behavior. Abusers carefully control their actions, choosing who and when to abuse. I'm not so sure she consciously decides when she will abuse me. It seems more spontaneous, which is why I keep referring to it as a volcanic eruption, sometimes starting with her emotional engine idling until she takes it to the max with 340 horsepower. There is definitely a "Dr. Jekyll and Mr. Hyde" personality at play, for

I have so often seen her calm, erupt, and reverse to calm and contrition or lack of knowledge about what she has done. What was incredibly interesting was the "myth" that if the victim doesn't leave, the situation must be tolerable. Oh, boy! Do I deem it tolerable? Largely, no. As I have said, things go along well for a time, then something snaps and she loses it. It's no fun being on the receiving end of her accusations and venom. It hurts, it stings, and it sucks. So, if I am only moderately tolerating her behavior, why am I sticking around? I've already said no one in my family went through a divorce, so it seems anathema to me. I don't want a divorce. So, I deal with "it". And there's the children, God bless them. I want to keep the family intact, but I also know in some cases it is best that divorce happens so as to protect the children from seeing, hearing, experiencing the negative behavior of their mother. If I'm gone, she has no one to bitch at. Hold that thought, because it's not a truism. Anyway, the research I read suggests that the myth about tolerating is destructive because it diminishes the severity of the abuse and implies the victim must be comfortable with it. I'm not, but no divorce. Just a thought - - if I'm not there, do the children receive the brunt of her negative behavior, do they become the victims of domestic violence, or abuse?

One night shortly thereafter, with the kids in bed, I bring up the topic of her abusive behavior.

"Carla, we need to talk about the behavior you unleash on me. It concerns me and I feel it is inappropriate and uncalled for. I can't begin to describe how it makes me feel." I'm using the tack learned from the counselor when we had our first and only joint session that, as you will recall, blew up in my face, literally.

"Sure. But you bring it out of me."

"I what? How?"

"You often ignore me. Like I'm not around. And we don't have sex as much as we used to."

"Oh, boy. I'm sorry if it seems I ignore you, but we're together and around one another every night and pretty much all weekend. Sure, I'm sometimes reading, and if I'm watching TV you are normally doing so, too." I don't respond to the sex part. We still make love from time to time, but no, not as often as in the early years. That was before the demands of two children and now longer work days for me with a longer commute. What I don't want to tell her is that my reduced desire for lovemaking is somewhat attributed to the emotional trauma missiles she has launched at me and my lack of desire because of that. The feeling is not the same. Something has been lost, and it manifests itself in lower sexual appetite towards her.

"The other thing is, I'm here alone all day with the kids. You're at work, with adults you can talk to and be with. I'm talking to two small children. But you wanted these children quickly, even though I was still very young. It's your fault. We should have waited longer to have children."

I was expecting that. What she said was basically a true statement. "Okay. I see your point. But I didn't want kids too late in my life when I couldn't be active with them in sports and such."

"Still, we should have waited. I think the emotional outbursts are due to post-partum syndrome. Having gone through two pregnancies and having two children to take care of is challenging, and something chemically or mentally causes me to lose it." This is a new one to me, and I don't know how to respond.

"Well, we need to do something. How about I call some day care providers to see if they have openings for maybe two or three days a week. We can take turns dropping them off and picking them up."

"That would help," she replies. "That way, too, I can spend some time with my neighbor friends up the street. I love you, Dave."

"I love you, too." Uh, huh. "The other possibility is you returning to work and us finding full day child care."

"No. I do not want to do that. I need to be with the children and not let someone else be their parent five days a week."

I found a KinderCare with some openings not too far from where we lived, so it was convenient for me to drop the kids off and continue on to the office on days I drove to work, and pick them up on my way home. Other days, Carla got them to and from day care. She was able to spend time with her friends, which helped her feel better. Along the way, she learned of and told me that one of the ladies, Fran, was cheating on her husband with the landscape contractor. Oh, geez. I didn't need to hear that, nor did I really care, for it was their personal business.

The bell tolls for marriage demise.

1983

CHAPTER FIFTEEN

Dave was at the office and would not be getting home earlier than the normal five-thirty to six o'clock. Carla could be certain of that, for he never got home early. And he would be picking up the children from KinderCare.

She was sitting at her make-up counter in the bathroom, putting on lipstick, eye shadow, all that stuff to help her look pretty.

Her neighbor friend, Fran, had called earlier that morning in a good mood. Her husband was on a business trip and she wanted to have some fun. Carla had an idea to what she referred, for she knew Fran was fooling around with their landscape guy, as Fran went on to describe how this would be different. Carla was initially apprehensive, but with a little prodding from Fran had agreed to participate.

As Carla got herself ready for this little adventure that Fran had proposed, she gave the matter some more thought. Was it okay to do this? Of course it was! She was certain that Dave was fucking one of the ladies in his office. At noontime no less. He vehemently denied it, citing he didn't have the time nor money to do something like that, emphatically denying he would ever even think of doing such a thing. Right, Carla thought. I don't believe him. She decided against a bra and panties and put on a sexy dress. The more she thought about it, the more excited she got. She could already feel it down there, the tingling sensation, and she had convinced herself it was okay to join Fran. If she felt good about it, it was okay. It wasn't wrong. At least that is how she rationalized it.

She was ready. Out of the house and up the street to Fran's house she walked. She wasn't worried about being seen by her neighbors, for most everyone was working, but she could just be visiting a friend.

Carla rang the doorbell, and moments later Fran opened the door to her with a big smile.

"Hi, Carla. Come on in. It's time to party!"

"Hi, Fran." Carla could tell Fran had been smoking pot, and she could probably use some herself. Fran read her mind and offered her a hit. "Ooh, that's nice."

"Let's go meet my friend. He's out back."

"Okay." As they walked outside into the backyard Fran offered Carla another hit. Carla's slight apprehension was lifting like the fog in San Francisco. She felt emboldened.

The ladies soon discovered that Fran's friend was already in the pool. He gave them a big smile as they approached.

"Carla, this is Stan. Stan, this is Carla. There!"

"Hi, Stan. I'm pleased to meet you," she said with what she thought was a sexy smile.

"The pleasure is all mine, Carla." He had a deep, smooth voice.

"Stan has many talents, so I prefer to call him Stan the handyman," Fran giggled. They all got a good laugh out of that, and Carla was starting to feel more relaxed. She tried not to stare at Stan. He had rugged good looks, short, curly dark hair, and broad shoulders accented by a good tan. Well, that's all she could see of him as he stood in the shallow end of the pool. She observed, too, that he was not wearing a swimsuit. Oh, my, this is going to get interesting, she said to herself.

Since Stan was naked in the pool, Fran made the next move. "I don't know about you, Carla, but I'm getting out of these clothes and jumping in the pool!" With that, she pulled her dress over her head, shed her bra and undies, and screamed as she jumped into the pool.

Carla was ready, too. The pot had her feeling mellow already. Off came the dress, and into the pool she jumped.

"Oh, Carla," Fran shrieked, "you go, girl! You are ready, honey!"

And they all were. Stan got an eyeful of two lithesome bodies cavorting in the pool, splashing and giggling. They frolicked in the pool, some touching here, a little more there, exploring bodies and boundaries, of which there wasn't much of the latter.

After a while they helped one another towel off as they passed around a joint. No one was feeling any pain. They adjourned to the bedroom, where they all became "handy", continuing to explore one another's bodies with different positions.

Two hours later, all quite satiated and exhausted, they got dressed and Stan headed for the front door to depart and hop in his company work truck to head back to the office. Fran told Stan, "Don't forget to put your entire time here on the billing worksheet."

"I won't Fran. See you tomorrow as I try to finish up your project." He laughed as he headed out.

"Oh, my, that was fun," Fran exclaimed. "I could do that again. How about you, Carla?"

"Yes, that was quite an experience, but I think I'll wait a while before I do it again."

They finished off a joint and Carla walked home. She had a few hours to kill before Dave returned home with the children, so she decided to take a short nap. Maybe because of her buzz from the pot, or maybe because that's how she was, she still didn't feel bad about participating in the threesome. Under the circumstances, it wasn't wrong. Dave will never find out, anyway, and that's what he gets for screwing the lady in his office. All is status quo, although she had to admit she had no proof he was fooling around, but she felt he was, so that's all that matters. So it's all his fault, she reasoned.

Carla dipped her toes in adultery.

1977/1978

CHAPTER SIXTEEN

I enjoyed my house in southern Maryland and the fact that I was not on the Field Rep road ninety percent of the year. I lived next door to a super couple that had me over for dinner on a frequent basis. Rick was a Navy Criminal Investigative Service Agent on the Navy base, and his wife was a very sweet lady. They were a very religious couple, and well-grounded. They probably viewed me as a "project", and we sometimes did get into religious discussions.

It felt wonderful to have some roots and a place I could call home. My weekend routine was to sleep in a little later, go for a long jog or do some pushups, and let the day come to me. My jogs took me down less travelled two-lane roads and on a dirt path that lead to the Chesapeake Bay shoreline. The only glitch with the dirt path was an occasional battle with horse flies. On rare occasions I had to jog in the snow, but that was not a problem. Being in southern Maryland also allowed me to frequently visit my "Dad" when he was off the road. He and his wife, Norma, were such hospitable friends. We joked about the time I was house-sitting for them and had the additional duty of taking care of their youngest son, Bobby, who was occasionally a handful. In fact, I was so busy in my new home that I didn't even own a TV. Reading, writing verse, visiting friends, not to mention work and the business travel, kept me very well occupied. I had no girlfriends at the time, so I would often drive south into the more rural areas and hang out at some redneck bars, sometimes sitting outside on the stoop watching the lovely sunset over the woods bordering the Patuxent River. If I didn't hit a rural bar, I went into town to try my luck meeting ladies at the very few bars there, like at a Holiday Inn downtown. Normally, there wasn't much action, for Pax River was a small place and single ladies did not abound in large numbers, or go out to the Holiday Inn to meet guys.

When spring hit I put a beach chair in the Porsche, put a few beers in a cooler, and drove down Route 235 to Point Lookout State Park where I parked my butt on a beach chair in the late afternoon sun and slowly consumed beers while reveling in the picturesque, peaceful beauty of the Potomac River. It was so relaxing that I had great difficulty leaving to return home. So peaceful and tranquil, especially after a few beers.

On weekends I often drove to the city to spend time with my IU friend, Wally, and we would do some bar-hopping in Georgetown and in the financial district. Wally and a girlfriend had also exposed me to Old Anglers Inn and the canal area out past Potomac Village. Visits to the city were remarkably enjoyable, and I gathered many wonderful memories of single life in Washington, D.C., not to mention rural southern Maryland with its redneck bars and miles of two-lane country roads through dense forest land bordered by large bodies of water.

I say this because in that late spring of 1978, about the same time I was recruited to a headquarters job in the city, I met this cute little brunette that in so many ways ended up turning my life upside down.

My new job was in Rosslyn, across the Key Bridge from Georgetown, and that is where I was fortunate to get an apartment through my IU buddy, Wally. One of my first dates was with a stewardess that a visiting Happy Valley College friend and I met while bar hopping in Georgetown. Shelly was home-based in Atlanta, was the daughter of a Navy four-star admiral, and had occasional layovers in Washington. We saw one another a few times, but it fizzled out. I dated a number of other girls I met in the city, and my dating life was quite satisfactory.

On a gorgeous fall day, I decided to drive the Porsche out through the high-rent Mcmansions area around Potomac Village and make a stop at Old Anglers Inn. The leaves were in full color mode, and the sky was a cloudless Carolina blue. I sat outside with a cold beer and engaged in my nostalgic, adult version Peter Pan syndrome reflections, a microcosm of the single life, a deliciously lived part of my life to that point.

My four years at Happy Valley College were the best four years of my life, with many wonderful lifetime friends. It was also when I met lovely, fun Debbie.

That was followed largely by active duty Army service, doing my duty, driven by the emotionally gut-wrenching death in Vietnam of my Army Basic Training Drill Instructor, Drill Sergeant Woolford, the true patriot who unfortunately paid the ultimate price.

Graduate school at Indiana University followed, and the three semesters there took a real close second to the best years in my life. The Big Ten with its big-time sports. Attending a world-renowned large university. Being immersed in the Midwest culture. And the camaraderie of a neat bunch of guys, the Brew Crew.

I had been blessed with an amazing amount of Navy official

travel in the United States and living in paradise, Hawaii, my "Shangri La". My overseas travel took me across the Pacific to Japan and Taiwan, and out the Aleutian chain. Travel across the Atlantic included Italy, Spain, Sicily, England, Scotland, Iceland, Ireland, and Canada. It took me into the Caribbean island-hopping to Navy sites in Eleuthera, Grand Turk, Antigua, Barbados, and even Cuba. And all along the way, so many Navy friends and women I met. All told, the people were so special.

If there is such a thing as living a "perfect life", that was it, the first five years of my Navy career. I couldn't possibly have asked for nor dialed up a better one. I was truly blessed to live and enjoy the single life I had been offered.

Wonderful reflections of an enchanting life.

And then there was Carla, the cute little brunette that entered my life. It had all started in Norfolk, Virginia, when I contacted a Navy colleague and he and his wife asked if I was interested in a blind date. While I was still dating in Washington, I started seeing more of Carla, so it turned out that my getting an apartment in Georgetown to settle down and enjoy the many benefits of living in the city might be short-lived.

The cute little brunette was becoming my steady girlfriend. There isn't really much else to say about the courting and dating. Nothing unusual or noteworthy. The relationship simply "developed" as the year 1978 wound down.

Great life reflections before the fall.

1984

CHAPTER SEVENTEEN

We were spending a weekend with her parents, and her brother Jim and his wife and family had come to the house. Carla was chatting with her mother and Jim's wife in the den, so Jim and I excused ourselves, grabbed a cold one, and went outside to relax and talk on the back deck. Jim and I didn't communicate very often. I really had no reason to call him, and vice versa. I liked him. He was civil, friendly, non-argumentative, and just an overall good person. He and Carla could not have had the same parents or DNA, could they? The conversation would be quite enlightening.

A few sips of beer to relax and loosen the tongue, and I said, "You know, Jim, I heard the tail end of that phone conversation between you and your sister about your parent's property and assets. I know it is none of my business, but I do feel your pain, believe me."

"Oh, yeah, that. Wow. Out of nowhere. It was not fun."

"I don't imagine it was."

"The good thing was, once she hung up and our life returned

to normal my wife and I had a good laugh over it. I mean, come on, sister, do we really need to talk about that sort of thing? Do you really need to get so obsessed with it? She was like this attack dog or a bulldog with lockjaw!" He chuckled.

Those comments told me a lot about Jim. He definitely was not like his sister. "Oh, man, I know what you mean. You're fortunate to live two-hundred miles away from her. I'm under the same roof."

"I pity you, Dave. I honestly do. She can be like a wildcat on steroids at times, and docile the next."

"Thanks, Jim. Can I share some thoughts with you? They may not be pleasant to hear."

"Certainly. I don't think much of it will come as any surprise, but please, I'd like to hear what you have to say about dear 'ol Carla."

"She is incredibly difficult to live with. She can be loving and fun one moment, feeling on top of the world, and can be this vicious, attacking cougar, or suddenly erupting volcano spewing hot lava the next, pick your analogy."

"I've experienced it, trust me."

"And after she unleashes with her venom, and calms down, it's like she is unaware of her behavior or the mayhem she had just created, and she'll wander off to go rest or sleep."

"I witnessed that behavior in our house when we were growing up. She would truly go bonkers about something, wanting her way, and just flip out. I mean, to the floor, where she would scream and yell, at least until dad heard it and would come rushing to the scene to yank her off the floor and physically restrain her. It was not pretty."

"Would she act that way toward both your parents?"

"Heavens, no. Normally just to mom, who I honestly believe

was afraid of Carla as Carla got older. She definitely had a way about her when it came to getting what she wanted."

"That's Carla. That's essentially what I live and deal with, except for the hitting the floor. She hits me instead."

"She could be intimidating, and scary, which really troubled my mom. Mom worked part time, so she was frequently at home. Dad was often at work, so he didn't see all of it."

"You know, she uses different tactics now. I know I shouldn't be telling or burdening you with this, but this beer has loosened my tongue and I want you to know what I'm dealing with if you don't mind."

"Go ahead."

"It's the screaming and yelling. It's the false, baseless accusations, being relegated to the den couch to sleep, the cigarette smoke in the face when I'm trying to get some sleep, and the now more frequent relegated to a nearby motel to get away from her insanity. It's crazy."

"Damn, that's a boatload of issues."

"Plus throwing spaghetti in my face and using profanity as she tells the children false information about me. I'm sure one of these days she will pull a knife on me and threaten me with it to get my attention or scare the crap out of me." I was on a roll and couldn't stop.

"That's ridiculous. How the hell do you put up with it, Dave? Why do you put up with it is the bigger question?"

"I don't know. The verbal assaults are rough enough. The fist pummeling is another matter. I want to strike out at her, but I can't nor won't do that. I do my best to tolerate her Jekyll and Hyde personality. We tried counseling, but that failed. I don't want to file for divorce for a number of reasons. I just try to take the bad days with the good, and hope the latter outnumber the former. I haven't called the police. I may have to, but that will create a new set of problems. There's no easy answer."

"I couldn't deal with that. I saw some of it, but was not part of it, if you know what I mean. I know mom and dad talked about it, and they may have seen a medical doctor, because I remember some discussion about bipolar disorder. But they knew something was not right. Problem was, I doubt Carla would have agreed to any treatment. She always thought she was right and was okay, and she may have talked her way out of treatment, providing some assurances she would do better."

"So, maybe bipolar? I thought about that, and as you inferred, when I broached it with her, she blew it off and said she was experiencing the results of post-partum abnormalities and that it was temporary."

"Right. Not temporary, I'm afraid. There's something else, and she's not going to change. I really have as little to do with her as possible. It seems like we always end up arguing about something. It doesn't take much to set her off. She has to be right, be in control, manage things. It's useless to talk to her in a logical manner. I avoid her."

"Yep. You know, I remember the look on your father's face as Carla and I left the wedding reception to go on our honeymoon. He had the biggest smile on his face. Just beaming."

"No doubt about it. He was a new person after she married. Much more relaxed. Quieter house. And mom's blood pressure went down. You were very observant."

My suspicions were confirmed. The family knew Carla had issues, not that they did much about it, but they passed me some "damaged goods", gave me their problem. Never mentioned it to me. How about that? They had a strong suspicion that their cute little brunette daughter may have been afflicted with bipolar disorder, the condition that transported people between highs and lows, with disastrous behavior emanating during the lows. Post-partum my ass, and good luck on my convincing Carla she needed medical attention. Well, at least I now knew what I was dealing with. Wouldn't necessarily make it any easier, but when her emotional engine was akin to the start of a NASCAR race, when the celebrity announcer yells, "Drivers, start your engines", I knew what the hell was coming. Unfortunately, I could not get out of the way, for I was part of her tantrum.

"Lucky me. Changing subject, the other thing that has more frequently raised its ugly head is your old neighbor, Billy."

"Oh, yes, lucky you," he chuckled. "Billy the outlaw. What a piece of work."

"Do you know him very well?"

"Thankfully, no. He was younger, Carla's age group, so I didn't hang around with him. He's quite a mess. The misdemeanor and the felony conviction. Prison time. And now not much of a future. You know what they say about recidivism. He's a good candidate."

"I went away for a few days, and found out from the kids that he had visited and they stunk up the house with pot smoking. Carla, I'm sure."

"Oh, no. Not good, Dave."

"Yeah. And Carla wasn't too thrilled when I told her he was not welcome back into the house. The only good thing was I caught her off guard, so she didn't get violent. She saves that for when she's beating up on me."

"Sounds like it."

"And she told me that when she made trips to the prison to visit him she was giving him money."

"Damn."

"I put a stop to that, too. She's really been full of surprises, Jim. A real handful. So, were they real close friends?"

"I would say so, although I had gone away to college and was not around as much during their late teen years. I know I probably shouldn't tell you this, but in the spirit of honesty and knowing what you're going through, I found out that my mom caught them in bed together one time. Holy cow. That must have been a scene. She said my father really laid into her when he heard about it. I think he wanted to kick her out of the house, but where would she have gone? Plus, she was still in school, and mom wouldn't hear of kicking her out."

"Nice. So our little visitor had a fling with my wife when they were in high-school. Neat. Well, that certainly reaffirms why I don't want to see him in my house again. Do you know what he's doing now?"

"Well, my parents and his parents are very close and socialize on a regular basis. I'm told that he's working for his father in construction, but also that he's taken up with some of his unsavory friends. I'm sure he's heading back to trouble eventually, especially since he's on probation."

"You're probably right. Well, before we go back inside to the ladies, since I'm sure Carla is wondering what we've been talking about all this time, I have to tell you about a story I recently read about a pro golfer. He had finished the third round of a pro tournament and had done poorly. The poor guy returns to his lodging where his mother, wife and children were staying, and the wife, who had been drinking, gets into him about his poor performance that day. She yelled and screamed at him, berated him, told him he was a loser and a pussy, and threatened to leave him and take the kids. I guess the mother got involved, and the ensuing altercation, which from what the golfer said is a frequent occurrence, ended up with the wife physically assaulting the mother and the husband! Both had blood on their clothes. The police were called, and they charged the wife with domestic battery. They also charged her with resisting arrest because she did everything possible to prevent the police from putting her in a squad car, and once in it, apparently damaged it. And all this stuff was in front of the children. And the golfer made a statement that he felt the judicial system would address it and that his wife should be cleared."

"Hmmm. Too close to home, yes?"

"My thoughts exactly. A lunatic wife, engaging in domestic assault, berating her husband, doing so in front of the children, and the husband seems to at least tolerate, if not minimalize, the behavior and altercations. That sounds too familiar."

"Yes, it does, from what you've told me."

"And from what you've told me, I don't trust Billy."

"Don't. I'll keep you posted if I hear anything of interest."

"Let's go and see the ladies."

With that, we walked into the den where everyone was congregated.

"Hi," Carla says. "You guys were out there a long time. Just chatting up a storm, huh?" She meant for it to come out as a cute remark, but I could sense the sarcasm and biting tone as only I could.

"Yeah. Just chatting up a storm about our favorite sports teams and athletes, and who was to finish on top in college football. Benign stuff."

"Okay," Carla responds, but she's giving me one of her evil looks. She knows, and I will catch hell from her later.

To myself, I say, "Screw you, dearest."

From a line in a poem by the Irish poet, Robert Browning…

… on the dangerous edge of things.

1985
CHAPTER EIGHTEEN

In early summer that year I was to attend a Navy conference in Europe, where I would make a presentation while representing my boss. Reluctantly, but realizing it was the safe thing to do, I suggested that Carla join me in Spain before returning to the states. She was good with that, and excited.

I first flew to Sicily to make a courtesy call at the Navy base there. A short two-day visit. I recall two things about my time in Sicily – I had turned on the TV, was channel surfing, and what did I come across but an Italian game show that required the contestants to shed clothes when they lost a round of questions, all the way to their underwear! That was it, no other clothes. I was glued to the tube. It got my attention so I watched it all the way through. The second thing, and no surprise, was when I called Carla to tell her I arrived okay. She was in a bitchy mood and the call sucked, as usual. No sex talk or I miss you, none of that. Damn, how I hated calling her during a trip! Things got a little squirrely the next day when the Navy van I was riding from the main base to the second site was stopped en route due to a strike by Sicilian union workers. They had blocked the only road connecting the two bases and the van had to return to the main base. Unreal. I made the trip the following morning, so I had to accelerate my work to catch my departing flight for our base in Sardinia. I flew into Olbia and was met by a local Sardinian base employee who drove us to the ferry that would take us to the Navy base on LaMaddalena. It had a submarine tender that serviced U.S. Navy submarines transiting the Med. On the drive to the ferry landing I looked out on the Tyrrhenian Sea. I got up early the next morning, went for a short jog through the local village and along the waterfront, which I believe was the Strait of Bonifacio, then after a shower and cooling down, wandered up the street to find a small tavern serving breakfast pastries, juice and very strong espresso coffee. I conducted my Navy work with a long-time colleague, Ralph, and later in the day retired to my hotel. Regrettably, there was no time for sightseeing. Before dinner, I found a phone facility for an overseas call, which I made, and it was simply yet another phone call from hell. Geez, she never changes, I thought to myself.

The next day the Navy driver drove me back to Olbia to catch my flight to Rome and on to Frankfurt, Germany. In Frankfurt, I remember the taxi driver speeding along the autobahn in his big Mercedez as he delivered me to our conference site hotel. I got the crappy part of the day out of the way by calling Carla, then sat on my hotel room terrace drinking a couple beers. It was a wonderful feeling being in a new place, my first time to Germany. I jogged the next morning through neighborhoods with lovely homes, attended meetings all that day, and in the afternoon explored the local business and retail area on foot. I bought a couple local beers at a store across from the hotel, said screw calling Carla, and sat on the terrace again before having dinner downstairs in the hotel.

After another day of training sessions, I said farewell and took a taxi to the airport for flights to Glasgow to conduct courtesy calls at Navy bases in Scotland. In Scotland I visited our base at Holy Loch, site of a homeported submarine tender, and enjoyed the experience of driving in the left lane as I made my way south to a small base at Machrihanish, near Campbelltown, between the Sound of Jura and the Firth of Clyde, stopping off along the way to visit Inveraray Castle, home of the Campbell Clan. I then flew to Spain where Carla was to meet me for a few days in lovely, enchanting Espana after conducting my visit to our base in Rota. I rented a car and drove to Herez to meet Carla's flight. Alighting from her plane ride she looked perky and happy to be there. We checked into a hotel just off base, and had a nice time roaming around Rota and other venues. Took in the bodegas, had our share of tapas, spent a day in nearby Puerto Santa Maria and Cadiz, and did a day trip back up to Herez to take in the sights. Fortunately, only one night was ruined by a Carla temper tantrum that of course voided out the day.

Spain conquered, and a trip out of the United States for Carla successfully accomplished, we returned home to assume our normal routines, and by that time, the occasional bullshit.

It didn't take Carla very long to settle into her destructive Jekyll and Hyde, "second goose", it's the post-partum blues I'm going through and causing me to be overly emotional, routine. A few weeks after a nice trip out of country, she decided to bring up the office ladies, my Taiwanese fling long before our marriage, and my Fort Bragg dancing episode, and this one got way out of hand. She did the usual yelling and screaming, the accusations, the "you sonofabitch" ranting, throw in how I didn't defend her with my mother, from that dark and regrettable event, while she's flying around the kitchen looking for something to grab and possibly throw at me. I'm thinking, "Help, help me, Rhonda".

"I hate you," she screams. Fortunately, I've positioned myself on one side of the chopping block, with her on the other. It's interesting that all of her tirades seem to start and exhaust themselves in the kitchen, well, except for when she's blowing cigarette smoke in my face while I'm trying to sleep on the den couch. "I know you're fucking someone at the office. You fucked that Taiwanese lady. You probably fucked one of those softball players in North Carolina. I could go on and on." I wanted to tell her that she was correct on one of the three, but I don't think it would have served any useful purpose and would have stoked the flames.

"Calm down, Carla. That was either before I knew you or are totally false accusations, as usual. Hell, you were in high school when I was in Taiwan." That did not resonate. "Why can't you get over this stuff and stop the imagination that's beating you up? You're being ridiculous and causing unnecessary anguish for both of us." I'm trying to remain calm, but it's tough. There is no stopping her once she puts her foot to the emotional pedal. I hope things don't get worse, but they do in a totally unexpected way.

"Bullshit. It's all your fault. And I'll show you how I feel about it and you." With that, she opens the knife drawer, pulls out a decent sized steak knife that I know is very sharp and could do some harm, and comes at me, screaming, "What do you say about this, huh? I could really hurt you with this!" She's now right next to me, her face curled and contorted, nasty in fury, a scary look for sure, the knife blade at times just inches from my face when she thrusts the knife at me. She's waving the damn thing around and I'm afraid it wouldn't take much for the knife to find a home in me. Holy shit, it's yet another dimension of her lunacy. There is nothing I can do. I try to back up some. I put my arms up to say stop the madness. Enough. "Stop it, Carla! What the hell are you doing? What has gotten into you?"

"Trying to scare the hell out of you." The knife is still in her hand and close to my face.

"You have succeeded in doing so. Now, put it back in the drawer."

"I will, but you're not staying here tonight. I want your ass out of here."

"Okay. Just put the damn knife down. I'll get my things." Should I have cold-cocked her? That would've created more problems I didn't need after the police arrived. Or, the opinion that this was just another one of those husband-wife spats, you know, what they are beginning to call domestic violence, or abuse. But no one talks about that, right?

I head down the hall, pack some work clothes, and I'm gone. I'm at the motel, wondering what the hell should I do? I'm living with a lunatic, a maniac. Something has to give. Why shouldn't I use that as the impetus, the final straw, to file for divorce? Why not? I can't answer that question. It is all too hard to digest and comprehend. It comes back to the seemingly illogical and indefensible posture not to divorce, that maybe things will get better. I'm lying on the motel room bed, staring at the ceiling, thinking about the shambles my life has become because of this wrong marriage. Life is no fun. One person. With all the possible mates that could have spilled from the Pachinko machine of relationships, I get her. That's all it takes, just one damn person that can screw up your life. I finally fall asleep.

The next day after work, returning home, I tell Carla I'm going to talk to a friend of mine at the office, ask him if I can move in with him temporarily while Carla and I decide what is going to happen. I'm so tired of her BS, but I'm still not, amazingly, thinking divorce. On the other hand, any passionate love for that woman is history, buried deep underground like pre-historic animal remains.

My friend, Ray, single, owner of a townhouse in Alexandria with an extra bedroom, was cool with my request to move in for the short term and it worked out well. I did my own cooking, and stayed out of his way when I could. I tried to minimize my presence, as difficult as that was in a small townhouse. Carla and I talked on the phone every couple of days and the calls did not result in shouting matches. We tried to talk through the issues. As I think back, I wonder to myself why I didn't call the police the night of the knife waving threats to report what surely would be construed as spousal abuse or domestic violence. But I didn't. I think people were expected to work out their marital issues with their counselors and attorneys. A lot of good it did me. Looking at the other side of it, obviously in hindsight, what if I had called the police and filed a complaint? Would they put her in jail? I doubt it. Would she still be living in the house, with thoughts of the abuse complaint constantly simmering to a near boil? Yep. That sounds like fun. And then, what would happen when she went before a judge, assuming I pressed charges? Oh, that would be fun, too. Imagine all the BS she would lay on a judge as she explained her emotional tantrums. I could just see the judge going dizzy and rolling his eyeballs, telling the two of us to get counseling and work it out, and oh, Mrs. Pedersen, keep your hands off knives unless you're cooking. Ciao, and we head home, with her berating me and screaming in my ear all the way home. Lovely.

So, in retrospect, my mental gymnastics came full circle. Like my college gymnastics floor exercise routine, I started at point A, thought or imagined myself through a number of moves on the mat, and finished with a double flip, half twist, landing squarely on my feet, back at point A.

And so, a few weeks after moving in with Ray, I returned home to re-unite with my family. Oh, I was so excited! I was running red lights to get home. The drive home was somber, mechanical, with the car and my soul like on automatic pilot. Hi, I am so happy to be here, back under the same roof as "Carla the Tormenter". Call me naïve, a fool, or maybe even an eternal optimist, they all would fit. Or, maybe just call me stupid (you can – it doesn't bother me) for staying in a loveless marriage with Carla. I had obviously decided, or defaulted, to live with the devil, or with the Greek myth figure, Hecatoncheiries, three monsters with 50 heads and 100 arms, representing the cataclysmic forces of nature. Carla was the cataclysmic forces of marriage. I had cast my lot with her and it was crushing me.

Sometime after "re-uniting" with Carla under our roof, I was scheduled to attend a Navy-wide meeting in San Diego. She wasn't happy about it and let me know, but I kept telling her that this particular conference was being held in conjunction with another Navy meeting that dealt with my specialty field. I had to be there. No, I wanted to be there. This was what I worked for. My God, I'm thinking, do other husbands go through this same shit every time they need to go on business travel? I didn't know, but I sure as hell hoped not. I mean, she just wanted to pulverize me like a hunk of meat going through a meat grinder. How did "travelling salesmen" survive? Or, the more current term, sales reps. Understanding wives, obviously.

I did my thing at the meetings and was glad I was there and participating. I was also able to make a presentation to all the Navy Fleet and Force Master Chiefs, one of which helped me later in a career move. They were good people to know, especially if they liked you.

One particular evening our Navy group had a live band in an area on the hotel grounds. Beer was available, and I was partaking and feeling good, particularly because I was away from Carla and, because of the time difference, had already executed the requisite phone call home to listen to her bitch at me and eventually say goodnight. I don't recall telling her I loved her. Shame. Anyway, I was having a great time with my Navy colleagues and ended up bending the ear of one of them about my personal situation.

Tom was one of the stars in my specialty field, and we went back many years, having collaborated at some previous Navy shipboard symposiums. He was a solid, sensible person, mature, and a retired Navy Chief Petty Officer. I had no one in my life, other than by phone calls to California, to family, to talk to about my marriage issues. With a couple of beers in me, Tom was it.

"Tom, can I talk to you about some marital issues I'm having?" I asked, hoping he would be willing to listen. I needed to get some things off my chest.

"Sure. I can be a good listener."

"Thanks. I told him about the frequent false accusations about the women in my office, the yelling and screaming, the emotional outbursts, the episode with Kyle when she repeatedly turned on his bedroom light when he was sleeping, the pot of spaghetti thrown in my face, the Jekyll and Hyde behavior on so many things, never knowing when her next volcanic eruption would be, the sleepless nights, the occasional fear for my own life, the cigarette smoke in the face when I was already relegated to the den couch, the profanity around the children when berating me, the things she tells those small children about me, encounters with the neighbor, her worthless friend Billy, and last but not least, the incident with a knife in my face, threatening and putting the fear of God in me.

Tom was incredulous. From time to time he broke in to say no one should be subjected to that type of behavior, and frequently shook his head in disgust. "I will say you never should have told her about some of your past. A mistake."

"I don't know what to do, Tom. I don't want to go through a divorce, and yet, it appears more and more it is my only way out.

She's not going to change. She is what she is. She has some screws loose, and I end up getting the brunt of it."

"You need to get out of the marriage, Dave. Counseling hasn't worked, and you're an optimist to think things will get better. I wouldn't put up with it if that were my wife. I don't know what else to tell you. You've obviously been subjected to a lot of emotional abuse. I hope for your sake she stops messing with a knife to make her point. That's crazy and dangerous."

"Well, I appreciate your listening, good buddy. Let's put this aside, rejoin the others, and have some fun.

"Amen."

It felt good to unburden my emotions and vet them with poor Tom. I'm sure he didn't want to listen to all my marital problems, but he was a good sport and friend in doing so.

As you can see, in 1985 things were getting progressively worse. She had graduated to a sharp instrument to get my attention, and quite honestly, there were some nights when I could not get to sleep, listening so intently in the event Carla was sneaking up on me with a knife in her hand, prepared to do harm. Would she do that? Probably not, but perception became reality.

And then, about that time, a job opened up in the Norfolk area. We would be closer to her parents. I'm sure they would love that! Maybe this would help her emotional state. She was excited about the prospect of leaving the city and returning home. Interestingly, at the exact same time, my Navy colleague, "Dad", contacted me at the office to tell me he was in lovely San Diego, there was exactly the same job opening there, and that he had "greased the skids" on my behalf. The director there was all in and ready for me to apply. I called him and told him I was interested and thanked him profusely for his interest in accepting my application. For me, living and working in San Diego, at that particular base, would be a dream come true. Great city. Great weather. And back home in California, closer to family and friends.

But not so fast, Dave. When I broached it with Carla, her immediate stance was, no way. I'm not moving to California, so far from my family. Okay. That takes care of that, I thought to myself. I didn't push it. Knew better, for it was a "fight" I would not win.

Onward I pursued the Norfolk job. Did my politicking with senior Navy personnel I knew, and was fortunate enough to get the call to my office one day asking if I was still interested in the job. I was on my feet, standing behind my desk, not wanting to talk on the phone for this important call sitting down. I wanted to be fully engaged and enthusiastic.

"Yes, sir," I exclaimed, thrilled for the moment.

"Well, the job is yours, Dave. Everyone that reviewed your application was very impressed and agreed you were the right person for the job. Congratulations."

"Thank you, sir," I again said. "I can't wait to report for duty." We discussed pay, which was at a level I had hoped for, and a reporting date, March of 1986.

I called Carla right away, and she was excited, saying she was going to call her parents. She fixed a nice, celebratory dinner, and all was good. I put in my resignation notice and the office had a very small, informal farewell function for me on my final day. It was nothing special – a cake, sodas, about a dozen people crammed into my boss's office to partake of the treats and to talk. There were some nice things said to and about me by senior leadership, and I made a few remarks. They gave me the standard plaque indicating my years in the headquarters office, and that was it. Again, nothing fancy.

This was followed by something quite normal. Carla had called the office and I told her about the farewell event, emphasizing it was small, short and simple. She lost it, madder than a wet hen. She couldn't believe I didn't invite her, and refused to listen to my rationale. She told me that she expected me to leave the office early, which I did, saying goodbye, telling the boss something came up at home, and catching an early bus to a different location where she picked me up, continuing to lay into me. I'm not so certain why I neglected to invite her. It was largely a combination of the simple ceremony and that I had a lot on my mind in terms of moving, selling the house, and taking on a new job, new place, new boss, along with house-hunting down there. Or, maybe it was more instinctive, subconsciously deciding I didn't want her there among my office friends and colleagues, and especially the ladies she still frequently accused me of screwing. Probably the latter. Knowing Carla, I would not have been a bit surprised had she taken the opportunity to lay into at least a few of the women in the office, a farewell in her own style.

You see, there's something I really have not come out and shared with you. Oh, I've suggested that Carla's abuse had an effect on my feelings, emotion and passion for her. When you are frequently put through an emotional knothole, something has to give. I did not love Carla with a passion. Did I love her at all, which begs the question, when does the love stop? When do you not care? When do you feel like life is hopeless? It even forced me to wonder, was I truly capable of loving someone? (Yes, someone other than "a Carla"). I wasn't going to file for divorce, so I certainly put up a pretense of a loving husband. Is it possible she saw through that? Sure. Would it have now contributed to how she treated me? Sure, but the abuse doo-loop started a long time ago. I had simply decided I was in this marriage for better or worse (wow, how's that for some irony and realism?), that I had made this decision or choice, right or wrong, and was going to endure it. Tolerate it. Make the best of it. Continue to put up with her crap, in the name of keeping the family together, or any other way you want to rationalize it. You want to torment me? Go for it. You also want my love? Pound sand.

No, what you may not know about me is that I am fiercely independent. All those single years unattached were figurative notches on a belt, testimony to a good life and to being able to make it on my own. There were days during my marriage when I so missed those carefree days and the many friends I had, most of which were living in California and literally were out of reach. I couldn't see or be with them. My nostalgia was often overpowering. All this no doubt contributed to a sense of loneliness and quiet desperation that in turn caused me to be "distant" or lacking in affection. So, along with my own soul-searching of what I had gotten into, like why did I make this huge life course change, there was the double whammy of her verbal and physical abuse. It was a damn good thing I exercised every day and had a good job, both of which were my equilibrium, although not knowing when that proverbial "second goose" would come certainly kept me a bit on edge and weary.

We did the happy prospective relocation thing, making a couple of weekend trips to stay at her parents to house hunt. We found a new two level house in Chesapeake, not real far from where her parents lived, and signed a contingent contract. Our house in Burke was on the market, so we were now in the waiting game of selling the house so the contingency would be removed from the new house.

With assurances to Carla that I would return home each weekend, I reported for duty in March. New boss, who I already knew fairly well, and new colleagues. There was a lot to learn in that large department, and the staff was very supportive. My boss had received an okay for me to live temporarily in the Bachelor Officers Quarters (BOQ) until the house business was completed and the family could move into our new home. The biggest change for me was that I could walk from the BOQ to my office! How about that? The days of the early commutes to the city and hoping for a parking spot within a mile walk to the office were gloriously behind me. There were large, open parking lots on the base near my office, so when I did start commuting I would be able to find a parking spot maybe within a hundred yards of my office building. Later, my boss gave me a parking space outside the back door of our office.

I made the dutiful weekend trips home and things were okay between us. We were a little bit stressed waiting for a buyer on our house, and of course Carla was taking care of the children single-handedly, with no help other than from my weekend visits. We were both excited about the move and the new house, although I will say we were leaving a very nice house within which we currently lived. We even went out to Old Anglers Inn one night, had a nice dinner, got chatting with people at a nearby table, and were invited to their house for after dinner drinks and socializing.

I was visiting her parents one summer mid-week night when the bomb dropped.

The phone rang and her father got up to answer it. Of course, I could only hear his side of the conversation, which was not much other than an occasional "okay", or "you're sure about it?" More silence, then, "It's your life, Carla, and your decision. Does Dave know? Oh," followed by, "Dave, Carla wants to talk to you."

"Hi Carla," I said, judging from what I heard spoken from her father that she had something important she wanted to tell me. She did.

"Dave, I'm going to make this quick and I don't want to talk about it. I've seen an attorney and filed for divorce. You'll be receiving the separation agreement in the mail, so I need you to call me back later to give me a good mailing address."

"Wow, Carla, I must say I am surprised by this announcement and decision by you." But I must admit my initial thought was, "Thank you, Lord". I didn't want to talk about it either, especially in the presence of her parents.

"Just call me with an address, a good one to ensure the mail gets to you." Ever the person wanting to be in control and manage things. She had to run the show. And with that, there was a click and our connection was broken, in more ways than one. Well, it was already broken in a manner of speaking.

While I was on the phone, her father had told her mother of the news. I hung up the phone, looked at them, and all I could say was, "Well, how about that?" I didn't want to discuss it with them, and I'm sure the feeling was mutual, for they had heard often their daughter's side of the story about how "bad" things were in the Pedersen household. I said goodnight and found my way out. I wonder if her father's first thought was, "Oh, hell, she's coming back home. Change the locks on all the doors."

The divorce process itself was unemotional and somewhat anti-climactic. The house was sold, we divided the proceeds, and I cancelled the contract on the new house in Chesapeake. So, I'm sure you're thinking life after the divorce would be smooth and uneventful, a piece of cake, a walk in the 'ol park, no issues, with Carla essentially out of my life and some well-deserved peace of mind in my future with proper ex-etiquette. Just another divorce. Not so. Things got ugly, for a long, long torturous time, and it truly was like being bitten by the head of the dead venomous snake, with Carla injecting her venom in multiple permutations of anger and torment.

From lunatic wife to maniac ex-wife.

1986

CHAPTER NINETEEN

Make no mistake, this was not similar to my breaking off the engagement with Carol in 1976, or to a lesser degree the "Dear Jane" letter to Kathy in 1977 from Sicily. Those were "relationships" consummated by two adults that, good or bad, ended up in the emotional dustbin. Over. Done. Life goes on. This filing of a separation agreement by Carla started the process to end a marriage that had been made official by a man of the cloth, in this case, a Methodist preacher. Contrary to when I walked out of Carol's apartment building after assisting her with move-in and had jumped up in glee and kicked together my heels, this was agonizing and torturous, and painful, even though it started the process of Carla exiting from my life. But not exiting enough. Not friggin' near enough.

While there certainly are a butt load of emotions one experiences during either a separation or divorce, the two overarching emotions are guilt and confusion. Oh, granted, there's plenty of anger and frustration to mete out to the other spouse, and heated exchanges are often the rule when two people are together, but when the spouse is alone and thinking through all the reasons how the marriage went to shit, much of the quiet contemplation reverts to feelings of guilt – what did I do wrong, what could I have done different, how could I have prevented the dissolution of a marriage that seemed so right on the alter, is it too late to reconcile and try to make things right? If you're thinking all that, you're on emotional brain overload. Plus, it's normally too late for the personal introspective Monday morning armchair quarterbacking (or in my case, Sunday morning since my first love is Saturday college football and not the Sunday professional variety). If the counseling was tried and failed, you're left to the two of you to figure things out, and believe me, that's asking a lot when you're most likely on a course of marriage destruction. It's hard. You're asking not only for a lot of compromise, which might be to-able, but you're expecting some big time behavior modification, as the shrinks call it, and that's the really tough stuff. You're not going to change. You think I could have changed Carla, got her to stop the volcanic eruptions that were possibly beyond her control? Hell, no, and she knew it too. I just hung in there for reasons I've already explained. It was what it was.

And there's the confusion. I've touched on some of it already, but there are times when you don't know your friggin' ass from first base. What do I do? Do I make an effort to reconcile? Do I literally or figuratively get on my knees and repent and beg forgiveness, simply because I feel it is the right thing to do? Be careful with that. If you're not 100% all in to laying it all on the line to reconcile, you're asking for more problems now and again in the future.

It's so damn tough and agonizing. There's a part of you that feels you should do what you can to keep the marriage together. For the two of you, for the kids, for the family. But there is immutably a flip side that is telling you, hold up, not so fast, you don't know if things will be better in the future if you stay together. I kept visualizing all the damn, senseless emotional trauma, the gut-wrenching crap, and frankly told myself, no, don't do it, let that cute little brunette go her separate way. You don't want any more of that. You may as well be telling the dentist, "Oh, that was so much fun, can I please have a few more root canals, today?"

Your conscience kills you. All the feelings of guilt. All the bouts of confusion and uncertainty. All this stuff is going through the prism of your intellect and psyche, and normally realism wins out. You're through. Let the chips fall where they may. Go through the legal crap, the property settlement, the visitation arrangements, and be done with it. Get on with life and hope things are better.

The latter is where I was wrong, and of course, as we now know Carla, it was wishful thinking on my part to have a "smooth" divorce and happier life thereafter. You see, the fallacy is that you cut the cord on the marriage, one person goes one way with their new life, and the other goes another way and nary shall the two meet. Wrong! I'm not so sure there was a conscious wishful thinking. I just know I wasn't going back to her and carried on. Goodbye. Ciao. She had other ideas.

And that is where I made my first bloody mistake. I was so thrilled that Carla filed for divorce and that she, for reasons I never really knew, started the separation process that I did not focus on the legal aspects of the separation. She had sent me the separation agreement, which I read thoroughly, a few times, probably still in disbelief that this was happening, that it wasn't me that filed, and it honestly sounded and read okay to me. Bam! Dave, you're not a friggin' divorce attorney! What was I thinking? Well, I wasn't, obviously. How would I know that the agreement "sounded and read okay"? I'm a reasonably intelligent guy, so why didn't I think to take it to a lawyer? Well, I didn't, so there. Chock it up to being so damn anxious to get her the hell out of my life, sayonara bitch, thank you, and where do I sign, that I actually signed the agreement and mailed it back to her. Done. No turning back, no changes to the separation agreement allowed now. I just had this myopic view and attitude that I was willing to sign anything to finally get rid of her. Hey, how's this? It has been said that alimony is the ransom a happy man pays to the devil. Well, there you go. I opted into the agreement arrangements and was stuck with them.

With the formality of the separation agreement done, I told my boss about the developments affecting my marriage. He suggested it would be a good idea to move out of the BOQ and into other lodging so as not to abuse the gracious decision of the commanding officer to make an exception by permitting my use of the BOQ. I found an apartment in Newport News, which was good because it reduced the rendezvous drive times, although it was a longer commute to the base for work. It was near historic Williamsburg with a full range of bars and restaurants catering to the William and Mary College crowd, many of which I availed myself of on my free weekends. My routine was to meet Carla every other Friday at a location off I-95 north of Richmond and bring the children back to my place for the weekend. Obviously, this happened after I moved out of the BOQ, for children were not allowed in those places. We would do the reverse on Sunday afternoon, sometimes eating dinner before I hopped back on the freeway to return to Newport News. You can say what you will, but having the children for two to three days out of fourteen did not constitute quality time and I frankly did not always enjoy that routine. Driving up and down I-64 and I-95 every other weekend, Friday and Sunday, became a chore. I'm sorry, but my heart was often not into making that drive, and to this day I dislike driving up I-95 toward Washington. It became more tedious after I willingly offered to drive farther north on I-95 for the "hand-off" to reduce her drive. Self-inflicted wound.

In the Spring of 1987, just over a year from when I had taken my new job and later commenced the bi-weekly rendezvous routine I told my parents that I thought I could handle or rationalize the guilt, bitterness, frustration, loneliness, and so on, but had trouble rationalizing, "What happened over the years"? How did I fall "out of love" with the woman I married, and why can't I get that flame back? (In Sanford and Son fashion, "The abuse, you dummy.") For so many reasons, I wish we were still a family, but the love and respect that is the foundation of a strong relationship was gone and scattered like the grains of sand in an Arizona sandstorm. There was just too much water over the dam, called all the abuse, plus being two-hundred miles apart, so it really was not going to happen. Totally unrealistic, so I just discarded the notion of ever loving her again. It just was not going to happen. Stop thinking about it and deal with the present, which became a handful in itself.

To make matters worse, she called me during the week all too often to complain and yell at me. So, we went from face to face verbal abuse to burning up the phone lines to do the same. I had no choice but to answer the phone since any one of those unwanted calls could be for a legitimate reason pertaining to the children. School, visitation, health issues, discipline issues, as if I could do anything about any of the issues being over two-hundred miles away! Same 'ol Carla. The conversation would start off on the calm, collected side and oftentimes gradually build to an emotional crescendo with yelling, screaming, threats, and so on. I kept a log, as if a lot of good it did, of her calls to me and there were many weeks with at least five calls from her. The emotional trauma continued, so that it didn't take long before I didn't even want to see her. Every other weekend was far too often. She had that same battering ram personality, bludgeoning me to death with her tirades over the phone. Pathetic. God, how I so despised that woman.

So, by the time I did my requisite calls to the kids to talk to them and see how they were doing, followed shortly by their mother jumping on the line before I could hang up, I was subjected to listening to her crap almost every day of the week. The only breaks I got were when the kids were with me. I was trying to live my life sans the cougar, but it just wasn't working out that way. She tormented me unceasingly. I came to hate telephones, for with every Carla call I was hit with telephonic hysteria and badgering. It wore on me. Part of the problem, I realized, was that I was still her primary connection to humanity, commonly known as those unfortunate to befriend her. So, while some of the phone conversations were unemotional, the majority were laced with venom. During the former, I could only sit with the phone to my ear and listen to her go on about this and that, stuff I had absolutely no interest in, but was being civil as "the dutiful ex-husband and father of her children". After a few nudges to get off the phone, I would finally say, "I've got to go. Bye." Plus, in those days you paid for long distance phone calls. Funny thing is, what she had to tell me was rarely about the kids. It was about her, which was totally contrary to the reasons that she and I had to converse – to maintain a parental dialogue. She just never understood that I could give a damn about her life, but I had to hear all about it regardless. Over the years, she would share with me much more than I wanted to know. Just a real chatterbox on all manner of topics involving her life, good and bad, and other people.

During one of her calls, she wanted to give me a heads up.

"Dave, before the kids tell you, I want you to know that Billy visits occasionally."

"Okay. Not much I can do about it, anyway, is there, Carla?"

"No, I guess not, but I just wanted you to know. I've told him he is never to put his hands on the children or raise his voice. He understands."

As only a convicted felon can, I thought to myself. "That's nice. So, what's he doing these days? I suppose he's having a difficult time finding work or getting into the mainstream of civilized society, or working for any government employer."

"Don't be sarcastic. He's living at home and working for his father doing construction work. Has been for a while."

"Good. I hope for his sake he keeps himself out of trouble." I've now inferred I actually care about him, which I do not and which is dangerous for I could hear more about him. But this was all part of Carla's passive-aggressive personality, luring you in with calm civilized discourse, and then using it against you later like snagging a fish and reeling it in. He's still a slime ball felon.

"He is, plus he's on probation and has to see his parole officer once a month. You know, it is tough being a single parent. It's no fun."

"I'm sure it's hard, but it helps that you're not working. You're right there for them every day when they leave for school and return."

"I'd rather be working."

"Then do it, and work out the child care like many other single mom's do, Carla, or move to this area so the kids are closer to me and your parents and I can help some, plus I'm sure the housing is much cheaper than the city."

"No. I need to be here for them, and I'm not moving."

"Suit yourself." The conversation has run its course, or so I thought.

"I need more money from you. Between the rent and other expenses, I'm having a tough time financially."

"No, Carla. I have bills at my end and I'm not in a position to pay more child support. Plus, you have the alimony."

"Damn you. You don't care about us," she screams. Here we go again. Her engine is revved up big time.

"I do, but you're not getting more money."

"You worthless piece of shit!" And with that, she slams down the receiver and there is silence, a silence I have come to love but always my hands are shaking and I'm sure my blood pressure is elevated. This is the sort of conversation that ensues after almost every phone call to the kids. I call to chat with them, hear how they're doing in school, about new friends, and I want to hang up, but Carla jumps on and wants to get chatty and then emotional. We may as well still be under the same damn roof. Separation has only spared me spaghetti and knives in my face, not the volcanic verbal eruptions. Well, not quite on the knives.

Same old torment from dear Carla.

1987/1988
CHAPTER TWENTY

It was my weekend for the kids so I asked the boss for a couple hours of leave and headed up I-64 and I-95 to a rendezvous point. First, I had to deal with the usual traffic back-up to get through the Hampton Roads Bridge Tunnel that seemed to materialize earlier and earlier, then race up the freeway.

Pulling into the Sally's Country Kitchen parking lot in Doswell I received the expected.

"You're late, Dave. Thanks a lot."

During my face to face encounters with her I have learned that saying less is better. "Couldn't help it. Traffic back-up at the tunnel. Did my best to get here on time."

"Well, I've got plans back home, so this means I may run late." She's wired up.

"Sorry. See you here at four o'clock Sunday. Let's go, kids."

"See you then." She's gone, thank goodness. I probably should run late more often. Less "chatting".

The kids get me playing a game in the car as we drive to my

place. It's fun for a while, but I eventually tire of it. Instead, we talk about school and their activities, more so with Kyle since he's in regular school whereas Katie is in a part-day program.

We get to my place and they know dad's Friday night routine, which includes watching Dallas and Falcon Crest, two great programs that I enjoy. The fact that it's my Friday night staple is testimony to my very inactive social life. When I don't have the children, I'll hit the Officer's Club on the base or a bar close to where I live for a couple of drinks before going home to watch TV. I let them stay up to watch the programs with me, then I get them off to bed. I'm normally right behind them since I'm a morning person. The next morning we get up early, I have a couple cups of coffee, then we're off to a nearby park with a circular running track. They play on the playground equipment while I jog, keeping an eye on them all the time. After my jog, we play on the equipment together before heading back home.

For this particular weekend, I've decided to make the drive into Norfolk to visit a large entertainment venue on the Elizabeth River called Waterside. It's jam-packed with bars, restaurants, specialty retail stores like clothing and Native American jewelry, along with an ice cream parlor and a fudge factory. Cool stuff. All good fun. We wander around, have Chinese for lunch, and go outside to lay under the sun on the expansive lawn surrounding the venue. We also walk over to the marina where visitors have tied up their boats and marvel at the beautiful yachts. Nearby is a waterfront park at which Friday night events are held, along with concerts and other shows. We play a little Frisbee on the lawn, and I'm hoping Kyle doesn't in his exuberance send the Frisbee into the drink. On some weekends there is a visiting naval vessel moored alongside Waterside, and the ship is open for visitation. I've seen German, French, British ships, and during an annual event called

HarborFest, one may also see immense tri-master naval training vessels from Norway and other countries. Remarkable.

We head back home in time for a late Saturday afternoon college football game. They know I love football, and enjoy watching it with me. I make it feel like we are at a game – I have appropriate snacks and beverages for them, and I pretend I'm at a tailgate party and have a couple beers. All fun. Today I'm able to watch my Indiana University team go up against a far better Ohio State team. Guess who won? Dinner is one of their favorites I learned from my mother – tuna fish placed atop an open English muffin half, then a big slice of fresh tomato, all covered with a slice of cheese, then put in the oven to bake. We all love them, so it's a good, simple, easy night of cooking for me.

While we're sitting over dinner, Kyle says, "Daddy, you know Billy visits, don't you?"

"Yes, I do, Son. Your mom told me he visits occasionally."

"Yeah. Whenever he does there's a strange smell in the house. I hate it. It smells bad."

"You know, Kyle, there's not much I can do about it. It's your mother's house, and she can pretty much have anyone there she wants and do what she pleases. I'll talk to her about it, though, but I can't promise it will stop." I don't ask him or Katie any other questions for two reasons: One, I don't give a damn about their mother's personal life, and two, she will never be able to accuse me of drilling the kids with questions about her. So, it's very simple. When around her, I don't ask questions, and again, I don't ask questions of the children. This way, too, I minimize conversation with her.

On Sunday, I put the kids in the car to buy a Sunday newspaper that I enjoy reading with my coffee, and we have breakfast. By the time we hang out in the apartment and they watch cartoon programs on TV, it is time to start working our way to the rendezvous with their mother. I take my time, getting off the freeway past Williamsburg to take a rural road, Route 60, to Richmond. We stop at a roadside rest area for snacks and soda, then push on. Carla arrives shortly after our arrival at Sally's, and as we have become accustomed to doing, we have an inexpensive dinner there together. The kids are telling their mother about our Saturday activities, and I can tell Carla is trying to converse more with me, to tell me of her woes. I do my best to ignore her and reduce any dialogue with her. Talking to her is like slowly removing a well-adhered adhesive strip off the skin, but seeing her, being with her, is excruciating and painful and is like suffering a hundred stab wounds. I can't stand it, and I want to get away from her. But, there is dinner to eat before I can do so, and because I feel some guilt about the whole bloody situation and her being a single mom, I hold on as long as I can before saying "Uncle".

"Carla, I've got to get out of here and back down the road. I honestly have to go so I can get home at a decent time and get ready for work tomorrow."

"We haven't been here that long. You can stay longer." A statement vice a request.

"No. I really need to hit the road." With that, I start to move out of the booth and everyone gets the idea and follows suit. At the car it's a quick, short mechanical hug, and hugging the kids, telling them I love them, and I say goodbye. While I hate saying goodbye to the kids, I always feel immensely better and somewhat exuberant as I drive down the road heading back home because it means the physical presence of Carla is in the rearview mirror for the time being. I know I don't have to see her for another two weeks, and I don't think about the incessant phone calls that whip me back to a past with her I am trying to forget. Good luck on that.

A couple months later I am reminded of the emotional pull

that I explained earlier – the guilt and confusion that can sit on your shoulder and talk you into doing something you do not really want to do. The daughter of my Navy colleague, "Dad", was getting married in Washington, D.C., and I responded to the invitation that I looked forward to attending and seeing "Dad" and his family for the first time in quite a long while. I also made a call to another Navy colleague, Barbara, whom I had known for a number of years and who lived in the city. I had always wanted to spend some time with her but never had the opportunity. She said she'd love to see me and I could crash in an extra bedroom at her place before heading home. Sounded great. An enjoyable Saturday was shaping up.

Unfortunately, Barbara contacted me, apologetic that she would be unable to see me. No elaboration, so I don't know if something came up that prevented my visit or that she had cold feet about the offer to let me crash at her place. So, I attended the wedding, and when in the city contacted Carla to ask if she and the children would be home. She said yes, and invited me over, of course. We had a casual, relaxed get-together, and there were admittedly some overtures or suggestions about reconciling. I spent the night, but nothing happened sexually, whether that was on her part or mine. The next morning, having slept off the few drinks that loosened my no-reconciliation tongue, commitment and perseverance not to go back to her, ever, and subject myself to the pain through which she had put me over the many years, I realized the somewhat compromising situation within which I had regrettably and stupidly placed myself. I had a quick breakfast and got the hell out of there, heading home to my quiet, peaceful abode, where I belonged.

You know that she was a talker of the first order, and was more than anxious to tell me just about everything in her life to my chagrin. It bored the heck out of me and I was frankly uninterested in her drivel. The next time we talked on the phone she did it again.

"I finally met my neighbor downstairs."

"Oh?" How's that for expressing interest?

"Yeah. He's a neat guy. He's middle-age and lives by himself. I don't think he's ever been married. At least, he hasn't said anything about being divorced or a widower."

"That's good. Nice that you met someone you can visit and talk to." Especially the opposite sex!

"I asked him what he did for a living, but he didn't say much except he worked for the government, travelled a lot in his job, and couldn't tell me much about it other than it dealt with international relations." Vague.

"Interesting. He could work for any number of international relations agencies. There's a large number of them. Between the State Department, NSA, the military services, and countless others known and unknown to the general public, he could work for any one of them."

"Yeah. That's what I was thinking. We have some good discussions that sometimes go for a long time, so it's a good thing he is just below me so I can quickly check on the children from time to time. I also help him with his paperwork."

Stunned, I stammer, "His paperwork?"

"Uh, huh. I help him with his travel claims. All I see is that he travels to places overseas. I help him figure out the financial stuff."

"Oh, wow, that is interesting." I'm still a bit surprised and taken aback that someone in his position would allow a friend to help him. Must have a good reason.

"It is," she replies.

"And being as he's a government employee, I'm sure he doesn't partake in the pot smoking you engage in, right?"

"First of all, that's none of your damn business, and secondly,

I don't smoke pot or cigarettes anymore. I'm trying to take care of myself. I want to try for an acting career."

"Okay. Good." I've already talked to the kids, so I start making overtures that I need to hang up. "And good luck on the acting. I need to have dinner, so I'm hanging up." That usually works. The need to hit the rack also helps. Hey, whatever works to get her off the phone.

"Bye," she responds.

This is the routine we go through for the next few years. She's there. I'm down here in Newport News. She writes a check twice a month for child support and alimony. We do the every other weekend rendezvous' so that I can have the children for the weekend and give her a break. I'm hating every drive up and down I-95. She frequently gets wound up talking to me on the phone and the calls become disastrous and very uncomfortable due to her yelling and complaining. That part of my life is like a broken record, the emotional trauma playing out over and over again. Instant replay of the most horrendous type. The best moment of any given day is when I finally can hang up the phone on her. The worst damn part of each evening is when the phone rings, knowing who is on the other end, and immediately shooting up my blood pressure. I have no choice but to answer the phone, since it could be something important about the kids. The calls I just love go like this …

"Dave, this is Carla."

"I know."

"Kyle's messing up in school. His grades could be better, and his teacher told me today he's the class cut-up. You need to talk to him. Here he is." She's off the phone, then I hear that soft, child's voice that suggests he's already been tortured by his mother.

"Hi, daddy."

"Hi, son. How are you doing, little guy?" I'm calm. I'm also two-hundred miles away and both of us, Kyle and me, know there is not a whole lot I can do to "punish him", which is what his mother expects me to do.

"Oh, I'm fine. Mommy told me you wanted to talk to me." The poor child sounds like he is about ready to cry, so I'm gentle on him.

"Yes, she did. She told me about your school work and your behavior in school. You know that daddy's not pleased with that."

"I know, daddy."

"You and I talked before about how important your school work is. I want very much, for your sake, for you to do well in school so that you can continue to do well each year and go to college like I did so you can have a good job to take care of yourself." I know it's a long time from now, so just planting the seed.

"I know."

"Tell me you'll work harder, Kyle, and make me proud."

"I will, daddy. It's just not easy sometimes."

"I know, son, but I know you'll do better. I love you, little guy."

"And I love you, daddy." As soon as those wonderful words are out, his mother has snatched the phone from him like she's grabbing at a hundred-dollar bill.

"What did you say to him?" she demands. God, what a total bitch.

I tell her the gist of what I said to him. She heard everything on his end. What am I supposed to do, hop in my car and drive two-hundred miles so I can punish him or say the same thing I just told him?

"Okay," she says. "I hope that helps. Otherwise, I'll let you know so you can do something about it."

"Got it, Carla. I'm sure he'll try harder. I've got to go. Bye."

She slams the receiver like she's pounding a hammer and the

reverberation bangs around in my ear for a while. You would think that she would understand that there is very little I can do, at any given moment, to discipline our children. I don't know what to tell her, for to attempt to advise her that she wanted custody and that meant she had the very predominant responsibility to raise the children and effect discipline as she deemed appropriate, would only result in a scathing comeback by her that could be heard even with the receiver held at arms-length from my ear.

That's just one small part of what I was enduring at my end. I was not living with my children. I was unable to watch them grow up, change week by week, month to month. I absolutely abhorred the idea of being married to their mother, but I sure missed my kids, plus the fact I had no idea what she was saying to them about me. I had read that one of the cardinal sins, or chief no-no's, in a divorce situation was one of the spouses bad-mouthing the other spouse to the children, and I knew damn well that was part of her slander campaign to undermine me. But back on point, I really wanted to be part of their lives, through school, sports, friends, dates, and all that stuff. I wanted to have a child so they would have an opportunity to enjoy the immense pleasures of life with which I was blessed. Well, until I married their mother, anyway. I wanted them to enjoy school. I wanted them to attend college and be able to say afterwards, "That was the best four years of my life, dad."

Now, that's all gone. How can you be a good parent and enjoy parenthood from two-hundred miles away? You can't, and don't try to tell me otherwise. It doesn't happen. What can you honestly achieve when you have a child two days out of fourteen? You're not the primary parent. You're the second team, and you only get called in when your team is down 49-0 in the fourth quarter and the situation is ugly. So much of their lives is past tense to you. That hurt, and it would be a feeling that would haunt me forever.

I knew, but I really didn't know my kids, you know what I mean? And to have a lunatic like Carla bludgeoning me verbally and emotionally whenever she could, just added to the despair I often felt about my situation. But just like my decision not to file for divorce to keep the family together, I put up with her continued crap so I could communicate with my kids.

It's not going to get better.

1988

CHAPTER TWENTY-ONE

I pleasingly came out on top during an incident that evolved from one of Carla's rantings on the phone, complaining about the kids and her life. In previous phone calls, she had made rather strong overtures that she was going to give me custody of the children. While at first that sent shivers through my body and soul because of my work routine that was demanding, along with my quiet, personal time, I concluded that I needed to be ready for that possible eventuality. I could make this work, and I would work hard at it. There was a large church very near my apartment complex that advertised day care. I visited and spoke to the person in charge, explained my situation, and was thrilled to hear her say they had openings. I just needed to apply as soon as I knew something. There was also an elementary school a few blocks away. I spoke to them as well, and to show good faith and help secure spaces for Kyle and Katie, I took them up on their suggestion that I do some volunteer work for them, which I did, spending a weekend assisting in the construction of a new playground at the school.

So I'm ready. It would not be easy, for sure, but having secured good day care was satisfying and gave me added confidence I could take custody. The next time she called she was ready to give me custody.

"They're yours, asshole. Good luck," she yelled.

"Okay, Carla, if that's what you want." I'm calm.

"It is. I've had it. You can take care of them!"

"Well, two things. Number one, you need to get with your attorney, since you filed, and have him amend the agreement that I have primary custody, and then have that filed with the court to make all this legal. We can't do anything until then, and I am sure your attorney would agree. Number two, the day I take legal custody I stop paying you child support." Holy macaroni, did she come totally unglued!!

"What? You sonofabitch! You bastard! You can't do that!" She obviously was not thinking clearly. If I have the kids, why does she need court-directed child support, right?

"Oh, yes I can. Why would I continue paying you child support if I have the kids?" I was trying to be logical, but that rarely if ever worked on Carla.

"Bullshit! I can't afford my apartment. What do I do?" She was hysterical, and I was enjoying every moment of this dialogue, but I remained calm because this time I was ready for her. Child care, school, she relinquishes child support. You see, it was the money part that stopped her dead in her tracks. It had not dawned on her that sans the children she could and should go out and get a job, but that wasn't in her lexicon nor the conversation that night.

"I'm sure you can figure it out. Let me know when the legal part is done and I will drive up to get the kids and some of their belongings and clothes." Silence, then …

"You asshole! You'll pay for this." She slammed down the phone. Conversation over.

And I never heard another peep out of her about changing custody. Well, not for a long while, anyway. She didn't change over time.

Even though I can sort of chalk one up for the good guys, I'm still feeling like the Greek Prometheus – as punishment, Zeus chained him in the Caucasus Mountains, where an eagle fed upon his liver daily. Amazingly, the liver was restored each day for more feedings. That's how I felt – Carla was constantly picking at me as though I was an endless diet for her ugliness.

In future months the kids tell me that Billy continues to visit, that the apartment stinks, and that she spends a lot of time visiting her neighbor downstairs. I figure Billy's looking for some commiseration from all his wrongdoings and jail time, and Carla wants the companionship and adult conversation of her neighbor, plus helping the poor guy out on completing his government travel claims. I hope they're not cooking the books on his claims, which could put him in deep kimchi with his employer should it ever be uncovered. But then, I'm just speculating, and it's not my problem.

To make matters worse for the kids, she was feeding them some misinformation. Poor Katie. During one of the weekends at my place, dear Katie said to me, "Daddy, mommy says there's still a chance that you might get back together. Is that true?"

Oh, man. My heart went out to this innocent young child that was being fed misinformation and hopes by her reckless mother. "Katie, I really do not think so. You're so young, and I can't and will not say much more than that. Please don't think about it."

"Okay," she softly replied, and gave me a sweet smile. I so wish their mother would not say such things to them. I had told Carla I was not getting back with her, period.

I knew she wanted to act professionally, but I was startled when she told me she was moving out of her apartment, putting things in storage, and following her dream to Las Vegas, where she hoped to meet the sort of people that could help launch her career. It wasn't Los Angeles, but there might be some folks that could help her, plus she had a girlfriend from the D.C. area who had moved to Vegas and offered to put her up for a while, including the kids. So, as she told me upon arriving in Vegas, she packed essentials for her and the children, loaded up the car, and drove out there. Pretty ballsy on her part I must admit, but that was how she operated. I really had only one emotion or feeling about her journey, and you probably know what it was. Would I miss the kids? Yes and no, for reasons I have explained. No, the overarching feeling was, thank you Lord for getting that woman away from the east coast and out of rendezvous range. I think she just needed a change in scenery.

There was one incident that occurred right after she left for Vegas and which was nice timing on her part, assuming she had anything to do with it. I came out of my apartment one weekend morning shortly after the "no shit" phone conversation with dear Carla about custody of the children and the financial ramifications that got her attention. As they say, follow the money. I was in a good mood as I entered the parking lot, but that went south as soon as I saw my car front windshield destroyed. No fallen tree. No airplane part that could have fallen out of the sky from nearby Langley Air Force Base or the commercial airport. Whoever did it certainly made the effort to do a thorough job. Like, there was no window remaining. Gee, I wonder who did this? The fact that no other windshields had been destroyed was ample testimony that my car was the sole target of this heinous act. Billy? Could have easily been put up to it by Carla, since he didn't live real far away. Her "secret spy" neighbor? Not him, but heck, he could have easily contacted a buddy, or some nefarious character with which he was "associated", and arranged the hit. Not likely, though, as it was small potatoes. No, if Carla had anything to do with it, it had to be Billy boy, or Billy-Bob, or whatever. I talked to the apartment manager and learned there were no cameras in the parking lot.

I used one of her initial calls from Vegas to discuss my vehicle conflagration.

"You know, I had the unpleasant experience recently of walking to my car in the apartment parking lot only to find it missing a front windshield."

"Oh? I'm sorry to hear that, Dave." She was smooth. Passive.

"Certainly not as sorry as me," I replied.

"Did you call the police?"

"No. There were no cameras in the parking lot so the police would have nothing to go on. Just a lot of broken glass around the car. And no one mentioned anything to the apartment management."

"That's too bad." She's not offering much.

I decide to hit her between the eyes, sort of.

"I think I know who did it, but there's no way I can prove it."

"Oh? Who?"

"I'd rather not say at this point. Let's just leave it at that. One of those unfortunate circumstances." And with that, she says goodbye and hangs up.

Any way you cut it, Carla was most probably showing her insidious self in yet another demonstrative way, and I was immediately wary of her and knew things could get ugly, or should I more pointedly say, uglier. And they did, with Billy's help.

When Carla's future calls came, it was all about what celebrity she had met, or what talent scout or manager she befriended. She apparently got in with the right folks, for there was talk of photo shoots and "hints" of being able to try out for some commercials or small roles, but none of that really materialized. Plus, it would probably mean she would have to move to Los Angeles.

For me, and obviously for Carla, the bubble burst after about three months in Vegas. By mutual agreement, Carla and her roommate agreed that Carla either had to find her own digs or return to Washington. Without solid prospects, she decided to drive back to D.C. and say adios to the Vegas dream. She would try another tack later.

Living with her friend, Carla had saved some money, so upon returning to Washington she bought a small three-bedroom townhouse in Manassas very close to where she used to live. One could think she was feeling more confident and comfortable about her life, having bought a home, but it didn't happen. I was in bed on a work night when she called and said something that came out of left field.

I picked up the phone, feeling drowsy, certainly knowing who was calling, only to hear that unmistakable voice say, "Dave, I'm going to commit suicide. I can't deal with my life anymore."

Holy shit, I'm thinking, what do I tell her? As a government employee, I had received some suicide awareness training, especially since the Military Services were experiencing a higher than normal suicide incidence rate. But this one was real close to home. "Just try to relax and take it easy, Carla. You know you really don't want to do this."

"I do. I can't cope anymore. I don't know if it's the kids, or what happened in Las Vegas, or what, but I want my life to end."

Well, don't get me talking about the kids and custody and all that crap, which would surely put her over the top. Trying to slow her down and distract her, I ask," Have you talked to your parents or your brother? Maybe they can help you."

"No, I have not, and I don't want to talk to any of them, for the same reasons I won't move back to that area."

Oh, oh, that hit a raw nerve. "Is there someone, a friend, you can call or see, someone nearby? I'm over two-hundred miles away and can't be driving up there."

"My friend in the old complex is out of the country, and I have no one else to call."

"Okay. Well, you need to try and step back and see what you're proposing to do. It's not the answer. The kids need you. You're their mother. They rely on you."

"Well, they'd have you. Plus, you'd have all the child support and alimony money."

"That's no way to look at it, Carla."

"Yeah, I know. I'm just having a tough time."

"If it will help, I'll try to squeeze out a few extra dollars for you. Maybe it will help."

"It will. Thanks. I'm going to bed. Bye."

So there it was. Suicide talk, and I end up cutting back and temporarily sending her some more money. Oh, well. Whatever. Things just get more jacked up. I realize the receiver is still in my hand, to my ear, after she had hung up. I hang up. What a mess. And as usual after her calls my hands are shaking. I know it will take some time to settle down, put the call behind me, and try to go back to sleep.

Good grief. To myself, "Why can't this woman go away, I mean, really far away, like overseas, forever? Just get out of my life. We're supposed to be divorced, and you're still banging on me like we were under the same roof when and where you had untethered access to me. At this juncture, allowing me to be your punching bag of choice and "counselor", I don't give a rat's ass if you do commit suicide. You would certainly be out of my life." I know that's a terrible thing to think, but let her do what she wants, even if it's killing herself.

And trying to understand Carla is a wasted effort. I had read that one of the four destructive behaviors that indicate a couple will eventually divorce is "criticism". Her variety may not have been pure criticism, but her constant accusations and verbal abuse represented a close second. Maybe it was even her insistence that we not go to bed or sleep until we had finished our "argument". Here again, she was essentially wrong, since it has been shown that when couples fight, they are so physiologically stressed, increased heart rate, cortisol in the bloodstream, etc., that it is impossible for them to have a rational discussion. It is best to take a break and come back to it later, even if that means sleeping on it. Then again, I think it is fair to say she started the distinct majority, if not all, the "fights", and resolution in her mind was not something I could achieve in view of her false accusations. How could I prove my point? Not possible. It was like the proverbial, mind-numbing query of someone that never laid a hand on their spouse, "When did you stop beating your wife?" I also read that counseling is not to salvage a bad marriage or sort out trauma. It's about revealing the truth about a relationship, which was what I conveyed to the Pastor. There you go – she did not want to face the truth about her behavior, thus the nix on counseling. So, we, or at least I, fell into that 80% of divorced men and women that cited growing apart and loss of a sense of closeness to their partner as the reason for divorce. No argument there. I had truly fallen out of love with her from all the trauma and torment.

I knew we would never get back together as a family. Too late for that.

And her colors never changed. On one particular occasion, I received a call on a Thursday at my office from a nurse at a hospital telling me that Carla was in the hospital and that I needed to get up there to take care of the kids. My boss understood, and off I went, but on the long drive up I couldn't help but think, how often or how many times could I realistically bail out of the office to travel two-hundred miles to help out? Crazy. You would think that she would have a close, as in geographically near, friend that could help her out in situations like this, but we forget that she didn't have or could keep friends since she eventually chewed them up. Apparently, her visit to the hospital was precipitated by a mix of medications and nerves.

By the time I arrived, she was convalescing in her own bed at home. I planned to stick around until Saturday morning, but I digress. Along the way, after I had taken her and Katie to dinner Friday night, I apparently failed to give her the desired response to a question she posed. As I recall, it went something like this ...

"So, Dave, you know I had a bit of success in Las Vegas in meeting some entertainment people and talking about a career for me."

"Yes. I recall that."

"Do you think I'm too old to start an acting career?"

Holy crap. Why do women ask men for their opinion about age, about how a person looks? That was bad enough, but add the fact that we were divorced and that I could care less about her looks. I was on soft, shaky terra firma on this, and needed to answer the question best I could or you know what would happen. "Well, you're still attractive. You haven't gained any weight. You definitely have a passion for what you want to achieve."

"So, what are you trying to say?" Building up a little steam, although she did manage to have a smile on her face.

"Just that you have a lot going for you. I can't tell you if your age or appearance would be a factor. That's for the professionals to figure out. Your age shouldn't be a problem, although you're probably getting a late start." That should work.

"Wow, I'd have thought you would be a bit more positive and encouraging."

"I thought I was." Can we please change the subject?

"Not really. Let's head back to my place."

Suited me fine, and I was looking forward to crashing on the sofa and leaving in the morning.

Kyle was staying overnight with a friend, and Katie went to bed.

The attack hit like a shark on blood. Without the usual slow build or preamble, she launched into me with a vengeance. It turned into a major, ugly, scary blowout, and it was traumatic for me. She was obviously under some pressure for a number of reasons, and she had the hospital experience the day prior, but good grief, should a person totally lose it that easily?

"You sonofabitch. You dick. I can't stand you. You're worthless. You couldn't even tell me what I wanted to hear, suggesting I was too old to start an acting career! I'm glad I divorced you. You fucked other women, I know, and you quit the Herbalife business." She was flying around her townhouse, throwing sofa pillows at me, and then headed for the dreaded kitchen to grab a knife. Deja 'vu.

"Knock it off. I don't want to argue with you. I came up here to help you!" I was trying to stay calm, but when you don't react to her level of anger that makes her more upset.

When she got close enough with the knife I took a downward swipe at her knife arm, startling her as she lost her grip on the knife and it fell to the floor. I didn't want to take any chances this time. I reached down and picked it up. Why did I do that? To prevent her from getting it, knowing all she had to do was make another quick trip to the knife drawer, or to gain leverage over her and possibly use it myself? "How would this feel, Carla?" I yelled.

"Fuck you!" She looked like she was working herself into a blackout. And she did.

I threw the knife to the floor and reacted with the requisite disgust over her behavior and called her an "asshole" as she fell to the floor. I didn't touch her or do a damn thing. Just sat on the sofa with my head in my hands wondering what the hell have I done to have been in a relationship with this certified lunatic and pondering what she has made me into? I could only think, God forgive me for this, but sometimes in my bitterness I declare you did a number on me.

She eventually stood up, quiet, the same old subdued behavior post volcanic eruption. She headed upstairs. I didn't say a thing and got the hell out of there to make the long drive home.

So herein lies the proverbial dilemma, and it all fits together with the feelings of guilt and confusion like a hand in a glove. When she is acting okay, as in not ripping my face off, I feel empathy and sympathy toward her, not love, and not enough to consider reconciliation, mind you, but it still sucks. You wear those emotions like a piece of clothing. It doesn't help when she's saying, "I can't believe you let us go." Who filed for divorce, Carla? And yet, this most recent traumatic event in her townhouse brought a more clear focus on why I don't ever want her back in my life.

Get back together for that?? Shoot me. Which is why I am also giving her more money than required – my way of "compensating" for this travesty and to atone my guilt.

And to further make my case as to how whacked out she remains, it was a number of months later when she did the "play it again, Sam" on me. On a rendezvous Sunday, I took my sister up on her invitation for me and the kids to stop over at her place in Ashland for dinner, which was en route to our rendezvous spot. I didn't bother to tell Carla about it, which should have been no problem. Wrong.

The call came in that night. "You asshole. Why didn't you tell me you took the kids to your sister's for dinner?

"Because I didn't have to. They were with me, and it was totally within my rights to do so. In one of my communications with an attorney, I was told that I could legally take them where I wanted while with me."

"Bullshit!" You know I don't like your sister. You are really a shitty father, and you're retarded because you had such poor memory in not remembering that you suggested I was too old to try an acting career." Oh, my. Talk about obsessing about something like a bulldog with lockjaw.

"You're ridiculous, Carla. You really are."

"And you know that you support me now because you felt guilty and you've blocked out your earlier negative attitude."

"Whatever, Carla." Sure I don't remember. I really don't give a shit about what I had said months earlier on the topic.

I needed to placate her so I could get her off the phone. "Okay, okay, I remember, but you misconstrued what I had said." That slowed her down, but she just changed subjects, telling me that I wasn't going to get a penny from her when she made it big. I told her I didn't care or want her money. Even with that, she yelled that she was going to bleed me money-wise just like she always said she would. Ah, that's gratitude for the extra money I was giving her. What a bitch.

A few days later it's another haranguing phone call.

"Hello," I blandly said into the phone, knowing there was a 99.9% chance it was her.

"You didn't call to find out about Kyle!" Within a minute she hung up.

I decided I had better call back, wondering what I had missed about Kyle.

All I got was more yelling. The weird, typical Carla part, was that she told me her babysitter's father told her he didn't approve of Carla staying out until four in the morning, and she wanted me to call him or write him to protect her honor. I kid you not. I told her, "No, I'm not going to get into the middle of your fights."

"I expected that reaction from you," she replied.

Click.

194

Called me back later, saying I was a shitty father and insensitive. She put Kyle on the line to ask me why I didn't call to see how he was doing. I explained that I should have called.

When Carla got back on the line, I told her I didn't call because I didn't want to talk to her.

Click.

I'm absolutely screwed. I can't get her to stop the calls. I can't not answer the phone, because I never know what call might be legit. She just calls and calls and wears me down, at least while we're on the phone. After the calls, while my blood pressure is higher, I can only hope there is a reprieve.

My body and soul at times felt like I was in a long ago "Twilight Zone" episode. I was losing it, all because I continued to allow her to have access to me. I remembered the episode when an "earwig" crawled into the ear of this guy while he was sleeping, worked its way in, and the guy awoke to the horrible realization that something had crawled into his head and was causing extreme discomfort. The guy sought medical attention, to no avail, and was forced to live with this agony. During all this, he became increasingly mentally unbalanced. Hell, maybe Carla had a bug in her ear, as opposed to her posterior. Anyway, the guy ultimately went insane if I remembered it correctly. The point is, Carla was that insect in my head that was causing me to occasionally lose my grip. Not always, mind you, but often enough, like with each phone call.

I decided to go for a long run, my equalizer, thank God. And you know what I thought about? Her death.

Did I ever consider ending her life? Hmmmm. Where was Paladin of "Have Gun Will Travel" when you needed him?

Nah, interesting but useless thought, so I'll pass. I'll just let her continue to torment and abuse me. The very sad part of this was the realization that I would even harbor such a horrific thought even though it spoke volumes of my despair, and I could not help but think about a long ago Kingston Trio song about a man named Charlie who got on the Massachusetts Transit Authority train one morning and could not get off. Around and around he went. Would he ever return? No, and his fate was still unlearned. I could not find a way off the Carla lunacy train.

And the hits just keep coming.

1989/1990
CHAPTER TWENTY-TWO

After a few years of a Playboy subscription and self-induced celibacy, things changed. The fact of the matter was that I was not interested in any new relationships, which for me and my romantic tendencies, could easily result in another serious relationship followed by another marriage. Plus, there was that guilt and confusion thing banging around in my head. On the flip side, I denied myself the platonic and carnal pleasures of female companionship. Not right. I decided to re-enter the dating world. Had some nice dates with very likeable and interesting women, and sure enough, met a lady that worked in the Langley Air Force Base Officer's Club and lived in nearby Hampton, Virginia. Being a member of a Navy Officer's Club in the Norfolk area entitled me to use other service clubs due to a reciprocity agreement. Maria was her name, and like the Maria in West Side Story, she was lovely and with a beautiful name. She had an olive complexion, with a slight figure and great legs, and actually reminded me of Natalie Wood, who starred in West Side Story as "Maria", the object of the line in a song, "The most beautiful sound I ever heard... Maria". And she smiled a lot. She worked crazy hours at the base club, so our dates were limited. We did, however, work to see one another often after she got off work.

In fairness to Carla, although I questioned why she would be entitled to know, and eventually the children, I told her I had met someone that was special to me and that I was seriously dating. To no surprise, it did not go over well at all. Crazy. This is the same chatty woman that had no reservations in telling me about her boyfriends, which I cared less about, saying to myself, "marry the bitch", who she was screwing, and was still routinely lashing out at me, yelling, screaming, accusing, verbally abusing, and doing everything that drove me farther away from her. She didn't get it. It was all part of her persona to control by fear and intimidation. What could she really do to me? Not much, but I got sucked into her vortex of abuses and bludgeoning.

So, the price I paid for confiding in her was, of course, more abuse. Go figure. I tried to assure her I would continue to meet my obligations, but I also told her she needed to back off the vicious conversations and the long, chatty calls. I told her I wanted to keep things on an even keel. Lot of good that did. But Carla doesn't know "even". It all has to be her way. My relationship with Maria simply became more cannon fodder for the lunatic ex-wife. Many subsequent phone calls with her were laced with venom, more accusations, and cute stuff like, "You're letting your dick do your thinking for you". Neat. I told her to knock off the trash talk, but that would never work. The calls often came to my office, and my boss was smart and supportive enough to tell me she was not allowed to call me there. That was great, but she burned up the home phone.

"Is she spreading her legs for you?" Really?

"Knock it off, Carla."

"Does Maria call you at the office?"

"It's none of your business, plus she's too busy with her own career."

"She's a slut."

I hung up.

I called the kids that next weekend. After a nice chat with them, guess who jumps on the line. "I'm going to tell them about Maria."

"Why don't you let me do that in my own way and at an appropriate time? As their father, I am responsible to discuss the matter of Maria with them. I will do that. I know you take great pleasure in telling the children things about me they should not hear, and I am again asking you to stop the bad-mouthing. It's not healthy."

"I'll tell them what I want to tell them!"

"I'm not finished. Rather than talking to someone else about these matters between you and me, I will talk to an attorney to find out my legal rights. That way it takes all the emotional B.S. out of the equation." Yeah. Good luck on that, Dave. And the attorney may say, "That was nice of your ex to rendezvous, but if she says no more, and you want to see them, you will have to go to Washington to do so."

"I'm sticking to my decision not to rendezvous," she advises me.

"Okay, then I'll do round trips Friday and Sunday to bring them down here. And Carla, I'm really tired of hearing your accusations and trash talk which achieves nothing. I can do without all of it. I told you I understood your concern, although I question the legitimacy of your feelings, but it's my life and I don't want nor need to say anything to you about Maria and my personal life. I honestly wish I didn't have to talk to you at all."

"Fine. I still think you're letting your dick do your thinking for you." Ever the same Carla.

"Enough. You make me weary."

"Good. You deserve it you asshole."

"I'll ignore the ranting. Good luck with your acting. I'll think this through and get back to you about taking the kids for a weekend. When I do, and the opportunity presents itself, they will meet Maria."

"Well, maybe we just won't be here when you arrive to pick them up." Cute trick.

"Not good, Carla. I've got to go. It's so much fun talking or trying to talk to you. It's time to limit the phone contact, especially if you're going to be cutting and nasty. Oh, just one more thing. Maria is a far better woman and person than you could ever be."

"Don't call me!" Click.

Works for me, although I know any respite from her calls or jumping on the line will be short lived.

With the passing of time, when I had the kids I often found a way to do something with Maria. I was falling in love with her and wanted to be with her as often as I could. We went on visits to homes of her colleagues that had young children. She stayed with the kids to watch me run in an 8K race one Saturday, and we all went to Busch Gardens theme park. The point is, the kids were getting to know Maria, and I was able at the same time to be with her. Right or wrong, that was what I wanted in my life, and I felt that the kids spending some time with Maria every few weekends was okay. Their mother didn't think so, but what was she going do to about it? Plenty.

Later in the year a pattern developed whereby I would take the children every third or fourth weekend, and would make the round trips to Washington on Friday and Sunday to pick them up and return them home to their mother. As you would suspect, a number of reasons contributed to this new routine. In fact, it later evolved to every fourth weekend. I had had enough of seeing her and subjecting myself, and the kids, to the horrors of I-95.

There were times when every third or fourth weekend would not materialize when she would call to exclaim, "Don't come up here this weekend, and don't call. Don't call the kids, either, if you care about how we feel. It's okay to write them. That way I don't have to hear your voice." Wow, talk about the tables turning, which totally satisfied me.

Actually, it was a really bad year altogether after advising Carla of my new relationship. Let's just put it all out there. If you can believe it, the calls became even uglier. Incessant screams into my ear that when I had the kids one Easter weekend I would take them to her parents for dinner vice being able to take them to friends of mine and Maria, or telling me she would not be home when I returned the children to Washington. She remains totally manipulative, vengeful, and it causes much mental anguish for Maria and me as well. In one ranting phone conversation she threatened Maria if she drove up with me. "I'll shoot her!" she screamed. Really?

Here is how the lunatic ex treats my livelihood and ability to keep her in some green. When I tell her to stop calling me at the office, she screams, "You're the assistant director. Stand up to that asshole! He probably wants you to. You can take phone calls from me!" I try to tell her for the hundredth time that she's overstepping her bounds. Doesn't help. What did help was a week later when she called and got through to my boss of all things. And she yelled at him! She honestly did, and boy, did it piss me off. Told him I didn't return her calls. Like hell I don't. My boss told her that she could call, but only to leave a message, telling her also that if I didn't return calls she should see an attorney. Of course, by now I'm sweating my job security, and my boss reaffirms that fear with some subtle suggestions about her being a distraction to my job performance. So, the next time I talk to her I let her know that neither of us would like the downside of my being fired. It fell on deaf, dumb ears, but at least there was a better protocol regarding her calls to the office. She also had to get in the last word by screaming the usual un-pleasantries when I confirmed that the office ladies were told to screen my calls. What an idiot. My secretary and the ladies in the office had also had enough of her calls. In hindsight, would a court order preventing her from talking to me at all been the right course of action? I'm sure there would have been downsides to that as well, more of not knowing when that "second goose" was coming. Could she deny me access to my children?

I actually, believe it nor not, reflected on this incredibly bitter, unhappy, poor excuse for a human being. She wasn't stupid. She could have done something useful with her life, but of course that would have required securing child care and working for a living. Instead, all of her energy was negative, nary a thought-provoking, logical response. It was all wasted energy, wasted. Accusations. Temper tantrums. So much emotion and juggernauts of no value. Sad. It became obvious she was making up for her shortcomings, and decided she would take it out on others. I happened to be the easily accessible prime target. Because of the kids, she had carte blanche access to me, 24/7.

There was no limit to her repertoire of topics. In one phone call she seemed to hit all the hot buttons. Said I was mean to her, that I should be paying her more because I didn't take the kids as often, that her family and others (huh?) hate and dislike me (I don't care), made reference to the shortcomings of our sex life (I know why that happened), told me to leave her alone (gladly, please!), that I never call her (right – I don't, I call the kids!), complained again about my bringing Maria on a drive to Manassas, that she had a great sex life (lot of good it was doing), and the kickers, that she was going to give me the kids as a wedding present if we got married (go for it) and that she was going to make life miserable for Maria and me (nothing new there). Holy crap, that woman can vomit a string of venomous diatribe. And for the most part, I have to listen to all this, until the end of that same "conversation" when she again called Maria a whore. I hung up the phone. So what can I do? See an attorney, right? Which I did.

The head of the snake prevails.

1990

CHAPTER TWENTY-THREE

Kyle and Katie were old enough to spend the night with friends and were out of the house.

Billy was visiting, and he and Carla sat at the kitchen table. A blue haze hung in the air like the ocean-induced haze on the Beach Road on the Outer Banks. The smell of pot filled the air, and Billy was downing a bottle of cheap whiskey.

There wasn't much talk. Carla was taking her hits, sucking in the MJ and getting mellower by the minute, and Billy's eyes glazed over from the booze.

When they weren't closed, Carla's eyes gave off that thousand-yard stare, looking at nothing in particular. After all, there really wasn't much going on at the moment.

Billy sat across the table from her, matching her stare into nothingness. He was making up for lost time while in prison, and was comfortable that he was safe here, in a house, walls protecting him from view, but knew he could not smoke pot in the event the authorities gave him a drug test in his parole status. So he needed to stay "clean", keep from getting screwed, being out of work, and without a legit source of income.

Carla looked at Billy across the table. He had a stupefied look. She knew he would do whatever she asked him to do. Anything. With that recognition, a shit-eating grin appeared on her face. Billy may have noticed, but that was unlikely. He was in a world of his own. Damn good whiskey, he thought.

"You know, we need to come up with some shit to fuck up Dave," she offered.

"Who? What?"

"You know who I'm talking about. My ex-husband."

"Oh, sure. Well, maybe. You know, I've never seen or met him."

"That's alright. Doesn't matter. Probably best. We can mess with him even if you wouldn't recognize him."

"Okay." He's not real interested, but this is his good neighborhood friend, Carla, so he'll consider playing along. He's wondering what she has in mind. He's not really into suggesting anything, plus he's got to be careful because he's on probation. No slip-ups permitted. But he's not very mindful of all this, for his brain is acting like the haze in the kitchen.

"You know." She giggles. "You know, we gotta do something to him."

"Why?"

"Because he's an asshole and I said so. He knocked me up twice and now I'm stuck with two kids. And now he's got a lady friend that I'm sure he's fucking."

"They're good kids."

"You're not helping me, Billy."

The whiskey "truth serum" took over momentarily as he burst out with, "Well, you're not helping much either, cause I'm trying to clean up my act."

"You'll get over it. Maybe messing with his car. Break a

windshield. Maybe go back a few months later and slice a tire. That sort of stuff. Mess with him. Fuck him up a little. Stuff you can do and not get caught, and there's no way he can prove anything."

"Well, you do remember I already did something to him last year. I broke his car windshield. Isn't that enough?"

"That's right. That was great, Billy. That's the kind of shit I'm talking about." She's beaming and smiling from ear to ear, like a Cheshire cat.

"Yeah, might work." He's not very enthusiastic.

"And if he marries that bitch, maybe we break into his house. Screw with his mind."

"Yeah." He's messed up and just going along with the gag.

"What might be a good idea is to eventually mess with her. Rough her up a little. Damn bitch. I hate her."

"Carla, you're my buddy, but you guys are divorced. Why do you want me to do all this shit? I have to be careful."

"I already told you. He's an asshole and I hate him and his little whore lady friend, Maria. I can't let it go. I just want to screw with him any way I can. Plus, I've got my brother, Jim, where I want him. He's afraid to talk to me. I want as much of mom and dad's stuff as I can get when they die. I asked my dad for some money, but he said no, get a job. Screw him. And I've got the kids convinced their dad is an asshole. They don't want to see him."

"Alright. You know what? I think you're a psycho."

"You're probably right, and don't you forget it. Come here Billy," she says as she slides her chair back and repositions it. She's thinking of herself as this evil enchantress.

Billy gets out of his chair, somewhat clumsily because he is really messed up. He walks over to where Carla is sitting. She doesn't say anything, but grabs him by the waist to pull him a bit closer. She unfastens his belt, lets it hang loose, then reaches out to his pants, unfastens a button, and deftly pulls down his zipper. Billy is in la-la land, wondering what's happening until she slides down his pants, pulls down his skivvies, and softly puts him in her hand. She's fondling him. He looks down at her face and sees the shit eating grin he missed earlier in his haziness. He almost feels like he could fall over, but Carla is kneading him, making him bigger, and keeping him upright in more ways than one.

"Hey, stand still!" she demands.

Billy's in hog heaven. He hasn't experienced this or felt this righteous since before prison. Was it that long ago? All of a sudden, she takes him in her mouth. He's ready to jump out of his skin. He can't believe he's getting a hummer from his old neighborhood friend. "Rocket Man!"

"Don't come, Billy."

"Okay," he responds shakily.

"That feels good, huh?"

"Uh, huh."

"I like you Billy, and I know you'll do anything I ask you to do, yes?"

"Yes." Oh, my. This feels soooo good.

"Good. I know you will. Okay, enough of this. Fuck me, Billy. I'm ready, and I know you are." Her intention was to go upstairs to her bedroom, but Billy barely makes it out of the kitchen before he trips and falls from his undone pants, Carla falling on top of him in a tangle, and they get it on. It was like "Ted Mack's Original Amateur Hour".

The next morning Carla reminds Billy that he needs to do some things for her. He doesn't remember all of the specifics, but dutifully nods his head and says, "Yes."

Carla holds Billy's future in hand.

1990/1991
CHAPTER TWENTY-FOUR

I received a good referral for a divorce lawyer and called to make an appointment. I was able to see her late in the day, thus precluding having to take time off from work.

Arriving at her office on time, I introduced myself to the receptionist.

"Hi, I'm Dave Pedersen and I have a five o-clock appointment with Ms. Wilson."

"Good afternoon," she replied, a pleasant smile on her face. "Please have a seat and I'll let Ms. Wilson know you are here."

"Thank you." I took a seat, and sat wondering how this meeting would go and what would I learn. Hopefully, something useful that will help me in my dealings with the cougar.

I didn't have long to wait. "Good afternoon, Mr. Pedersen. I'm Barbara Wilson. How are you today?"

"It's a pleasure to meet you, Ms. Wilson. I'm doing well, thank you." I almost was tongue-tied. I mean, she was knock-out gorgeous and very shapely, but I had to get that off my mind fast.

"You can call me Barbara. Can I call you Dave?"

"By all means, Barbara." Had to say her name right away to avoid forgetting it.

"Let's go to my conference room." I followed her into a very well appointed room, mahogany furniture, the right amount of plants and fu-fu. Quite comfortable.

"Very nice."

"Thank you. How can I help you today, Dave?"

"I'm divorced and my ex-wife lives with the children in the Washington suburbs. To say that she is a terror to deal with, is a thorn in my side, and is an extremely vocal and vicious lady is understatement. She continues to make phone calls which turn into ranting and tirades, and I'm sick of it."

"Well, you probably already know that because of the children, she has open access to you. That doesn't mean she can rip into you every chance she gets. You really have three options. Deal with it as best you can. Hang up on her when she goes overboard. Or we could execute a restraining order."

"I see. Not much I can do."

"True. If we go the latter route, that could create problems communicating with the children. And from what you've said, I suspect she will find other ways to torment you."

"She has and she will. I'll try the hanging up on her when things get real nasty, which is often the case, with name-calling about my new lady friend. Shifting gears, can she tell me the kids cannot see my sister, whom she does not like?"

"No. While they are in your custody, it's your call."

"Can she do the same with my lady friend, Maria?"

"Same answer. No she cannot."

"What about those instances when she tells me on the phone that she will deliver them to me for custody in four hours?"

"It must be done legally. Change the court order, and of course modify any child support directives. If you have the children she's not entitled to child support."

"What about medical bills? She claims that I must pay one-hundred percent of them, and she helps out on major expenses."

"It's moot. Major is not relevant. A medical bill is a medical bill."

"I've told her I'm going to start paying her on the first and fifteenth of the month vice bi-weekly. It works out better for my planning and budgeting."

"That's okay."

"She has told me she no longer is willing to rendezvous with me on the weekends I have the kids because she doesn't want to encourage a relationship between Maria and the kids."

"I can't help you there. It's your call. So, you either do not see the children or you make the necessary round trips to pick them up and return them to her. Sorry."

"That's okay. I won't be making many trips. It gets tiresome driving up and down I-95."

"Understood. That's your call, Dave."

"Last but not least, what can I do about the name calling toward my lady friend and threats to go to her house?"

"Well, she can name-call, and when she does you hang up, telling her the conversation is over. She can threaten to go to your lady friend's house. If she doesn't do it, it's moot. If she does, your lady friend can call the police and have her removed for trespassing. If she does something physical that's a whole different matter for the police to deal with. I would advise your lady friend to be prepared to call the police should any of that happen."

"Okay. My ex-wife has told me that she has actually been on the doorstep of my lady friend's house. She's scary."

"Yes. It certainly sounds like it, and I don't envy you one bit. Is there anything else I can answer for you?"

"No, I think that's it. You've been very helpful, and I appreciate it. This at least gives me a sound legal basis for my decision-making going forward."

"Good. Please let me know if I can help you. You have my card. Call me if needed. It's been a pleasure meeting with you."

"I will, and thank you again."

With that, we said our goodbyes and I headed out of the office to drive home, standing by for the all too frequent call from my bitch ex-wife.

Receiving some legal counsel helped me, but it didn't stop the phone calls or her jumping on the line.

Maria and I had been seeing as much as we could of one another, work schedules permitting. As best I could tell, she and the children got along well, with no help from their mother, of course, who I know did her very best to poison them on Maria.

We did pretty well at meeting up on Friday nights, when we would hit different local spots that had free appetizers. There, we would sip on a couple of drinks, partake in the goodies, and hold hands while we talked about our respective weeks and got to know each other better. It was relaxing. It was calm. It was certainly therapeutic, a blessed change from the ever-present, on-going calls from Carla, who continued to make it clear how absolutely incredulous she was that I would have a lady friend and forsake her. She flat out did not accept it. How many ways could I tell or write her to say we're divorced, the marriage we had is long over, I don't even like talking to or seeing you, stay away from my personal life, my calls to the kids will be limited because I don't appreciate you jumping on the line, and knock off the name calling. I told Carla that there were no secrets between me and Maria, she knows about the times I had taken her out for a meal, and the mean things Carla has uttered to the children about her. It just doesn't let up. In fact, Maria made a decision that she didn't want to be around the children until things got better and certain people stopped acting out with so much spite and anger. Where did that lead? It meant I made the conscious decision to see my kids less. Was I wrong? Given the totality of Carla's venom, I think not. And at that point in my life, where was my real source of happiness? Carla and the children? No. Maria. Carla made that bed, so everyone gets to sleep in it and suffer because of her dim-witted logic and vengeance. Oh, I also told Carla that Maria was not frightened by her threats of bodily harm or other manifestations of her visceral psyche. Bring it on. We'll deal with it.

Along with our Friday nights together, Maria and I enjoyed a few two-night stays in Nags Head, North Carolina on the Outer Banks. We're both beach-lovers, so staying at a hotel right on the beach was perfect.

It felt good to have a lady in my life again, and I emphasize "lady" for a lot of reasons. Carla was no longer a lady.

Well, things were mostly good, excluding the phone conversations with Carla. Similar to the windshield episode at my apartment, I came out one morning to find not only a flat tire but a sliced tire as well. I looked around and did not see any other vehicles in tire extremis, so deduced that I was targeted. I had a very good idea who did it, but how do I prove it? If I went to the police and suggested Billy, I'm sure he would have had a good alibi, either Carla or one of his buddies. Chalk up another Billy adventure. And the boy wasn't doing very well on other accounts. I don't know if it affected his probationary status, but "chatty Carla" had told me that back home he had been ticketed for public intoxication. That was Carla for you – she just had to keep me informed on her life, who she was dating, who she was no longer dating, a child care business she had attempted, and of course, Billy Boy, none of which I cared about and frankly told her so. She didn't listen. Nothing could shut her up, except for me hanging up on her when she got too ugly. She did tell me she and Billy were seeing more of one another. What she saw in him I don't know, but that door swung both ways. I just saw trouble ahead with that relationship. Who knows what it might spawn?

Carla and I had other disagreements, particularly with regard to our separation agreement. Without getting into specifics, I had met her more than half way on financial aspects, and she knew it. Child support, medical bills, payment methods. I did more than required. It was the guilt thing, plus she was in my ear and head multiple times a week. When she told me she had told people that she had walked all over me in recent years post-divorce, I decided it was time to put some things in writing to advise her we would be going strictly by the agreement in the future. She let me know she was not happy about it, but what the hell.

The problem I had with Carla was that it was absolutely, one-hundred percent, irrefutably impossible to have a civil discourse with her. Wasn't happening. Any discussion that started off civil eventually turned the corner to a vicious verbal tirade. End of discussion. So, I had to resort to writing letters, not that I had all the time in the world to do so, but that was the only method I had of communicating with her. Did it work? Largely, no, because she would read a letter, pick up the phone, and well, you know.

I wrote one letter shortly after my meeting with the lawyer to try and capsulize things one more time. In it, I told her that there was no reason why we could not keep a civil relationship through everything, especially for the children, and that it had been almost four years since our break-up. Things shouldn't get so emotional. Who the hell did I think I was communicating with, the sweet fairy Godmother? I added that the kids did not need to hear it. I reminded her that things were okay (I lied) until I got another woman in my life, adding that it was obvious the kids now harbored ill feelings toward Maria, who was always sweet and good to them. Contrary to what the kids were lead to believe, I went on to say, Maria did not come between Carla and me. I told Carla we were never going to get back together for the simple reason that, reaffirmed with almost every phone call or face to face encounter, I would not live with her again. I reminded her what my lawyer had told me about visitation and with whom I could have the children around. I re-emphasized that she, Carla, had no reason to comment on my personal life.

Do you think that worked? Hell, no. The opinions about Maria continued, as did the hang-ups by me, and I called the children less frequently and stuck to a monthly visitation. I also sent more letters, always much the same tenor that she back off and settle down. But, you don't change the stripes on a tiger. She was molded as a vicious, vindictive screamer, and that is what she would always be. She even felt it was okay to call my parents and occasionally yell at them, for God's sake. What a looney. I did threaten her with a restraining order on my parents.

I'll tell you what she deserves – Billy as a mate. Wouldn't that be a match made in heaven? I wonder how he would do putting her in her place, assuming he could. I wonder how he would respond when ultimately the knife was waved in his face.

Things did improve with the kids. I was seeing them monthly, and when I brought them to my place we often did activities involving Maria, as I had told Carla would happen. Maria had some good friends with children the ages of Kyle and Katie, so we often hooked up with them for a cook-out or day around a pool. Busch Gardens was nearby, and that was always a fun day. And we often played putt-putt golf. Actually, the kids seemed to get along well with Maria, and it appeared genuine. They formed their own opinion. How about that?

Maria and I dealt with the crazy phone calls that came to my apartment as best we could. To her credit, she understood that Carla was a cougar in disguise, not that it made matters that much easier for our relationship. There was no way around Carla. Maria and I discussed the situation frequently, and each time Maria assured me that she would not let the deranged ex affect us. A poem to Maria:

The beach is deserted
This wind chilled day
I am alone
At one with nature
 At its most benevolent,
With an incessant wind
And the constant crash
Of foamy surf roaring ashore.
Even the seagulls
 Are conspicuously absent.
Perched behind a sand dune
The wind rushing by overhead
I don't feel the cold,
For the sun in my face
And thoughts of you
Warm me throughout.
My mind drifts like the wind
Coveting
Image after image of you.
Your walk
 Your enchanting eyes
You in my arms
 Holding you close.
I am in ecstasy,
A new serenity found.

There's just one thing.
Like an unfinished masterpiece
This beach is incomplete
    Without you.
I wish you were here
At my side.
Today
Tomorrow
    And the next day too.
I wonder where the seagulls are.
I wonder.

Maria was special and I fell hard for her. No surprise. We had a great time together, enjoyed our sex, and it was during one of those two-night stays in Nags Head that I proposed to her. She said, "Yes", but I have to wonder what thoughts ran through her pretty head about Carla and her invasions of our privacy and lives. She had to think the antics of the avenging "ex" would continue. Wedding plans ensued, and it was to be a small ceremony.

Simply as a courtesy, I sent Carla a letter advising her of the engagement between Maria and me. As Yogi Berra was famous for saying, "It was deja 'vu all over again". In response to my letter she called.

"I got your letter. You're making a mistake." Oh, how I wanted to come back with, "You mean, like the one I made in marrying you?"

"No, you're very wrong, and beyond that, it is none of your business. You know about it, and that's that."

"Oh, it is my business, dickhead. We might move to Virginia Beach. If we do, I think I'm going to give you custody."

I'm thinking Billy is playing a role in this scenario since he has been visiting her. "Fine. We've talked about this before. You know what you have to do."

This always slows her down. "We'll see, you prick." Click.

From the perspective of dealing with Carla and having to take her phone calls, it's a relatively mild summer, if any period of time dealing with her can be labeled as such. The kids flew out to California to spend some time with my parents, and they spent a few weeks with Carla's parents, during which I took off some time from work so I could have them for a week. With that set-up, Carla has less reason to routinely lose it and call me, for her emotional quiver is near empty.

But all good things come to an end. The end of summer with the kids back with their delightful mother brought back the usual scathing remarks after I had talked to the children. Some things don't change, and unfortunately, hearing her lovely voice is difficult to avoid unless I opt to stop calling the children altogether. Tough to do. They're my kids, well, sort of.

One of the first things we did when Maria and I began cohabiting about a month prior to our wedding was that we got an unlisted phone number. That really sent Carla up a tree. Oh, my, was she hot, and the phone call to inform her of this change turned nasty. We simply did not trust her with our phone number, and Carla had continued to behave in a manner that showed the wisdom of that decision. I told her she could call me at the office to leave a message. I gave her three numbers, particularly in the event of an emergency. Carla got hysterical, claiming I was trying to put her over the edge. Look in the damn mirror, Carla. She had to be right and in control. But, here was the kicker from that conversation. She had the gall to tell me she would do something to Maria, face to face, or pay someone else to do something to her, adding, "I don't care if I go to prison!" Prison, or a mental institute, is where she needed to reside. Besides concern for Maria's welfare, I'm thinking two things: 1) Why me? Why was this evil, condescending, vicious person put in my life? What did I do to deserve her? It must have been all the hell I raised while at Happy Valley College. This was payback time, and I was sure that no other man on the face of God's earth had a wife and ex-wife like Carla. No way. There couldn't be two alike. And 2) I thought of dear 'ol Billy, Mr. jail bird felon, a person that was going in the wrong direction, and now spending more time with the lunatic. He definitely displayed a criminality streak and mindset, and I wouldn't put anything past him if his dear friend Carla asked him to do harm to someone. I wonder if he would share Carla's sentiment that she would not mind going to prison? Anyway, I simply reminded Carla that we had no choice on the unlisted phone matter in view of her vulgar call to us earlier in the month. So what did Carla do? She calls Maria's mother to bad-mouth me for an hour. Oh, my God, she just doesn't stop. Just a little Gatling gun of venom to any and every one.

It gets better. Carla did the requisite message at office thing two days later, and when I later return the call she tells me she also now has an unlisted number and gave me numbers of three of her friends (I was flabbergasted she had a friend, let alone three) in case of an emergency. I never used them. Not one. Hey, worked for me. She said she was glad I did what I did, so she could justify doing the same. Also told me she had talked to an attorney and friends, and the kids, and that "we're cutting you out." Thank you, Lord Jesus! It was a Mexican stand-off. And let me tell you, it was quiet for a while. I wasn't going north, and she wasn't calling. A few months later, however, she was back to her evil ways. We had made arrangements for me to drive to Manassas to pick up the kids for a weekend. Only guess what? The bitch was not at the house when I arrived! She did have the decency to leave me a note on the door saying she could not contact me without having my home phone number. The fallacy of her illogical explanation and excuse was that this was a Friday and she could have used an office number to reach me. Geez, woman, you can do better than that.

We talked a few days later, going in circles about phone numbers and visitation, and at which time she claimed that Maria and I were calling all the shots. Huh? What shots? Things should have been simple, and would have been in a normal divorce situation. She also was incoherent enough to say she was thinking about suing us for "abuse". Can you believe it? Talk about the proverbial pot calling the kettle black! Abuse? She knows and has defined abuse, like the dump truck load of it she had laid on me for so many years.

Maria and I got married in late September at a very nice restaurant in Hampton, on the water. Lovely place. My parents flew out, and we were joined by Maria's mother and stepfather, my boss and his wife, and some Navy and Air Force colleagues. We didn't tell the invitees the purpose of the event. It was simply advertised as a "celebration". So, after a period of time allowing our guests to relax with a pre-dinner drink, I positioned myself at the front of our catered area, thanked everyone for coming, and introduced the preacher that would marry Maria and me that very night. Our guests gasped with delight. It was a superb evening and everyone had a great time. The next day Maria and I flew to San Juan and embarked on a cruise ship for our honeymoon. It was the first time cruising for both of us, and we loved it. The ship sailed around the eastern Caribbean, making stops in St. Thomas, Guadalupe, Granada, and Aruba. We were dazzled by all the beautiful jewelry in so many shops in St. Thomas and Aruba. We saw some of the same in Old San Juan before being taken to the airport. Of course, one of the outstanding features of the cruise was that Carla could not reach us. This was Maria's second marriage as well. What I came to realize was that our two divorce scenarios were different as night and day. Maria and her ex-husband did not communicate. Zip. How splendid was that? So why the hell was I at one to five million odds, so lucky as to win the marriage and divorce lottery jackpot with an evil screamer as a wife and a lunatic, vengeful ex-wife? How?

The figurative "honeymoon from Carla" was over, as she picked up where she left off. Oh, did the royal shit hit the fan shortly after returning home. Oh, my. Carla was absolutely beside herself. The calls were frequent and ugly and things just got progressively worse. It was like she knew she had a license to torment, and added Maria as a target. The only good thing was that the calls were limited to when she left a message and I returned her calls. Maria and I were able to combine our resources to purchase a small house in Hampton in the Buckroe Beach area. It was large enough for us and the occasionally visiting children.

Getting married didn't affect visitation or having the kids for a weekend. By then, I was driving both ways, all the way up and back, and the visits were about every four weeks, sometimes stretching to five or more. Carla and I didn't chat as much as before, and the turnaround at her place was quick and short, the shorter the better. She still managed to get in her digs.

Her logic was disarming. "Did you and the kids spend a lot of time with Maria?"

"Well, yes. We're all under the same roof, you know."

"I don't like that. They shouldn't be subjected to your wife. The visitation time is for them to spend time with you alone," she countered. She was getting hot, but I didn't give a damn. In a few minutes I would be in the quiet privacy of my car rolling down the road, joyful that I would not have to see her for at least another four weeks. Screw her.

"Pretty tough to pull that off, Carla. We're all together. I'm not going to ask Maria to leave the house. And yes, we do things together. That's the way it is going to be, period."

Not what she wanted to hear. "We'll see." I'm gone and on the road. Ciao, bitch.

Truthfully, we all seem to be doing well at our house. It's now a fact of life. They appear to be comfortable with the fact that we are now together in the same house. Maria treats them great, and I think they respond accordingly. Maria is a loving person and she likes Kyle and Katie. But I really do not know for sure how the kids feel about Maria. I know they have been brain washed by their mother against Maria, so time will tell.

This is how things went for really the next year or two. On and off visitation. Returning phone messages left at the office, during which the conversation always ended up going south. Face to face encounters were blessedly reduced to a minimum. While she claimed she did so, I'll never know how many times she was on our doorstep and departed unannounced and unbeknownst to us. Or how many times Billy Boy may have done the same.

Maria and I got a much needed respite from Carla when she up and told me that she was going to take the offer of a high-school girlfriend living in New York City to go and live with her while she again pursued her acting ambitions. This was also about the same time she told me that Kyle said he would rather live with someone else if his mother died. Are you kidding me? Well, there you go. So, I guess I was wrong about the kids and Maria. Go with God, son. There's not much I can do about it. Carla's missed calling was to work in an interrogation chamber.

Please move far, far away Carla.

1992/1994
CHAPTER TWENTY-FIVE

Things weren't that quiet. Billy continued to be a perceived thorn in my side. I say perceived because I could never prove he was culpable for the windshield and tire incidents. His latest trick, and I'm confident it was him, although not one-hundred percent certain, was to tailgate me one night as I drove out of the neighborhood to hit a few stores. I must say, he had to be patient, for he had no idea I would be on the road that night. He must have been sitting and waiting on a side street near our house, and as luck would have it, I had to jump on the freeway. It didn't take me long to realize there was a vehicle right on my butt as we travelled at high speed. He hadn't made contact, but he didn't have to in order to scare the crap out of me. Where are the police when you need them? I tried speeding up, but he hung with me. I tried slowing down, hoping that would exasperate him and he would curl off, and that didn't work. He tapped my rear end once, and I thought he was trying to run me off the road and kill me. I was looking for an exit, but there wasn't one in sight. He would occasionally flash his bright lights to try to disorient me. My eyes were now seeing stars. All I could do was maintain speed, and when I finally came to an exit I took it. He obviously didn't want to take the chance of being identified or me getting his license plate number, so he continued on straight. It was too dark and he was now too far away for me to see his plate, or even get a good look at his car for that matter. And there was no possibility of facial recognition, for the same reason. But regardless, I had never laid eyes on that felon. Never met or seen him. I couldn't pick him out of a line-up of one. I pulled into the first parking lot I found, stopped the car, and exhaled. That was fun. What's next? It had to be Billy doing Carla's bidding.

Carla's calls continued, under the pretext that she was calling so the kids could talk to their father. If you believe that I have some waterfront property in Arizona I would like to sell you, as the trite expression goes, excluding the Colorado River and Lake Havasu. Not much left after that. One time the message was, "We may be getting snow in New York. Please call me." I kid you not. When I later returned the call, the subject was totally different, so the "problem" was a subterfuge to say something about my personal life with Maria. Stupid me for returning calls. Another time it was about Kyle's "D" in physical education. I called him to tell him he needed to clean up his act in P.E., then she jumped on the line to say she was ready to give me custody of the kids. Ho-hum. I told her to bring it on. The calls were sometimes every other day, depending on their "importance", and sometimes there might be a ten-day break. Another call informed me she was confused about her current boyfriend. A subsequent call a few days later advised me she was no longer seeing her boyfriend. Who cares? She took a dig at me saying, "You are someone that love comes and goes with, and you easily fall out of love." I said I had work to do. Goodbye. Our phone calls are one-sided. I listen. I don't opinionate. I try to wear her down. She seems to think the calls are okay since it is a way for me to more frequently talk to the kids in New York. Right. I didn't talk to the kids the two previous calls.

There were some good news calls, like the time she told me Kyle was doing better in school and about a ski trip on which Katie was going. During these calls, she tells me about her friends and the occasional progress she was making on gaining contacts for acting tryouts. She did tell me that the kids were in a commercial. Good stuff. Otherwise, her calls wasted my time, for I was tired of hearing about her life and issues in New York. I tried to tell her I was not interested, but she continued to abuse my conversations with the kids.

Summer arrived and that meant the children would be spending some time with their grandparents. This also allowed them to see their cousins. I took the kids on some of the weekends, knowing they would rather be with their grandparents and cousins. Okay. They're getting older and time with dad and Maria took a lower priority. And that would continue to be the case. Hey, I didn't blame them. I would have wanted to spend time with other kids my age, especially as teenagers.

It crossed my mind, too, that maybe some of their friends, especially those in New York and back home in Manassas, were also in divorced families, and maybe there was a kinship with other children of divorce. That may have played a role in their desire to spend more time with their friends. Children can also feel emotionally abandoned by their fathers. Was that me? How much a factor was the total disdain I had for their mother that certainly mitigated against me wanting to be around her and making those long drives to Washington to see them? I wanted no part of her. Of course, for now I was not seeing them on a routine basis since they were in New York.

I had read an excellent piece on the children of divorce. Divorce is not like any other family crisis. It's a man-woman crisis. The mother or father may resolve it, close one marital chapter and go on to the next. For the children there are no chapters, just one long continuum. The child sees an unhappy marriage (ours certainly was, although I had resigned myself against divorce. They certainly saw their mother's ugly behavior toward me). He or she lives through the brouhaha of divorce (especially by my living and working in Hampton Roads, Virginia, and the kids living with their mother in Washington), the stress of early post-divorce, the years after (I can imagine what they were told about me and Maria when my new relationship materialized), all of which they might take into their adulthood as they form their own points of view about relationships and marriage. I knew my children would have a totally different perspective on marriage than me, who had parents that seemingly did it pretty well and didn't have to divorce.

In hindsight, from everything I have read, you don't stay together for the children, so I was wrong there. Those who choose to do nothing whatsoever will come to regret it. Ignoring an unhappy situation may be the easiest course of action, but it is also the one most likely to result in a sense of wasted opportunity. It was best that Carla filed, for the children of unhappy marriages do terribly. Kyle's improving school grades might be proof. But Carla was breaking the rules of divorce by her many heinous actions that did not mute the effects on both me and the kids. I had come across an article on Ex-Etiquette that included suggestions such as putting your kids first, don't badmouth the ex in front of your children, not to be spiteful or hold grudges, and to prevent arguments. I did learn, however, that the affects can be muted when parents manage to keep their post-divorce hostility under control. Well, there you go. Carla got an "F" on Ex-Etiquette, to no surprise. Her vindictiveness and ugliness were non-stop, and the kids heard and saw most of it. Shame on her.

I tried yet one more time to put things in perspective for her, and it naturally had to be in the form of a letter. In that letter I told her I was still trying to come to grips with the realities of divorce, which I suspect was understandable. It would have been much easier if she had gone on with her life and stayed out of mine. I explained that in the first few years I felt a lot of guilt and confusion. No secret there, adding that confusion is no longer an issue. I'm re-married and very happy with my life with Maria. I told Carla that, believe it or not, in the early years I prayed a lot in and out of church. But God didn't "tell me" to reconcile with you. There are rare feelings of guilt, but they are becoming less frequent. I suspect the guilt emanates from seeing them try to carry on without a husband and father. Of course, how I was treated by Carla post-divorce, not to mention the devastating fights when we were still married, certainly played into the minimization of guilt and confusion.

Do the letters ever do any good, where Carla might take a pause and say to herself, "You know, he's right?" No way. She showed her stripes a long time back and hasn't changed.

I did have some fun with one of her phone calls. Of course, I had no idea where her friend lived in New York and where they were setting up their home. I assumed it wasn't a cushy Brownstone, and I hoped they weren't living in Bedford-Stuyvesant. She had called and left a message at the office, and I had returned the call as soon as work allowed.

"You left a message to call." Short and sweet.

"Yes. Thanks for calling back. I wanted you to know our address in the event you write to the children, and of course for mailing checks to me."

"Right. Lay it on me."

She gave me the address, and when I heard her say, "East 89

Street," I chuckled to myself and decided I would have some fun at her expense. "Do you have it?"

"Oh, yes. I have it. You know, I constantly find it's a small world. In the early 1970's I spent a few weekends on that very street, visiting and having a wonderful time with a girl named Laura that I knew from grad school. Nice girl, and she showed me around the city." I was trying to unload as much as I could before she had a chance to speak. "Yeah, I went jogging from her place over to Gracie Mansion, and did some neat bar-hopping and dining out around there."

Silence. It worked. She was speechless. "You prick," she exclaimed, and hung up.

My smile was ear to ear. There you go, Carla, you know about my Taiwanese lady friend, my Kiawah Island friend, and now my New York City lady friend, but there are many more that you will never know about. Iceland, Italy, Japan, and many places in between, including Washington. I didn't hear from her for over a week.

She and the kids were in the city for probably close to two years, but other than rubbing shoulders with actors and the occasional talent scout, things weren't breaking for her. Must have been too old, but I sure wasn't going to suggest that!

I had a feeling things were starting to unravel for her when I returned one of her calls to hear this.

"Hello. Dave?"

"Who else would it be, Carla? What's up? I'm busy here in the office."

"Tough. I have to tell you about something that happened to me last night."

"Go ahead."

"My friend and I got a babysitter for the kids and went out. We went out to dinner and rode the subway to visit some neat places."

"Get to the point, Carla."

"Well, we ended up in Greenwich Village Park, and there was hardly anyone around, so we smoked some pot."

"You did what? In public?" I was shocked.

"You heard me. Well, a narc caught us and we were taken in for drug possession. It was terrible. They took mug shots and finger-printed us. How disgusting."

"Yes, I'm sure it was. What's the outcome?"

"They let us go since we had a small amount and we weren't dealing it, but we will have to go to court. They were nice cops."

"Okay. Good and bad." I really didn't care about all this nonsense, but I played along. "When is your court hearing?"

"Next week. My roommate knows an attorney and she has already spoken with him. He assured her not to worry, especially due to the small amount and first offense."

"Okay."

"That's all you have to say?" She's incredulous.

"Yep. That's all. I'm sure you can take care of yourself."

"Thanks! The attorney said we will probably receive a fine. Will you help me by paying part of it?"

"Hell, no. You can pay it. I have no responsibility to help you in a situation like this, Carla. You're on your own."

"You prick! I knew you would say that! You don't care."

"No, I don't. Now, if you are done I have to get back to work so I can continue to afford to send you your alimony and child support checks."

That slowed her down. Money talk always does. "Follow the money", as the expression goes. What a truism.

"Goodbye." The phone went dead. Lovely sound.

And her life started to unravel.

1994/1996
CHAPTER TWENTY-SIX

The acting dream seemed more and more out of reach. No tryouts, no contracts, no stardom, no big bucks to deny me. Carla had to recalibrate her life ambitions, assuming she had any aside from making life miserable for me and then Maria. Maria and I talked about it occasionally, commiserating, for it was an equalizer we had in dealing with Carla's antics from far away.

"You know, it's sad," I said to Maria one Friday night over a glass of wine. "She has custody of the children, which is what she wants for a number of reasons, and she's smart enough to probably find a decent job. I'm sure she could find affordable child care."

"I'm sure she could, Dave, but she doesn't want that. Why pursue something like acting at this point in her life? That's not easy."

"No, it certainly isn't. The thing is, government and decent clerical or administrative, bookkeeping jobs are a dime a dozen in D.C. Why doesn't she pursue that? It's much more realistic." This was the pragmatic side of me talking. And sticking to basics.

229

"Because she wants to just live off your free money. It's easier."

Ouch. A bad topic. "Well, she needs to get her ass in gear and get a job, but I can't force her to. And she'll continue to play the "Woe is me" game and blame everyone else for her problems. And take it out on us, for sure."

The following week I returned a call from Carla.

"You called?"

"Yeah. I just wanted to tell you the outcome of our court appearance."

Oh, geez. "And?"

"The judge was pretty cool about it, and the arresting policeman was pleasant. Our attorney asked the judge to drop the charges and put us on probation, but the judge said there needed to be a lesson learned from our foolishness, so he fined us each five-hundred dollars and we were also put on probation."

"Okay. Could have been worse."

"Yeah. Expensive lesson from partying where we should not have been."

"Yep. I gotta go. Anything else?"

"I'm thinking about returning to Washington. Things just aren't working out here, and it's an expensive place to live. I'll let you know. If we do, Kyle will be able to start his freshman year of high-school down there. Good timing."

"Keep me posted. Bye."

That was it. She had to tell me about the pot ordeal. Whatever.

Carla didn't again mention returning to Washington, so I guess life in the big city was more accommodating than what she had let on about it in an earlier conversation. She wasn't mentioning Billy, either, so he must not have been making the long drive to New York to visit his dear friend, or maybe he was back in jail.

None of this changed anything for me, since she had figuratively placed a bulls-eye on my person for continued torment and torture. It never stopped. How could I be so unlucky? Thank God she wasn't living in the same neighborhood, or even the same city. Here's what I had to deal with over the next few years during the continuing saga of our ugly divorce.

The calls were steady. Same old shit. Did the hang-up thing when she got ugly, which was often. Some of the calls were a scatter-gun shot covering multiple hot-button subjects.

"Are you going to pay for Kyle's sports expenses?"

"That's what the child support is for, so the answer is no."

"You cheap sonofabitch!"

"You done?"

"No. I'm having trouble with my townhouse tenants in Manassas."

"Sorry, can't help you there, Carla."

She then launched into her life in the big city woes, how she was getting nowhere on her acting, that New York was a very expensive place to live, that she wasn't happy with the men she was meeting, and on, and on.

"Go back to Washington," I told her.

"I may be ready to give up the kids."

"You know what you have to do."

"Shit." That's all she could say or do.

"I have to get back to work."

But then she gets on the college expenses kick, even though it's four years away for Kyle, and six for Katie! "You're going to pay one-hundred percent of their college, you know."

"Carla, we've had this conversation. No, I will not. As I have tried to tell you, college costs will be a joint effort. We'll do what we can to take advantage of grants or loans due to our divorced status. I will certainly contribute as much as I can, realizing I've got a home and life to support here. And like I did when I attended college and grad school, the children hopefully will not find it terribly beneath them to work a few hours a day to help out. In fact, it has been proven that college students that work less than twenty hours a week have better grades."

"Bullshit! I won't have my kids working when in college. And I'll get an attorney after you to make sure you pay all of it." That worked. This is coming from someone who is absolutely clueless about college and has never set foot on a college campus, and who doesn't want to contribute a cent.

"Gee, then maybe they won't be able to attend college. How's that? No one can force me to pay for their education. We'll talk about it more at a later date. Good bye."

Her next call I had to return got much, much too personal, and suggested this woman of vengeance still had her sights on getting me back into her life, regardless of all my previous pronouncements that our marriage had ended eight years prior and that there was no way in hell I was going to do something so foolish, irrational and flat out crazy as to live under the same roof with her, ever. Ever.

"Dave, I'm in dire financial straits."

"Well, I can't help you. I send enough to you."

"I need more. You know, my phone bill this month is three-hundred dollars! That's crazy."

"Then stop making all those needless calls to me, like this."

"I can't help it. You're the only man I can talk to."

"Lucky me."

"Oh, you love it."

"Wrong. You can please stop calling me any time you want."

"Right. You know, we never should have divorced. I'd marry you again. Do you plan to stay married to Maria?"

What the hell? What is it with this woman? Why can't she leave me alone and get on with her life? She is an absolute fruitcake. I can't shake her. "Of course I do!" This conversation was making me feel very uncomfortable, and I tried to get her to hang up. She had to be high on pot.

"Damn it."

"Goodbye, Carla. Stop calling me."

A few months later, along with the many calls to talk about the kid's grades, school pictures, medical bills, always a fun topic, and Kyle's modeling success, she's back on me about my marriage.

"Are you going to be available any time soon?" I mean, just in case I re-marry and then you divorce. I wouldn't want that to happen."

She's looney tune and dangerous. "Don't plan on it, Carla. I'm very happily married. Please stop this foolishness."

"Well, I just wanted to check."

"Stop it. And please stop calling me about stuff like this. You continue to abuse my access to the children."

"Before I forget, you need to talk to Katie about her grades and tell her not to be influenced by her lazy girlfriends."

"I shall do that."

Out of right field, "You deserted us, and we think you should leave Maria and come back to us."

"No. Now stop it! Stop encroaching on my personal life." I think I knew where this was going, and it was not good.

"Then leave me and the kids alone. Stay away. (Huh? They're in New York!). And don't call or write. We're tired of you. I wish you were dead, asshole!"

I hung up on her. How much of this do I have to endure? If I stop taking or returning her calls, not talk to her at all, she has every legal right to have an attorney execute a court order against me, directing me to take every call. If I challenge it, guess who must make a trip to either New York or Washington? I can't win. I'm trying to stay somewhat connected to my children and must continue to tolerate her bullshit. I give up.

It didn't take long for her to get back on the beat up Dave wagon. Same topics, same ranting, same torment, and throw in some medical issues of hers and her theory that I could take the kids child support money after they turn eighteen and put it into college expenses. Said she'd take me to court if I didn't. Good luck on that. My explanations continued to fall on very deaf ears. Subsequent discussions on that topic would go something like this:

"I know you think you're going to get them to attend a state college. Well, I think Kyle ought to attend Georgetown University. That will cost you!"

To which I replied, "I don't care where they go. I'm paying the same amount whether it's Georgetown, Princeton, or George Mason in-state."

She got on a kick again about the amount of life insurance I had in her name, which was the required amount, threatening to get an attorney after me, some medical issues of Katie's, along with her school grades, and she even got on me about flying out to California to attend my parent's fifty-year anniversary! I told her it was none of her damn business. By the way, Maria and I had a wonderful time in San Francisco, at the Naval Station Treasure Island Officer's Club, a location I had arranged using my Navy contacts. It just seems like every other day it was something else involving the kids. Eye exams expenses, sports expenses, eyeglasses, tax exemptions on our returns, that I failed to call the kids about their school grades, and found it necessary to tell me she did not want Maria making the trip to take the kids back to New York at the end of the upcoming summer. In her words, she did not want to see the woman to whom I was married and sleeping with. She let it slip that she was upset that I was re-married after nine years and she had still not been able to re-marry. Gee, I wonder why? Was there some other guy out there stupid enough to ask for her hand in marriage? She also told me she learned that Maria was a

GS-12 with the Air Force. I wish! Who could she have heard that from? I told her it was none of her business, and that Maria was graded lower than a twelve. Did no good, calling me a liar until I hung up on her.

Things really got whacko when she asked my advice about her returning to Washington. She came up with twisted logic that since I was paying for the kid's college, that they did not want to attend college in New York, then since I would benefit from paying for in-state tuition in Virginia, how about me paying for her move back to Virginia? I told her absolutely not. She simply told me what I had heard a hundred times already, "Well, screw you. I'm not paying for any of their college! Oh, I'm going to Florida next weekend. Please call Kyle and Katie to check on them and say hello. Bye."

Another good one – the proverbial question, from her, "Are you going to buy Kyle a car for college?" I told her, "No, I am not. Buy my son a car for college? On my budget? Get real. No one bought me or my brother a car for college."

She was full of these wild ideas involving my money. She called one time to ask if I was going to fly the kids to Spain. Huh? She added that it would be so nice for me to escort them to Spain. Another resounding "No, and No."

"You cheapskate. I'll let you tell them you won't fly them to Spain."

"No problem, Carla. I'll be happy to, and I feel sorry for them if their feelings are hurt."

"Good, you sarcastic sonofabitch." She continued to badger me about Spain. I finally reminded her that she got about one-half of my paycheck, that we had financial issues at our end, and it was totally unrealistic for me to find that kind of money. "You guys make a lot. I want to see a copy of your paystub."

"Don't count on it," I told her.

"I'll have a judge find out what you make and edict that you pay for their trip," to which I again told, her, "Good luck."

"You're cheap and greedy and obviously don't love the children if you won't send them to Spain. The kids and I have talked about how cheap you are." Oh, shit, that was hitting below the belt. If I had been face to face with her I would have given very serious consideration to punching her lights out. Ungrateful bitch. As it was, I simply said, "Goodbye" and hung up the phone. It's the only thing I can do. Endless torment. Endless demands. Shaping the kid's heads about their father. I was on the losing end, and frankly, it was getting old and tiresome, not to mention cruel.

The next battle royal was about Kyle's sixteenth birthday, wherein she asked me to go in financially. You might think, slam dunk, sure, do it, but I held Carla off by saying I would think about it. I dragged my heels. When I later returned a call to her, she lit into me about something else.

"You shit. You didn't call to check about Kyle's medical visit."

"I'm sorry. I simply forgot about it." Or, maybe I intentionally forgot, for it would be one less time I had to listen to her.

She explained that the tests were negative and that he was okay. "Have you decided about his sixteenth birthday contribution?"

Maria and I had discussed this, and we had differing opinions. To digress, all this Carla crap was wearing on Maria, and I couldn't blame her. She was tired of Carla's repeated requests for this and that, and there was the time that, since we had relented and given our home phone number to Carla, that Maria overheard being bad-mouthed by Carla during a call. Such bullshit we had to put up with, and it created tension in our marriage, which I am confident was Carla's objective. Ever the manipulative schemer.

"Yes, I'll contribute," I told her, exasperated.

"Good. Oh, I have some medical bills I'm sending you."

"Right. Just as long as you know I'm only paying half. The

medical office can go after you for the other half. That's the way it is, Carla. Sorry about that."

"Damn you. You cheap bastard. And you still won't pay for the kid's trip to Spain. Well, I guess they're not going."

"That's right. It's not happening. I don't have that kind of money laying around."

"I hate you and wish you'd fucking die. You little shit."

"Ciao, Carla."

"I'm not going to call you anymore!" Uh, huh, how many times have I heard that?

"Promises, promises," I tell her.

"And I'm not going to tell you ahead of time if there is a change in the check amount that I write."

"That won't fly, Carla, since I send you blank checks trusting you'll insert the proper support amount. If you want to play that game we'll go back to me sending you a check already made out, and I know you don't like waiting by the mailbox for my check."

"Screw you." Click.

March of that year was certainly filled with lots of fun conversations with the viper, in her inimitable way, causing pain and discomfort. She even brought up Kyle's birthday again, and was furious I sent nothing else to him aside from the sizable contribution to his birthday night out. And she got on a kick about clothes that Maria and I sent lovely little Katie for Christmas. Going for the jugular in Carla fashion, she had the senselessness and audacity to tell me, "Katie doesn't like the clothes Maria and you send her. She and her friends use them to dress up as whores. And we still think you should send the kids to Spain this summer."

Oh, my God, this woman, this devil knows no bounds of decency. "Then return them," was all I could say, but adding, "You know, I so dislike talking to you. I may stop taking your calls at the office, and let things take their own course from there."

"Fine. As long as I have a way to reach you when something comes up about the children." You could tell she was smirking at her end. She had me by the balls on that count.

And then there was the call about Kyle's prom tux. I told her I would cover most of it. Enough.

In May we made arrangements for the kids to visit that upcoming summer. She also told me she was depressed, had money issues, townhouse tenant and management issues back in Virginia, various other personal problems like with someone she worked with, boyfriend issues, and the real kicker, telling me she was pregnant. Honestly, I did not ask for details.

"I know I shouldn't be telling you this, because you'll probably tell Maria (yes), but I found out I was pregnant."

"Okay."

"I can't believe it. I'm absolutely devastated. So, I'm going to have an abortion. What do you think? And I know what you're thinking. My boyfriend is going to pay for the abortion."

"I have no comment, Carla, and refuse to discuss it. That's your business and you should know we are long past conversing about your personal matters. Totally up to you what you do. I really do not care." I wanted no part of that topic, and told her so, trying to hang up, but not until she told me she was assaulted the night before.

"I know you don't care, but I was assaulted last night."

"Not good." Sorry, but I cannot act as though I really care.

"I knew you wouldn't care."

"Go ahead. You've already got me on the phone."

"I was relaxing by myself in a nearby park, close to where we live, when a guy grabbed me and started to wrestle me to the ground. I started screaming."

"That's not good. No mace for your nighttime stroll?"

"Hmmph. Well, luckily there were some people nearby and

they came running over to help me. The guy took off. He smelled terribly of alcohol, and it was a frightening experience."

"You were fortunate."

"It could have been so much worse. I'm so fortunate those people were nearby and heard my screams. I'm leaving and returning to Virginia. They can have this city. Billy's going to drive up and help me move." I wonder if Billy will find out about her abortion?

"I have to get back to work, but before I hang up, let me tell you something. You have no problem or reservations in dumping all your personal problems, including different bed partners and pregnancy, on me. And yet, I get a steady lady friend who I marry in the eyes of God, and you have the gall to blister and torment me about it. Stop calling me. Get out of my life. I've had it!"

"That's just the way it is. I will continue to torment you, so go to hell." Click

So, it appeared after their summer stay with the grandparents and Maria and me, I would be driving them back to Virginia. Gee, maybe I'll bring Maria along for the ride. I'll just need to get her a helmet and a bulletproof vest for the trip. Hit the Army/Navy surplus store. No big deal. But then, we would be coming face to face, or more literally, Carla's face to Maria's face in the car. Lovely. Would she come out with a gun, ready to shoot Maria?

Leaving Big Apple and acting dream.

1996/1997
CHAPTER TWENTY-SEVEN

It is early summer. Carla has returned to northern Virginia, living in her townhouse, and the kids are in Norfolk, having flown down from New York. I picked them up at the Newport News airport, not far from where Maria and I live, and drove them to their grandparent's house. I would be taking them for a few weekends, and for a week at the end of the summer.

We had some fun times. We rented an RV and the four of us went "camping" over a long weekend at a place west of Charlottesville, Virginia, called Sherando Lake. Lovely place. So relaxing. No phones, so out of reach of viper Carla, who may have been getting re-united with good 'ol Billy, and my morning coffee before a jog in the mountains was extra special. I liked getting up very early when it was still dark out and listening to the sounds of the woods and lake. We went on hikes, and tried our luck at fishing, but only caught enough fish for one dinner.

We also visited Busch Gardens theme park in nearby Williamsburg a few times when they stayed with us on a weekend, and even did the more educational outing by wandering up and down Duke of Gloucester Street in wonderfully restored historic Colonial Williamsburg. We did some socializing with friends of ours from work that lived in Newport News, and one of the couples in particular had children Kyle and Katie's ages, so that worked out great. As teenagers, they made friends quick, which I was pleased to see. It also gave the adults an opportunity to relax and chat over a cold beer or glass of wine. One day we made the drive to Kings Dominion Water Park just north of Richmond, having a super day frolicking on all the water rides. And even though it was a bit out of the way, we made a few trips to Waterside in downtown Norfolk, with all its shops and specialty stores and eateries.

That was blessedly the fun part of the summer, for even though the kids were in the Norfolk area, Carla still found it necessary to drill me with occasional phone calls on any manner of topics and do the devil's work, like telling me about her debts (I reminded her she could easily reduce her phone bill, but that went in one ear and out the other), medical issues, lack of success in finding a job (I found that hard to believe), men issues, and so forth. I listened to her, said as little as possible, and wore her down to having no alternative but to hang up. She did tell me Billy was visiting regularly. Lucky guy!

I drove the kids to their home at the conclusion of summer break and did my very best to minimize the amount of time under her roof before heading back to be with lovely Maria.

As the Christmas season approached, there were needed communications. I actually initiated a call to her, a first in many years, to ask if I could drive up Christmas day to see the kids and give them their gifts.

"Carla, this is Dave."

"Hi. What's up?" She was suspicious. "I can't remember the last time you called me."

"Yeah, it has been a while. I only need to talk to the kids when I call, as you know."

"Right."

"I called to ask you if I could drive up Christmas day to see the kids and give them their gifts. I won't stay long in the event you all have other plans."

"No. I'd rather you not come here." Okay.

"Okay. Guess I'll send their gifts in the mail."

"I guess so, Dave. Goodbye. I have to be somewhere." What a shame we could not talk longer. It's always so much fun.

I called a few days later asking about seeing the kids the upcoming weekend, and received another, "No. They have things they need to do." I guess I wasn't going to see the kids this Christmas. And the truth of the matter is, when she was behaving that way, I really had no desire to see any of them. Let them live their lives.

As usual, it didn't take her long to change her tune. In late January she called.

"Dave, this is Carla."

"I know who it is. No one else calls me."

"Oh, are we in a bad mood? Are you and Maria having issues?"

"Nope. We're doing great, Carla, much to your chagrin I suspect. What do you want?"

"When are you going to take the kids next?"

"I don't know. Let me think about it. You know I don't like making those two round trip drives, but I'll get back to you as soon as I can."

"Oh, you have to discuss it with Maria?" she asked sarcastically. More of a statement than a question.

"Maria and I discuss our plans. Yes."

And then she launched into the old diatribe. "Why did you do this to me?" I wanted to remind her that she had a nasty habit of ripping my face off, waving kitchen cutlery in my face, along with countless times she threw the evening meal out into the backyard, and the many other vicious actions toward me, and that she was the one that filed for divorce, but I didn't. It just wasn't worth my time at this sad juncture. She continued. "Did you put sperm in me? (well, yes, and it does take two to tango). Don't you care about your kids? (Yes, and I put up with your crap in order to continue to communicate with them). I hope you're unhappy" (I'm not!). She then got onto money issues from sixteen, seventeen years ago, of all things. When she said, "Maria is a fucking bitch," I hung up. Screw the whole family up north. It would be a while before I showed my face to pick up the kids.

In classic fashion, she called me a week later. I couldn't believe the topic, but then, knowing her as I did, yeah, maybe I wasn't surprised, for I know she fed the kids a steady diet of "hate daddy and Maria" stuff.

"Dave, I'm worried about Katie. She told me she feels like she's going to have a nervous breakdown."

"Oh, no. I wonder what caused those feelings?" Probably got it from her mother, Miss Lunatic and "I'm going to commit suicide" herself.

"I don't know, but I think it's all your fault since you haven't been to any of her sporting activities."

"That's tough for me to do, Carla, and you know it. I don't get away from the office during the week and you do live, by choice, over two-hundred miles away."

"Bullshit. I don't care about your work. If Katie does something to herself, like commit suicide, I'll kill you!"

"Calm down, Carla, and stop the threats."

"That's a promise, asshole. And goodbye!"

She called a day later to say she was taking Katie to a Psychiatrist, adding I would pay for it. I told her we would discuss it later. Before she hung up, she repeated that since it was my fault, I would pay. Oh, boy. I learned over the next few weeks that Katie was okay, that she just needed to talk to someone besides her mother. In the meantime, I had read somewhere that if the parent gets counseling, the kids won't need it. Parents are their children's life lines. If you are disorganized, hurt, sad, and as a result, depressed, don't be surprised when your children manifest some of the same emotions. I wanted to tell Carla that little gem, but I knew she would refute it.

The following month Carla called to tell me her mother unexpectedly passed away due to a stroke. I knew she was a smoker, and suspected that was a factor.

I called her brother, Jim.

"Hi, Jim, this is Dave."

"Hi Dave. It's been a while."

"Yes, regrettably. I just wanted to tell you how bad I feel about your mother and offer my condolences."

"Thanks, Dave. I appreciate it. Wow, what a surprise. So sudden. Seemed to be fine the day before when I talked to her, then, boom, has a stroke and she's gone."

"I know. That must be awfully hard on you and your father. Your mother was such a kind, loving and unselfish person. The kids absolutely loved her. I'll miss her. We all will."

"Yes. It just won't be the same without her in that house. I'm sure dad will have a real tough time. I probably shouldn't be telling you this, but it's not a new topic. Carla has already called to remind me about the household possessions that she expects to receive when dad passes away. Can you believe it? How greedy can someone be? It's my own sister, but I can't forgive her for what she's doing. And I know from talking to my father that he takes

244

a very dim view of her not working, or making more of an effort, especially to find a government job."

"Are you kidding me? The abject height of greediness. Of course, I'm not surprised, and I refuse to bring you into all the craziness in my life brought on by the divorce and your dear, vengeful sister."

"I know. I understand, Dave, and believe me, my heart goes out to you. I get bits and pieces from her from time to time. She seems to stay on a warpath with you and to take every opportunity to bad mouth both you and your wife to our family."

"Thanks. It isn't easy. I can't shake her. I won't say more, Jim, for she is still your sister."

"I am not so sure about that, Dave. I think I lost my sister a long time ago. Hey, shifting gears on you. I heard Billy is spending more time at Carla's, like frequent visits."

"I had not heard that, although I knew he was visiting. Normally, Carla's like an open book, telling me everything going on in her life, and I mean everything. Stuff you don't want to hear."

"He's still working for his father, and I'm assuming staying out of trouble."

"Well, we'll see how long that lasts. Thanks for the info, Jim. Keep me posted, okay? And please pass my condolences to your father. I plan to attend the viewing."

"Good. See you then. Hope you can make it. I know he would like to see you."

"Bye, Jim."

Same old Carla. She doesn't change.

Maria called me at the office.

"Dave, I just got home from work and the back door is ajar, like open, and I see wood splinters in the door frame and on the floor."

"Oh, no. The house has been broken into, hon."

"What should I do? Can I go into the house? Do you think it's safe? I don't see Missy, who always meets me at the door into the utility room."

"I would think it's safe at this point. Do you hear anything, like any sounds from the other end of the house?"

"No, it's real quiet. I need to check on Missy."

"Well, I'm heading home. If you want, keep the phone on and talking to me while you walk through the house. But, if you don't feel comfortable doing so, go back outside and call nine, one, one to get the police there."

"Okay, I'm walking through the house." I hear her calling Missy, our beloved Bichon, then I hear her say, "Oh, here you are girl." She tells me, "Dave, Missy has a small wound near the top of her head. I'll bet the intruder struck her."

"Damn it. Is she alright?"

"She has a little blood showing, but otherwise she's our little Missy and is okay."

"Oh, good. I'm on my way. Call the police."

I arrived home to find, as Maria did, our back door messed up. It appeared someone put a size twelve into the door and busted it open. I looked outside, and sure enough, the old rickety gate was broken as well, not that it would take much to get through it.

I found Maria and Missy, and they were okay. Walking through the house it was obvious that the intruder created some mayhem by "tossing" much of the bedrooms.

"He took some of my jewelry, but he didn't see the money I had in an envelope in my top dresser drawer," she told me.

"Hopefully, that's the worst of it. We'll file an insurance claim for the damages and losses."

The police arrived. Nice guys. Took a report, and one of them dusted for fingerprints. I know it was necessary, but I had no idea the mess the dusting made on all the doors and furniture. It was a real booger to clean afterwards. They told us to hope for a set that they could try to match against their database, and that unless a neighbor saw anything and could provide information on a vehicle, license plate, or description of who might have broken in, the chances were slim that they would make an arrest. They said they would check with local pawn shops to see if any of the jewelry showed up there.

We secured the damaged back door that night as best we could, cleaned up the mess, including all the fingerprint dust, and tried to calm our nerves. There is no way to describe an experience such as that, for you feel violated and vulnerable. The next day I contacted our handyman, who came over later that day to fix the back door. He replaced some of the door jamb and installed a dead bolt with a long bolt to give it more resistance.

My next project was to find a security company to install a house security system. After talking to a few companies, we made a selection, requesting they also install a camera surveillance system. While I could not prove it, I had an idea who may have broken in, although it could have been anyone, and wanted it on tape if it ever happened again.

During our next phone conversation I told Carla about the break-in. As with the car incidents, she showed scant interest. I wondered what else was on her "To do list" to screw with me and Maria.

Carla is digging a deeper hole.

1997

CHAPTER TWENTY-EIGHT

The next year went by rather quickly. My time with the children was limited since the arduous double round trips on I-95 were less and less frequent. I stayed in contact with the kids by phone, but that's not the same as being with them. But then, that door swung both ways – either my reluctance to make the drives, and their desire as teenagers to spend time with their friends. I missed seeing them and being part of their lives, but it was partially a self-inflicted wound. I was incredibly busy at work, with lots of demands from my senior officers. There was never a dull moment. This Admiral wanted this change at our golf course, and this Admiral wanted a change in policy at the officer's swimming pool behind Flag Row. The wife of another Admiral was teaching aerobics in one of the base gyms on Saturday mornings, so guess where I was on those mornings? Between ensuring my staff had the support they required to meet our mission, visiting our facilities on a routine basis to check on things, doing the best I could to take care of my commanding officers, and in my spare time drafting position papers on countless subjects, I was busy. And yes, my job came first. It was a work ethic thing.

I requested leave from my executive officer from time to time so that I could depart work around mid-day to drive north and attend some of Kyle's gymnastics meets and Katie's field hockey games. It made for long days, attending a late afternoon event, and then turning around to drive back home. Having our house in Newport News helped a bit, as it meant I didn't have to drive through the Hampton Roads Bridge Tunnel to get home. Both Kyle and Katie were doing well in their athletic endeavors, and Kyle had improved his grades, good enough to help him get into college. In New York he had occasionally been in honor society, but somewhere in between he got sidetracked. Hopefully, he'll keep his grades up now. Katie was not all that scholastic, so she needed a gentle nudge from time to time.

The point is, divorce and family separation sucks. Of course, it was made much worse by Carla's antics and behavior, and mental trauma she inflicted on me, and later Maria, and the relationship should have been more civil. Her "Ex Etiquette" sucked. She broke all the protocol rules. She had sole custody and called the shots. The kids lived under her roof, so they heard what they heard. There was no joint custody and very little "joint parenting". Geography contributed, for how can you be a good parent, really positively impacting the lives of your children, when you see them maybe two days out of thirty, or fewer? Good luck on that. The interesting thing was that Carla remained reluctant to relocate to the Norfolk area where she had friends and family. I'll never understand it. Had she done so, I obviously could have played a larger role in the lives of the children. Didn't happen. Her call.

At the same time, as Jim had told me, Billy was spending more time with Carla. It did make me wonder if there was more than a childhood friends-thing going on, like a romantic relationship.

Maybe that's why it seemed like the angry, venomous calls were less frequent. Don't get me wrong. The calls were still there, just fewer and farther between. After all, the kids were still with her, and by virtue of that alone, there were calls. They normally started off okay, but true to form like over the now so many years, somewhere in the conversation a fuse would light and here came another volcanic eruption. Name a topic. It was like deja 'vu. But anyway, maybe Billy's visits kept her somewhat distracted, and it certainly gave her another man to talk to vice me.

Jim called me to give a most interesting heads up.

"Dave, how are you?"

"Oh, pretty good, Jim. Things are a bit quieter and calmer for me and Maria, if you know what I mean."

He chuckled. "Yeah, I know."

"What's up?"

"Well, I thought you might be interested in something my dad told me last night. He had been out golfing with Billy's father, who shared with him that he was able to use his contacts in the construction world to get Billy a construction job in northern Virginia. Apparently, it's with a large company that recently signed a number of big contracts to do some major developments off Highway Fifty in Fairfax County, along with a number of other jobs."

"Well, good for Billy. May help him keep his nose clean. I wonder if he'll move in with Carla or get separate housing."

"We'll see, but the door is certainly open for him to live up there closer to Carla."

"Time will tell, Jim, and thanks so much for the good intel. Give my best to your father. By the way, how's his health?"

"I will. He's having some issues. It's not keeping him from golfing or fishing, but I can tell he's having to slow down a little. I'm keeping an eye on him."

"Well, I hope he'll be okay. Bye, Jim."

So there you go. The felon is moving to northern Virginia to be with the cougar. Wonder how that's going to turn out? I can only imagine the possibilities.

Meanwhile, Maria and I continue to stretch a dollar as best we can. My support payments ate up a lot of my paycheck, so there was normally not much left over at the end of the month after paying our bills down here. When I needed a new car, it was basic, no frills models, often without air-conditioning and radio. The air-conditioning I could manage without, and I would transfer the old radio to the new car. That always got a lot of laughs and guffaws from people when I would tell them, particularly my brother-in-law on Maria's side. Work kept us both busy, and we got so much pleasure out of our Missy. She was a member of the family, and went everywhere with us, including sneaking her in to the motel during our much too infrequent two-night getaways to Nags Head on the Outer Banks. Unfortunately, there just wasn't room in the budget for travel. Another downside of divorce – finances. I found out the hard way that divorce, and supporting two households, takes a huge financial toll. I lived paycheck to paycheck, and that sucked. Carla always claimed otherwise, that we had plenty of money, but that was not the case. We had mortgage, car payments, repair bills, and the normal necessities that eat up household funds, but Carla was relentless and always seeking more money from me above what I was legally obligated to give her. Needless to say, it was a topic that she made high-charged, over and over again, revving up that 340 horsepower anger engine of hers.

In a way, life for me and Maria was sometimes dull. We didn't have money for travel, but we did make up for that by visiting the nearby beaches and going out for a few drinks at local establishments on a Friday or Saturday night when our schedules permitted. We both had an interest in racquetball, so we occasionally got on a court at the nearby Air Force base and played each other pretty close. Those were fun times, and always followed by a cold beer. It also helped Maria get her mind off Carla's entreaties and indecencies.

But make no mistake, the albatross called Carla the viper loomed large in our lives. We even got to the point that we refused to utter her name in our house. God, we hated her. I know it is wrong to hate, but I'm sorry, she made it all too easy to do so. Forgive me, Lord.

I took off a few hours early one midweek day to make a round trip to northern Virginia so I could take in Kyle's gymnastics meet. He was still competing in trampoline and floor exercise, but to my delight and surprise, he had filled out some in his upper body and was also now doing the horizontal bar. It was obvious from his hi-bar and tramp routines that he had no fear. I was proud of him, and certainly proud of him being on track to earn a varsity letter.

Carla could sniff me out from a mile away. I tried to hide but was unsuccessful. She found me.

"Hi, Dave."

"Hi. Kyle's doing great stuff. I'm sure you're proud of him as well."

"I am. How are you doing?"

"Great. And you?" The fewer words the better. Don't lob any openings.

"Okay, I guess. You know that Billy has moved in."

"No, I didn't know that. Hope it's working out alright."

"Well, yes and no. I think I love him. He's usually very good to me and we get along really well."

"Usually?" Shut the hell up, Dave.

"We have our disagreements. Some yelling back and forth. That kinda stuff. He definitely knows how to dish it back out to me. There are times when I can't handle him, you know? He gets a little rough."

Oh, Lord, what do I say to that little gem of knowledge? To myself I'm saying, hey, that's great to hear. A little comeuppance for the viper. Tables turned. Getting some of what you put me through, heh? Normally, I could give a rat's ass about her personal problems, but this had my interest for obvious reasons. I therefore feigned an interest, knowing she would divulge all, or most of the gory details anyway. "Oh? How so?"

"Well, it's usually when the kids are out of the house and I've been smoking some pot and he is drinking his cheap whiskey. We sometimes get argumentative. We might push one another, and he ends up pushing harder, but there's no hitting. Just a lot of yelling. We're okay the next morning."

"Ah, so you spare him the striking, the knife thrusts, and sending him to a motel. Nice."

She was silent. Maybe she didn't remember all those cruel things she laid on me. The whole bipolar disorder, or was it post-partum syndrome? Whatever. "Well, take care of yourself. I'm sure everything will turn out okay."

"Yeah, I hope so. We've talked about marriage." Oh, my goodness, here it comes. The ideal match. The felon marries the viper.

"Good." She needed a new man in her life. Something told me that regardless, she would still find ways to talk to me, via the conversations with the kids, or about children issues.

Kyle completed his final routine, and shortly thereafter the meet was concluded. Kyle placed top three in all his events.

"Bye, Carla. I'm going to catch Kyle before he heads for the locker room so I can chat with him for a few minutes before I head back south. It will be a long day."

"Bye, Dave. I might be visiting my father soon."

I snagged Kyle, we talked, I told him how proud I was of him, said I loved him, and I was on my way. I wish our meeting could have lasted longer, but I could tell he wanted to get with his teammates, and I had to bust out of there. Sad, but that's the price one pays with divorce and separation. You get to see your teenage son in a sports activity for about an hour each month, at best. It hurts.

I wasn't the most consistent at checking the tapes from our surveillance system, but fortuitously happened to do so one Sunday morning. Oh, what a surprise. Well, not really.

Smile, you're on candid camera, Carla.

1997/1998
CHAPTER TWENTY-NINE

There, in plain view, as big as Dallas, was my ex-wife, Carla. On the screen, vivid, her face scrunched up and contorted like she was unsure of herself or what the hell she was going to do now that she was planted squarely on our doorstep. She was obviously on a mission and she undeniably was a maniac, but I rather doubt she knew what mission. Like, okay, now that I'm at the front door of my ex-husband and his wife's house, what do I do? What can I do? I'm sure she ultimately deduced that there wasn't much she could do with walls and locked doors facing her. It was about two in the morning and there wasn't anyone around or outside that would spot her. She certainly wasn't going to bang on the door, for if she was smart, she would figure out that I would be calling nine-one-one. She could be arrested for trespassing, and I would demand those charges in a New York nanosecond. No, she was there to be there and to play out her demons. She had it in her misaligned, confused head to torment me in some other manner, but she couldn't because she was frozen in in-action on the doorstep. Poor child.

The tape indicated she was there no more than about five minutes, which to her probably felt like an hour of mental agony, assuming she was capable of the mental part, or even the agony, but long enough to realize nothing was going to come of her bonehead move.

I told Maria about it when she alighted from the bed.

"Oh, my goodness, Dave. What are we going to do?"

I had thought about it. "Nothing," I replied.

"Nothing? You're not serious. That woman is a whack job. We don't know what she might do, especially in view of all the threats she has made against both of us."

"Exactly. I know. But we were safe in the house, and she knows I would call the police in a heartbeat if she made a scene. No, I think the best thing is to preserve the tape for possible future use. I want something more serious she or Billy might attempt on the camera tape to try to put an end to this crap from her. I know it's a bit of a risk, but I think we're okay for now." Little did I know that was how it all would play out and be her un-doing.

"Okay, Dave, but she scares me."

"Me, too, hon, but let's see what happens."

Sure enough, Carla called the next week. The normal stuff about the kids, although we did talk about me taking Kyle on a college visit tour since he was a senior that year. This would be a good time to visit some campuses and help whet his desire to attend college. Get him excited, as I did whenever I was at a Cal or Stanford football game and on their campuses in my high-school years. But she also had to share some info about her neighbor for whom she had helped with some travel paperwork and was presumably still doing so.

"While Billy was at work yesterday I visited my good friend

from downstairs where I used to live. He told me that his accounting and auditing office was looking into his travel claims. He's worried they may see some inconsistencies. I'm worried for him, too, because depending on what they find and charge him with, he could really be in some trouble. I'd hate to see him lose his job or his pension. That would be terrible."

"Well, it sounds like he has plenty to worry about." I didn't want to bring up her possible role in this monkey business. She knew what she had done, and then again maybe not, if in fact he provided the numbers and she just filled in the blanks on the travel claim form. I doubt any charges could be brought against her. Also, he might not implicate her. What would be the value? He knew what was going on, so would probably take any hits. We would see. Stupid stuff, for sure.

"Yeah. This makes me so nervous. I'm a wreck. He's a nice guy and friend. I hate to see this happening to him."

Well, then you shouldn't have been cooking the travel claim books, or helping him do so. "Time will tell." I decided to hit her with the surveillance camera fiasco as a Doug Flutie Hail Mary pass to put her in her place. "You know, Carla, during the many recent decidedly one-way phone conversations you failed to give me an opportunity to tell you something." As much as I did not want to alert her to it, I felt she would probably forget I told her.

"What's that?" I had her attention.

"After the house break-in I installed a security system with a surveillance camera."

"So?" Ah, in classic Mad Magazine, Alfred E. Neuman-style, "Who, me?"

"I was checking the tape and it revealed your ugly, conflicted mug from last weekend. You are one messed up woman. Please leave me and Maria alone and do not bother us, particularly by descending on our property."

Click. Hopefully, that might somewhat mitigate the madness. Wishful thinking.

Carla's world was unraveling or had been in a continual state of chaos for a long time. It seemed like the bad stuff was coming at warp speed and piling on her like a good 'ol Army barracks "blanket party". The lack of success in New York. The pot citation. The assault. Her mother's passing. Her pregnancy and abortion. Her neighbor's travel claim issues. Her developing relationship with Billy that also brought her some domestic issues. Her ill-conceived, reckless, pointless drive to our house to plant herself on our doorstep at two in the morning. Her angry calls to her brother to greedily demand certain possessions of her parents. And of course, all those countless, yes hundreds of calls to me consuming copious amounts of negative energy and emotion to unleash her fury over the many years to viciously attack me verbally and torment me, not to mention the lunacy during our marriage. She was helpless and hopeless, mentally adrift, obsessed with me and wanting to harm me, and Billy could have her, God bless him. And, of course, there were Billy's efforts, I assumed, to wreak havoc on my life, or more particularly, my vehicles and home. I'll never be able to prove he was culpable, but it had to be him. And I have to think Carla put him up to it, for on his own I seriously doubt he would want to play Russian roulette with his parole officer. And yet, things would get progressively worse for Carla.

Carla's downward glide slope of life.

1998
CHAPTER THIRTY

Late fall. A typical year had elapsed, all the way around regarding Carla and her obnoxious calls, limited visitation with the kids, and Maria and me trying to live our lives. My work was becoming more demanding as the Navy established study groups, on which I served due to my senior manager position, to assess and ultimately execute a regional apparatus for our Norfolk-area installations. With that, every nonsensical phone call from Carla was an unwanted, unwelcome intrusion and I had zero tolerance for them, even with the oft-stated preamble that she needed to discuss children issues. They morphed. They twisted. They turned. They often became vicious. But then, what would you expect from someone bent on revenge?

A cascade of events occurred in somewhat rapid, chronological succession, followed by more events that literally turned our worlds and lives upside down. Looking back, the succeeding nine months were pivotal in the lives of all of us. There was no way I could have foreseen or speculated on the events that would unfold. So much of it was a result of that truism that everything happens either at a good time or bad time. Things were catching up on Carla. Good 'ol timing and fate for some overdue comeuppance.

I had driven up early in the summer for Kyle's high-school graduation. Where had the time gone? I missed so much of his life for obvious reasons, and it really hurt that he grew up without me. He came out okay, thank goodness. Maybe there was some truth to the opinions of experts that children in an unhappy marriage usually fare better when mom and dad separate, in other words, cleanse the house of much of the toxic behavior. There was time after the graduation ceremony to locate him outside the arena to shake his hand, give him a hug, and tell him I loved him. He was happy to see his remote father, but he was also consumed with celebrating the momentous occasion with his buddies, which was only natural and a hell of a lot more fun that being serious with dad. I didn't cling to him or attempt to extricate him from his friends. I know where his priorities lay at that moment in time. He was all smiles and laughing, and I did wonder if to himself he was thinking, "Hi, dad. Good to see you. I think I saw you about a month ago, and maybe a month before that. I can't say I really know you that well. It's too bad things weren't different for us, but that's water over the dam. Maybe I'll see you some while I'm in college." As if reading his mind, I said goodbye, told him we would be talking college, headed out into the arena parking lot with its appropriate nighttime shadows that characterized much of my life with my children, and made the long, lonely, introspective drive home. Damn it. It should not have been that way. I should have been able to enjoy and help my children as they grew up, not be two-hundred or a thousand miles apart.

There wouldn't be that much to discuss about paying for college, fortunately. The discussions with Carla had been bitter, but along with her vacuous emotional opinions she had nothing of substance to offer, nor financial means other than Kyle staying with her on school breaks. It would be like trying to get blood out of a turnip. We were finally in the reality phase. I had executed the necessary research into grants and loans, and Kyle was fortunate to land a low-cost federal loan and a couple small grants. I would essentially be paying the difference, although I strongly encouraged him to look for part-time work on campus. I reminded both he and his unbelieving mother that he could manage a couple hours of work each day. Contrary to my situation in college where my buddies and me worked and participated in intercollegiate sports, along with carrying a full academic course load, Kyle would not be engaging in any sports. He was attending Old Dominion University, which had a Business College of good repute, not far from where Maria and I lived, and regrettably, they did not have a men's gymnastics program, thus no athletic scholarship possibility. Nowadays, that men's sport was normally only found at the large, more well-financed universities in the bigger conferences, and while he was a good gymnast, he was not athletic scholarship material at a Penn State or Ohio State. Kyle, bless him, had offered to live in our house and commute to ODU, but I told him, hell no, you're going to college and you're going to live on campus and get the total experience, starting with living in a dorm. When he was born I told myself I would do everything humanly possible that he might have a college experience like his dad's. Well, not totally. I'm not so sure I wanted him to do an instant replay on my Happy Valley College years.

A few months after Kyle started college, his grandfather, Carla's father, passed away. Of course, Carla had called to tell me the sad news. I called her brother.

"Hi, Jim. Carla just called about your father. I'm so sorry to hear of his passing and saddened by it. I hope you're doing okay."

"Thanks, Dave. I appreciate it. We'll miss him, and his golf and fishing buddies will as well."

"I'm sure you will. He was a nice man and I liked him. If I could ask, did he die of a broken heart from your mother's passing, or were there medical issues?"

"I think it was a combination. He so missed my mother, and that in itself may have contributed to some medical issues that flared up recently. He really went quickly."

"I'm sorry to hear that. Well, I know you're busy, and I suspect you're the executor of his will, which I'm sure will be an additional burden on you."

"I am, and he and I talked about it at the end, so I have a good understanding of why he executed his will as he did. Very interesting. Because you were understandably not included in the will, and have no vested or financial interest, I will share with you what he told me. This will of course all come out at the reading of the will by his attorney, and I know you'll keep it to yourself. Plus, I know you have no desire to discuss anything with my sister," he added with a chuckle. "She is going to be totally shocked and I know will go high and right at the reading, but my father told me he instructed his attorney to keep her largely out of the will. No money, but will get some household furniture, and very little. No jewelry. That's it. He was not happy with her, and in fact shared with me that there were some heated phone conversations with her, and that the ugliness was always precipitated by Carla. So, don't feel too bad. Dad took some shots, too."

"Wow. That is surprising and remarkable, on all counts. Trust me, it will remain in my confidence. Not a word to anyone, and I appreciate your candor and trust. Well, take care of yourself, Jim. I hope to be talking to you again when things settle down for you. Maybe we can relax and chat about more pleasant topics over a cold beer, and maybe I'll wipe the dust off my golf clubs."

"Sounds good. Bye, Dave."

Oh, my, you could have knocked my body over with a feather. The news certainly made me light-headed. Comeuppance. Carla was getting hers. Her outspoken greed came back to bite her in the posterior. Oh, to be a fly on the wall at the reading of the will. Actually, maybe not. Regardless of the audience and the solemnity of the occasion, when she hears the attorney announce she was not to receive any inheritance funds from her parents, she will go absolutely bonkers, ape-shit, and hysterical. I can hear her, because I have been on the receiving end of her vicious behavior for more years than I want to recall. Yes, I try to block it out, but there's no way. And to this day, every damn time my telephone rings, no, make that every time I hear any phone ring, my blood pressure spikes, my skin crawls, and I am on the defensive. I can't help what she has done to me, and I will forever immensely dislike her and the ground she stands on – in a figurative and literal sense, her grounds of greediness, exacting fear and intimidation, belittling, arguing points with vitriol and viciousness, her maniacal behavior, and just plain outright tormenting and ugliness. That's her in a nutshell, and I was the ready and willing victim. She is a psycho.

Shortly thereafter, I received the inevitable call from Carla.

"Dave, my father left me out of his will. No money. Just a few pieces of furniture. I can't believe it." I loved the furniture piece, as it was surely poetic justice. It was what she wanted, after all. She was already zooming along using all 340 horsepower of emotion, and I would have no part of it. I told her so.

"Carla, I don't want to hear about it. I don't care. That's a matter between you and the estate. I'm busy, so goodbye."

"You shit. I knew you would say that." Click.

And you have a wonderful day as well. I mean really, why call me? What could I do about it? What would I want to do about it?

Yell at Billy. She was right. I didn't care. I was just glad I was able to dump her off the phone so quickly.

In December she called to tell me she and Billy got married. Oh, my, let the fun and games begin! For here was a marriage made in hell, or Hades of Greek Mythology. She also told me they were moving to Virginia Beach. Billy wanted to work for his dad, which probably made perfect sense, and Carla finally decided she wanted to be closer to what was left of her family.

It didn't take long, and of course chatty Carla had to tell me all about their move to our area and some stuff regarding her and Billy, which I unsuccessfully told her I did not want to hear about.

"Katie, dear, I need to have some privacy for a few minutes, okay? Thanks," I heard her say.

"What Carla? Please make it quick. You know I'm not interested in hearing about your personal matters. I've told you this before."

"But I have to tell you this so that someone knows. In case something happens to me, you know?" The ultimate drama queen.

"Tell your brother."

"No. I'm already starting to feel like a battered wife."

"You mean like you used to do to me, Carla?" I had to get that in, for I had learned to be frank with her. What could she do about it, right?

"Shut up."

"Hmmm. Not nice."

"I'm sorry. Let me finish so we can hang up before Billy gets back. He's mean and he beats me occasionally, and none of the fights are my fault. When it's over, he apologizes and tells me he loves me. I know he does. It's always when Katie is staying over at a friend's house and we've been partying. We haven't been married that long, and I really do love him. I can't get myself to do anything about it other than try to talk to him hoping he'll change. The last thing I want to do is call the police and file charges. That would only make matters worse. I don't know what he would do. I'm kind of afraid of him." Oh, my, Carla's a victim and getting a taste of what she used to dish out to me.

"He's not going to change. You're involved in the classic case of domestic assault and violence. Things happen. Someone gets hurt. But the victim is reluctant to do anything." Gee, I wonder how I became such an expert on domestic violence and could speak so fluently on the topic. First-hand experience. Lived through it to know about it.

"Great. What do I do?"

This was over the top deja 'vu. The only difference was that Billy apologized after the negative behavior, while Carla went to sleep and forgot about it, unless she was sending me packing to a motel, ready to do battle or effect that proverbial "second goose" from the golf joke over and over. I wanted to say, "Plastics", like that line from the movie, The Graduate, but she would not have understood. "Counseling. And that's all I'll say, Carla. I've got to go. Goodbye." And I purposely didn't add, "Good luck", because that would infer I cared, which I did not.

I relay some of this to Maria, including the part about the will of Jim and Carla's father, since I heard it from Carla post the reading of the will, so it was official and fair game to discuss with Maria. We had some very interesting discussions over a drink at happy hour, as you might imagine. Pinot Grigio for her, an ice cold Yuengling for me. When we reflected on the mental trauma she had inflicted on our lives, not to mention years of it on me, and the shenanigans I'm sure Billy pulled, we were entitled to take some small pleasure in some of the events Carla was now experiencing as the little self-centered world of this person with no redeeming qualities unraveled big-time.

I told Maria one night that I hoped these issues with Carla would end and that this long playing soap opera she created in my life, and Maria's to a degree, would also come to a close. It had been tearing up my life for almost twenty years, and something had to give. I also told Maria that I honestly did not know how and why I allowed a relationship with Carla to develop to the extent of marrying her and paying a hell of a price for my irresponsibly poor judgement. How did this happen? How could I have married this person that became a stark-raving lunatic?

How I handled Carla, or did not properly handle her, was a point of discussion and angst between Maria and me. I often wondered about my own frailties. Was I normal in how I treated the entire, lengthy episode with Carla? What could or would I have done differently? For certain, I could have filed for divorce, but that did not happen. I tolerated her in our marriage, and failed to do "something" to change things. The divorce years were a different matter, especially after Maria entered my life. But even before then, was I weak? Did I tolerate her in the sense of accepting status quo? I had to keep communication lines open, which was to my peril. Or, was the overarching issue that I tried to avoid confrontation? It would be easy for me to rationalize that Carla was like a verbal battering ram, a personality force that, once in her grips, pushed your butt into a corner. My problem was that I did not know how to come out fighting from the corner. I was that boxer in the corner taking a beating, hit after hit, gloves up in defense, and aside from a few "moral victories" with her, putting her in her place, so to speak, still came out on the wrong end of any confrontation with her. She was a bully, no two ways about it. And yet, again, what choices did I have? Very limited. I just had that gross misfortune of having to deal with a strong-headed, verbally abusive and aggressive, vengeful, venomous woman that knew what she could get away with.

I don't know if Carla sought counseling, and I certainly did not know if the counselor, had she gone through with it, had strongly suggested that Carla get Katie out of the house since she and Billy were predisposed to staying together in a less than harmonious, albeit loving, relationship. And thus, it happened.

"Dave, this is Carla."

"I know. Some things don't change."

"I have something very important to tell you."

"You're moving to Spain. Okay."

"I wish you would show more interest."

"Old habits are tough to change, Carla. What is it?"

"I'm giving you custody of Katie. I don't want to go into all the reasons. But Billy's doing okay financially, and I'm going to find work, so we don't care about forfeiting the child support for Katie. So, she's yours, whether you and Maria like it or not."

"Okay. When?"

"I've met with my attorney and he's working on a modification to the court order. We don't need to worry about Kyle since he's over eighteen. My attorney will have the change soon, but I don't want to pull Katie out of school before the semester ends, and Christmas is coming up, so I would say around mid-January."

"We can do that. What does Katie feel about all this?"

"She's not happy about having to change high-schools twice in her junior year, and she's upset about leaving her new friends, but I have been very blunt with her that moving in with her father is the best solution. I'll just leave it at that. I hope you and Maria are ready to do this and can support Katie."

"We are and we will."

"Okay. I'll call you when we're ready. You'll probably want to rent a small van for all her stuff, including a few small pieces of furniture in her bedroom."

"Got it. Let me know when its official and the time is right."

"Well, you got what you wanted."

"What?"

"You know what I mean. You got Katie and the money."

"Bullshit. I have never requested or demanded custody, and it's never been about the money. As I recall, you were the one to tell me the kids are mine, come get them. I merely said change the court order and by the way, if you don't have the children, you don't need the child support money from me. Made sense. And that's when you would hang up on me after some expletives, so maybe it's always been about the money for you until now."

"Whatever."

"Goodbye."

Oh, my. Life and its unceasing changes in trajectory. This was a total surprise, but from what Carla had shared with me, was best for Katie. I knew Maria would be cool with it. It would be good to have a new face in the house and have an opportunity collectively to help and support Katie. More so than Kyle, I knew she needed some help and tenderness, and some gentle shoves in the right direction. I wanted to see her attend college as well.

In mid-January, as Carla and I had discussed, I made the drive to Virginia Beach to rescue Katie from what was most likely an environment a bit too toxic for her well-being.

Maria, bless her, had gone to work on fixing up a bedroom for Katie, and it was coming along quite nicely. I had an idea of Katie's favorite colors, so gave the room a fresh coat of paint. I wasn't much of a plumber or electrician, but I could paint!

Katie and I didn't talk much on the drive to Hampton. I didn't want to force any conversation, and I figured that Katie had a boatload of thoughts and concerns banging around her young head. She would talk when ready to do so. One thing I did tell her, however, was that a few girls she had met during her summer visits were excited about seeing her again and anxious to get together with her, including showing her around the school during the upcoming weekend when no one else was on the campus. She gave me a little smile and said, "Thanks. I'm looking forward to it. They were neat girls and I liked them. This is going to be hard, dad."

"I know, hon. You're a strong young lady and we're confident everything is going to work out okay for you. We're here to help you. You just need to reach out to us so we know how best to make you comfortable, okay?"

"Okay, dad. I will." And with that, we drove in silence until arriving at Katie's new home. Maria wasn't pushy, and eventually that night the two of them were chatting about all manner of things. I stole away to another part of the house to let them re-unite and get to know one another better.

With Katie's mother living in Virginia Beach, Katie was able to spend the occasional weekend with her. And with Billy. When she returned home, we talked about various things. I never asked her any questions about her mother and Billy, and she knew I never would, but there were occasions when she offered up voluntarily that she didn't feel comfortable under the same roof as the two of them. She could sense a level of discord, of a lack of communication. I listened to what she said and didn't pursue it. I think I knew her mother pretty damn well.

So many life changes are underway.

1999

CHAPTER THIRTY-ONE

I was doing my normal routine one morning on a work day, up at about 3:40 am to feed Missy, have a cup or two of coffee and watch the Weather Channel, the very early edition of network national and world news, then leaving it on that channel to watch the local news that came on at 4:30 am. After watching the third complete local weather segment, I was either heading to the nearby fitness center to which we belonged or lacing up my running shoes to go out for a four to five mile jog on the neighborhood streets. I had been doing this routine for decades, so it was easy. It was habit. I had started a daily workout regimen around 1970 when I was living with my parents in Danville, California. I continued it when I went to grad school at Indiana University, and the routine was made quite easy when I started work for the Navy, for all the Navy installations had a fitness facility. And you can run anywhere. But enough of that.

I almost spilled my cup of coffee when the local channel came out with a news story from the night before. They termed it "breaking news" for the early morning crowd. It seems a couple in Virginia Beach was having a marital dispute, and the wife ran from the house, jumped in her car, and was driving down Virginia Beach Boulevard when she decided to seek safety in a shopping center parking lot. The only problem was her husband was apparently in hot pursuit, saw her enter the parking lot, and crashed his car into the driver's side of his wife's car. Did some damage to both cars, but no one was seriously hurt. The police were called to the scene and ticketed the husband for reckless driving and endangerment. I laughed when the TV news announcer provided the names of Billy and Carla Williams. What a hoot! Make my day! I knew the fun and games would commence when those two knuckleheads tied the knot.

I told Maria about it when she got up, and she was equally floored by it all. I went to work, and that night received a call from Jim, Carla's brother.

"Hi, Dave. I guess you saw the news story about Billy and Carla?"

"I sure did, Jim. Wow. Crazy stuff. Makes you wonder about their marriage, but it's not my problem."

"Yeah. Questionable marriage to say the least. I called Carla to see how she was and she told me she was fine. Just a little shaken up, and of course pissed off at her husband. She said they were arguing about something stupid, that he pulled out a kitchen knife and threatened her with it, and she ran from the house."

"Oh, my, gosh. A knife? She got some of her own medicine, for sure. In another time, it was her pulling a knife on me and it was me getting out of the house. And you know what, Jim? I wouldn't be a bit surprised if she initiated the fight and that she has driven him to that sort of reaction. He's probably feeling the same despair and hopelessness that I felt."

"Yes. I remember you telling me that. Well, she told me that their flail was a big misunderstanding, that they still love each other, and that she was not going to press charges. She's hoping Billy's attorney can convince the judge that the collision was an accident vice intentional. We'll see, and of course there might be the matter of his parole. I do not know how long he was to be on parole or probation."

"Right. Sounds to me like there are some domestic violence issues at play, and for whatever reasons, she does not want to bring charges and make matters worse. Who knows what he might do to her if she did bring charges. Could get nastier as he fights back." To myself, I was thinking that maybe the argument or fight was over her abortion she had in New York, but then, if she was smart she would not tell him about it. After all, she learned through me what ensued from honesty and candor in a relationship.

"I think you're right, Dave," he replied rather somberly. I didn't care, but she was Dave's sister, and he cared about her welfare, maybe at least to some small degree.

"I know you care, Jim, so I'll keep you in my thoughts."

"Thanks, Dave."

"Well, you have a good evening, Jim. Goodbye." With that, we hung up, and my first thought was, I really do hope I don't see another similar story on the news that involves them.

As things get crazier and crazier.

1999

CHAPTER THIRTY-TWO

Katie was now with her father and stepmother and no longer living with Carla and Billy. The blue haze from Carla's pot smoking filled the kitchen, and she was stoned and in dreamland. Billy sat across from her at the kitchen table, working hard on a bottle of whiskey. Carla was wary, for she knew of trouble that could emanate from their partying. The recent car crash fiasco was ample proof, not to mention the many times things got out of hand inside the four walls of their house when one thing lead to another and bam, they were yelling at each other, throwing things, fists might fly, and she would always be on the losing end of yet another knock-down, drag-out fight. And there was the physical hurt the next morning, even though they managed to "kiss and make up", or so she thought.

Carla knew they had issues. She was no dummy. But she wasn't going to seek counseling like Dave suggested, and she sure as hell was not going to call the police when things got out of hand. That would make things worse. She had no idea how

Billy might respond, so that gave her pause. She thought she still loved him, or did she? Or, was she simply afraid of him? Was it a mistake marrying him? Maybe. It certainly wasn't a marriage on the rebound. Hell, she had been divorced for over ten lonely years. She had the kids, but aside from the various flings, she did not have a man in her life, which was why she tormented her ex-husband relentlessly. The bastard. And then he ups and re-marries, to that bitch Maria. God, I hate her. She now received Dave's love, not me, she lamented.

She still wanted some revenge on Maria. Billy breaking into their house was no big deal. She wanted Maria to feel some pain, physical pain and hurt.

Carla sat there scheming while Billy got more shit-faced on his cheap whiskey. She wanted revenge on Maria, and she decided that while there was still at least some love between her and Billy, the marriage was going into the toilet and something had to change. Like, get him out of her life without calling the police after the next physical assault. What would calling in the police achieve anyway? He would get a slap on the wrist with a good attorney who would marginalize the assault or put some of the blame on her, regardless of his probation, and he would be back in the house to do it again. No, something else that would send him to prison, that's it. She rationalized that if he returned to prison she would visit him. That would make things alright in his eyes and in hers. That would be the least she could do. And she did not want to file for divorce. After all, he was just a lowly construction worker and could not bring any money to the support table.

The other thing that upset her was that their somewhat dysfunctional marriage caused her to have to give up Katie. She really didn't want that to happen. She was tough on Katie at times, but she did love her daughter, and didn't like Katie being out of her life. Yeah, that sucks. It was Billy's fault. He always started the fights. Well, most of them anyway. Okay, some of them. Carla knew his hot-buttons, and she used that to get him riled up, just like she used to do to that bastard, Dave.

Yep. Billy had to pay. She knew how, too.

"Billy, it would be nice if something happened to my ex-husband's wife, Maria."

"Yeah? Like what? By me? Will it get me in trouble?"

"No, you should be okay, but you'll have to do it quickly and get back here. Kind of a hit and run. I'm not asking or telling you to do it, just saying it would be nice if she met some harm."

"Okay. What dju want me to do?" He was slurring his words. The whiskey had taken its toll and he was not thinking clearly.

"Well, if you or someone wanted to do something, you would go to my ex-husband's house one weekend evening and try to catch his wife leaving the house for work. Then, beat her up a little. Rough her up some. Not a lot, but enough so that she hurts."

"What if he has a camera system on the house?"

"That cheap bastard? Hah. No way."

"Oh, man, that still sounds risky, and I am trying to clean up my act and be a better person. I need to stop the crazy stuff."

"Yes, a little bit, but you could probably do it without getting caught. If you decided to do it, I'll treat you real special when you return." She gave him what she thought was a sexy smile. Like before, she knew she could manipulate him to do what she wanted. "No more after this."

That got his attention, but he's thinking, yeah, right. "Okay, Carla, because I love you." Poor Billy. He thought doing Carla's bidding was a right of passage to her heart and psyche.

"Good. We'll talk about it later." Carla was scheming big time and thinking that it was very likely Billy would get arrested. She never told him that her ex-husband had installed a surveillance camera at his house after the break-in. As long as it was turned on and recording, Billy's assault of Maria would be on tape, and she would kill two birds with one stone – hurt Maria physically, and get Billy out of her life for now. She didn't know if she would divorce him. She would have plenty of time to think about that. She wasn't overly concerned about her role in this matter. She rationalized that if she did not actually ask him to harm Maria, merely suggested, but he more or less did it on his own, she would not be implicated if and when he was arrested. On the other hand, if she told or asked him to harm Maria it might mitigate charges against Billy and lessen his sentence, but she could be implicated. This was complicated, and it was almost too much for her hazy thought process to digest that night. She was hoping he would do this trick on his own volition.

She then had an afterthought. Maybe it was too late, but she would try to get him in a sexy mood before he got nasty and wanted to fight. "Let's go upstairs and have some fun."

"Okay, Carla. I think I'm ready."

Carla had one problem that she did not anticipate in her ill-conceived quest for revenge. This scheme of hers could backfire on her.

Carla continues to play with fire.

1999

CHAPTER THIRTY-THREE

After dinner one night in the Williams household.

"I'm going to meet a friend and have a couple drinks, Carla," Billy says with a questionable measure of confidence.

"What? And leave me alone?" she retorts. Her engines are revving.

Billy is somewhat taken aback by this reaction. "Hey, no problem. I'll just be a couple hours, that's all." He's in defense posture.

"Like hell. I don't know where you're going! For all I know you have an old girlfriend on the side that you're still screwing," she counters.

"Oh, Carla, give it up, please. I wouldn't do that to you and you know it. I just want to see an old prison mate that's now living in this area. Damn."

"Right. Well, go ahead you scumbag! Thanks for deserting me tonight." Full throttle on the emotion engine. Jeff Gordon screaming around the number two turn at Dover Raceway, heading into the straightaway.

"Bye. I won't be long. Plus, this is the first time I've done this since we got married. It should be okay for me to get out of the house once in a while, ya know?" Billy thought it best to leave the house now before things might get physical and ugly. He actually wondered to himself if this was how she treated her ex-husband.

Carla did not respond, knowing she could not control him as she wanted, but simply turned around and headed upstairs.

Billy drove to a local bar in Chesapeake not far from the house. There, he met up with Stoney, a guy he met in prison. Stoney was laid back and a good person, notwithstanding the DUI involuntary manslaughter episode that landed him in prison.

They each ordered a glass of the house whiskey and were relaxed as they talked about their prison time and what they were now doing with their lives. Billy was a whiskey guy now. No more of that pot stuff. Let Carla do it if she wanted.

"You know, Stoney, I'm having a tough time with something my wife suggested I do. She didn't come right out and ask or tell me to do it, but she sure as hell suggested in kind of a strong way."

"Oh, and what is it she suggests you do?"

"Well, she still has a burr under her saddle over her ex-husband, and now his wife."

"You're kidding me," Stoney replies. "Really? Her ex-husband? And I'll bet she never even sees the guy anymore now that she's married to you."

"Right. She has no need to see him. Both of the kids are now out of our house."

"So, tell me, what does she want?"

"She wants me to do a quick whack job on the guy's wife. Slap her around a little. Do a little physical harm, but not much, you know?"

"You're kidding me, right? Billy, that's bullshit. You can't be doing that shit. If you get caught, you're back in the slammer. Damn."

"I know, but she thinks I can get away with it. Quick hit outside their house at night and scram before anyone else sees me."

"Wow, that's too risky, buddy. I don't want to see you back in prison. No way."

"Yeah. I'm trying to straighten out my life, Stoney. I have a decent job with my dad. I'm learning new carpentry skills. Someday I'd like to go in business for myself once I'm farther removed from the felony charge and prison time. We have some marriage problems. Carla and I get in fights once in a while, but she starts them. I think she does it on purpose, just keeps pushing me until I can't take it anymore."

"Then why would you even think about doing it? No, don't answer me. Love. You love your wife, and as crazy-ass as her suggestion is, you want to please her. That's it, huh?"

"Yep. That's it. If I don't do it, I'm sure she'll remind me of it on a regular basis. She'll find a way to bring it up and hammer me about it. She's just so damn manipulative and forceful. She has a way about her. If she thinks something is right to her, that's all it takes. She won't let me forget it. I know what she suggests is wrong, but I really want to keep our marriage intact."

"That's a tough, unforgiving situation you're in, pal, and I'm thinking you haven't been married that long. I know what I would do."

"What?" Billy asks, knowing the answer.

"Don't do it. It's not worth it, Billy. Let her beat up on you and torment you for not doing it, but don't do it. Prison would be far worse, especially since you seem to be turning your life around."

"Oh, man. I know what you're saying. I gotta think about this. I don't know what I'll do. Maybe I can pull it off without getting caught. And then again, if I'm caught I'm toast. If I do this, this is the last time I do something like this for her. Never again."

"You got that right. Think about it, and don't do it!"

"Okay. Hey, let's talk about something else. What are you up to these days? Staying out of trouble?" Billy says with a smile and a chuckle.

And with that, they shift gears to more fun topics like race cars and women.

Think twice before doing Carla's bidding.

1999

CHAPTER THIRTY-FOUR

The three of us, Maria, Katie and me, were getting along well. Maria was super helpful to Katie, and I knew Katie appreciated it. Carla was moderately quiet, at least there weren't nightly or even weekly calls. She called to talk to Katie, and I was occasionally caught on the downside with Carla wanting to be her chatty, tell-all self. It was moderately tolerable. And Maria was no longer on the receiving end of Carla's vicious attacks. But that didn't mean anything, for Carla had made her feelings known often about how she felt toward Maria. I didn't see that changing. Maybe it was the quiet before the storm. And then again, maybe Carla was preoccupied. I was even able to talk Katie into visiting some Virginia colleges, so we took a few days on two different occasions to visit some campuses and, where possible, talk to college admissions staff and some students. It was an eye-opener for Katie as she saw the possibilities. Katie didn't have the best grades when she came down to our area, but we worked with her, encouraged her, and her grades were improving. She liked the Longwood College and Virginia Commonwealth University campuses, interestingly two very different campuses, one in a rural setting in central Virginia, and the other in downtown Richmond, Virginia.

And then, a terrible thing happened that spun out of control into something horrible. Luckily, Katie was at a girlfriend's house for the night, so she was spared the ordeal. It was late spring and dark out as Maria was leaving the house one weekend night in the early evening hours to check on an important catered event at the base Officers Club when she was assaulted in the driveway of our house. I heard a scream and I rushed outside. I could tell she was hurt.

"Maria. Oh my God! Are you alright? What happened?"

"I think I'm okay. Just feel a bit beat up, you know? Someone jumped me from behind and pummeled me."

I dashed back in the house to call the police, then came back outside with a blanket to keep Maria warm. "Here you go, hon, this will keep you comfortable." The way she described it to me as we waited for the police lead me to believe that the attacker was hiding in some nearby bushes, hoping that Maria would come out of the house. He obviously had good timing, although we'll never know if he frequently made a habit of being on or near our property.

"I had my key in the door lock when I was suddenly grabbed from behind. He had one hand over my mouth and one arm around my waist. I was able to wrench my face loose from his hand and screamed to alert you. He was strong."

I was shaking my head in disgust and disbelief. "What happened next?"

"He threw me to the ground and started hitting me. I curled up in an attempt to avoid some of his hits. It had to be Billy, but I wouldn't know since I've never seen him."

"You're probably right. Carla probably put him up to it."

"I was thinking and trying to come up with something to say to him that might get him to stop pummeling me. He was starting to hurt me. So I took a chance and yelled at him, "You must be Billy! You know what? We have a surveillance camera system pointed on to the driveway. And Carla knows we have cameras, you fool!" All of a sudden he stopped. He looked at the roofline and I'm sure he saw the equipment. He said, "That damn Carla." And off he ran, around the corner. I heard a car start up and it laying some rubber as he took off."

"Oh, my, gosh. You thought to say that to him? You're brilliant. I can't believe he used Carla's name. He must have been too shocked from what you said." Maria was quick on her feet, well, on her back, too, but that was a masterful stroke that would have a yet unknown effect on Carla and Billy. "How are you feeling, hon, are you going to be okay?"

"I think I'm okay. When the police arrive let's ask them to radio for an ambulance to get me to the emergency room. I feel rough from his hits. Damn him. I guess I won't be checking on that function at the base."

The police finally arrived after what seemed an eternity and Maria explained what happened. An ambulance also arrived and took Maria to the hospital. I told her I would go to the hospital as soon as I finished with the police. I told the officers that I had a camera system.

"Well, let's take a look." We went into the house and watched the tape. "Very good," one of the officers stated. May we take this?" I told them it was theirs for safekeeping. This was all taking time, valuable time in my opinion. I thought that assuming it was Billy, and I of course had no reason not to suspect that it was, he was in the next county by now. Finally, the police contacted the Virginia Beach police seeking their assistance in possibly apprehending

Billy. More time of course as they processed the request at the Virginia Beach end. The officers assured me that they would collaborate with other police departments to verify Billy's identity and seek an arrest. Along the way, I had also provided some much abbreviated background on the disaster that was Dave and Carla's marriage and her post-marriage lunatic behavior over the many recent years. They got the picture, and the tape. I had provided Billy's name, telling them he was a convicted felon and on parole after serving prison time, as well as information I had from Carla and Billy's crazy behavior in Virginia Beach. They thanked me and said they would check their data base as soon as possible for a match, and reminded me they would be working with the Norfolk and Virginia Beach police as well for some history from their files on Billy. Getting a mug shot would be easy.

I drove as quickly as I could to Maryview Hospital on J. Clyde Morris Boulevard, a major Newport News/Hampton area hospital, where I was able to check on Maria. She was still with a doctor when I arrived, so I waited anxiously in the emergency room waiting area, hoping for some good news from the doctor.

I didn't have to wait long, which also suggested to me that they got her into a doctor very soon after her arrival. The doctor walked over to me. She was young, awfully young it seemed. She was either doing her residency or had just completed it. She introduced herself.

"Mr. Pedersen?"

"Yes, doctor."

"Hi, I'm Doctor Oppleman. I was tending to your wife."

"Yes, doctor. How is she?"

"Oh, she's going to be fine. She's very strong-headed. A few superficial wounds that require some bandages for a few days, but that's the extent of her injuries. She is quite sore, and will be for a few days before it wears off. I've given her some pain medicine that she will hopefully use judiciously. She needs rest."

"Her head is okay? You know, her skull? Any concussion?"

"No, no. She's fine. She's a real pistol, telling me all about it. And she really thought fast in that traumatic situation."

"Oh, good. Whew. I'm so happy to hear the injuries are relatively minor. Thanks, doctor."

"My pleasure. I'll go check on her again. Oh, by the way, I'm recommending she stay here in our care for the night so we can keep an eye on her. She wasn't too thrilled about that. In fact, she made a funny expression that her fun meter was ticking." She laughed, then before leaving, said, "When she gets home tomorrow try to keep her calm and quiet. No strenuous activity for a few days, and definitely no jogging, and she'll be back to normal."

"Will do, doctor." And she was gone.

I visited Maria in her room and filled her in on my discussions with the police. I told her about giving the tape to the police and providing Billy's name. We chatted for a bit, both in shock and disbelief that Carla was still vicious and dangerous, still inflicting pain, like a bite from the head of a dead venomous snake. I told her goodnight, that I loved her very much, that I felt horrible that she had to endure the physical assault, and that I was proud of her for her quick thinking. With that, I returned home to feed our little Missy.

I drove home, rather in a mental and emotional fog, trying to get my brain around what had happened, fully realizing I was not surprised that Carla could be behind it. She was an evil woman and continued to show that in so many ways. I took care of Missy and read for a bit in a very quiet house. I loved reading novels and always had a good book going. I had lots of favorite authors, so it was no problem finding a book at the local library. At the time, I was working my way through novels by Jack Higgins. And in fact, the only TV I watched was the Weather Channel and morning news before my workouts. I caught the local and national news early in the evening, then the TV was turned off and I was reading. I went to bed at a decent time since my days started very early. Before I fell off to sleep I pondered on Billy's whereabouts. Who knows where he took off to during the elapsed time between the assault and police marshalling their resources to try and find him?

The local news the next morning was shocking and horrific, and certainly informed me of Billy's whereabouts after the assault. I sat stunned as I listed to the morning anchor tell the audience of a tragedy that had unfolded the night before.

"Last night during a domestic dispute a local lady, Carla Williams, was shot to death. The police have in custody her husband, Billy Williams. The incident took place in a shopping center in Virginia Beach on Virginia Beach Boulevard. From what the police have told us, Mr. Williams was driving his car in pursuit of his wife, who was driving her car. She drove into the shopping center seeking help, but before she could do so, Mr. Williams rammed her with his car, got out of the car, and shot his wife multiple times. She was later declared dead at the scene. But that is not all of the story. The police are not able to say very much since the full investigation has not started, but a reliable source said that Mr. Williams is also the suspect in an assault that occurred in Hampton earlier in the evening. There, the wife of Mrs. Williams' ex-husband was attacked in her driveway. She is recovering at Maryview Hospital in Newport News.

Our news team was first on the scene last night and also went to the Virginia Beach home of Mr. and Mrs. Williams where they were able to talk to a neighbor. The neighbor's townhouse is next door to the Williams unit. We have a clip from that interview by our Channel Thirteen reporter, Dave Rockinson." The clip followed. "The neighbor, Paul, prefers to be off-camera and provide only his first name. Sir, did you have any indication of a domestic dispute last night in the unit belonging to the Williams'?"

"Oh, yes. It was very evident. There was a lot of screaming and yelling by the people next door. Normally, you don't hear much through the walls, but this time was different. There was a lot of noise."

"Sir, could you make out any specific comments made by your neighbors?"

"Yes, I could. The man was yelling that his wife knew there was a camera somewhere and that she set him up. All I could hear from her side was that she didn't know anything about a camera. Then he yelled, "You liar!" I heard some crashing of things along with some more yelling. Then I heard him say, "Put that knife away!" I heard her say, "Yeah, I set you up, asshole!" Then I heard some more screaming, and him yelling, "You cut me!", and then it was quiet until I heard the front door slam and someone running down the stairs to the parking lot. I heard car doors slam twice and saw the cars racing out of the parking lot."

"Thank you, sir, for your time." The reporter turned to the camera and said, "Back to you, Fred. This is Dave Rockinson reporting for Channel Thirteen."

The news anchor then said, "We will continue to provide you more information on this tragic story as it becomes available. And now, a check on the weather and traffic on this beautiful April morning …."

I received a call from the Hampton police the next day. They had been collaborating with the Virginia Beach police for their investigation. The officer asked how Maria was doing. I thanked him, told him she was doing well and would recover fully, and that she was due home later today when I could pick her up.

The officer told me that Billy had remained at the scene of the shooting and that, on the advice of his attorney during initial questioning, had not admitted to killing his wife. He had taken a defensive posture in telling Virginia Beach police investigators that his wife put him up to a number of activities he had taken against me and Maria, including the vehicle damages, the tailgating incident, and the house break-in. Before they were married, she had actually paid him to commit most of those criminal activities. Billy also admitted to the assault on Maria, I suspect because he knew it was on tape. Billy made it clear he was simply doing her bidding out of his love for her, that she repeatedly told him how much she hated me and actually wanted me killed. She must have been a real whack job, the policeman had added. I told him he didn't know the half of it. No, make that ninety-nine percent of it over the past twenty years.

Don't take a knife into gunfight.

EPILOGUE

One year later. I needed closure and one way to achieve it was to attend portions of Billy's trial until there was a verdict. I just needed to know his fate and what he told the jury about Carla's impact on him. It wasn't because I was necessarily a fan of his, for I most certainly was not, but he was someone that in a very different way got caught up in Carla's maniacal web. I sensed a pattern. Me, Billy, her brother Jim, and you may as well include her mother and father. Lord knows how many other people found themselves on the wrong side of her.

Billy had a damn good lawyer, and I sat spellbound through much of the deliberations I could attend. It wasn't many, for I had a job, but I took some annual leave on occasion to sit in that courtroom in Virginia Beach. The first thing I noticed was the jury, which was predominantly male, and on the somewhat younger side at that. I presumed the prosecuting attorney, mindful that the victim was a female, would strike for as many women as he could manage. By the same token, the defense attorney would try to minimize the number of women. It appeared he was successful. My guess was that the jury might be more favorable to Billy. We would find out, of course. The ebb and flow of the proceedings was fascinating, as were the witnesses asked to testify. One of the persons to testify was the neighbor of Billy and Carla that was interviewed on TV, and it was obvious that he was a key witness for the defense.

Billy had pleaded not guilty to Second Degree Murder, a class two felony in the Commonwealth of Virginia, which carried a possible sentence of from five to forty years in prison, most likely advising the court through his attorney that he could provide ample testimony and proof that Carla was an accomplice and co-conspirator, if not instigator, behind many of his crimes. His attorney based his case on temporary insanity and heat of passion, and knowing Carla as I did, I could certainly appreciate his strategy. After all, any good attorney, with the right psychologist, could make a strong case that there was a fine line between sanity and insanity. We've all heard that expression. Interestingly, Carla made that statement to me on occasion during her countless rants. I suspect that Billy's attorney knew quite well that he was not going to get his client acquitted of any and all charges, so he was after a voluntary manslaughter verdict, a much lesser offense, and certainly one that was in the realm of the possible due to various mitigations. But, you don't shoot people to death, and Billy did have some baggage, so that would undeniably be a factor.

This case did have some mitigations, namely that during the ensuing yelling and screaming in their townhouse upon Billy's return from assaulting my Maria, Billy testified that Carla was first to produce a sharp steak knife from a kitchen drawer. She threatened him with it, waving it in his face, and ultimately cut him a couple of times. That sounded all so familiar, and you might wonder why I was not on the witness stand. That was discussed among and between the legal teams, and it was decided that my being on the witness stand to testify might create some complications deriving from the concurrent charges against Billy for assaulting Maria. Having me on the stand might have been a risky proposition. The prosecution might not want to hear what I had to say about Carla, while the defense might wonder how I might come across since Billy had also allegedly assaulted my dear wife. Quite a conundrum, so I was on the sidelines. Billy also testified that Carla intentionally did not warn him about cameras at our house, and had actually told him during their argument that she wanted to set him up to get rid of him. Nasty stuff.

Well, apparently Billy had also armed himself with a knife in self-defense. It also turned out that an emergency room doctor testified that Billy was treated at the Virginia Beach General Hospital for multiple knife wounds to his body. I doubt Billy would have had the mental wherewithal to cut himself. So, there you go, a possible self-defense testimony, even though matters were resolved in a shopping center parking lot distant from the house. Which brings up a good point. What may have been a purely self-defense argument inside the townhouse walls became a "heat of passion" defense for what eventually occurred in the remote parking lot. The killing was not deemed premeditated, but derived from the brouhaha in the townhouse and the chase. Billy's attorney made a strong case for Carla's evil persona, viciousness, manipulation, and strong suggestion that she wanted harm to come to both Billy and Maria.

So, the verdict was guilty of voluntary manslaughter. It was a mix of self-defense and in the heat of passion, with much lighter jail time associated I'm certain, and was straight out of the law code – intentional killing in which the offender had no prior intent to kill, such as killing that occurs in heat of passion – the person became emotionally or mentally disturbed. I had read up on the

Virginia Criminal Code, and it went something like this … On the spectrum of homicides, voluntary manslaughter lies somewhere in between the killing of another with malice aforethought and the excusable, justified, or privileged taking of life that does not constitute a crime, such as some instances of self-defense. Federal law defines voluntary manslaughter as the unlawful killing of a human being without malice upon a sudden quarrel or heat of passion. After all, Carla wanted to put his butt back in prison. Also, heat of passion generally refers to an irresistible emotion that an ordinarily reasonable person would experience under the same facts and circumstances. I doubt very much that Billy returned to his house with the notion of killing Carla, but her pulling the knife and striking him with it ultimately caused him to grab his gun and chase her when she ran from the house. In the meantime, he "lost it". The sentencing portion was scheduled for a month later, which I attended. After the prosecution and defense presented their aggravating and mitigating factors, it was left to the judge to decide the sentence. I heard the judge sentence him to four years in prison. I didn't quite agree with that sentence, for Carla was in control all the way, having put him up to a good number of criminal activities. I was thinking a shorter sentence than four years, but I suspect there's ample precedent in these types of cases, and again, he was a convicted felon with prison time, on probation, and had committed a number of other crimes against me. In my discussions with the attorneys and prosecutor I advised them that in view of the outcome of the murder trial we were dropping the assault charges against Billy. I think it was the least we could do under the circumstances. The guy would pay his debt to society, and Maria was okay.

I did visit Billy in prison. Just once. I certainly did not like the man. After all, he did a pretty good number on me and on Maria, but there was a sort of kinship. We both dealt with the dark side of Carla. I came out of it okay, oddly enough, because Billy shot her. He solved my problem. Billy's in prison for a long time. He told me she could be sweet one minute, then come unglued and be very ugly to him, with criticisms of his construction work, his time behind bars, his friends, and berating him for some of his actions during his younger years. That was Carla. He told me he just lost it with her. Yep. She could do that to you. We had an emotional talk. With tears in his eyes, he also told me he really was trying to clean up his act, to make amends, and be a better person. Carla made it tough for him to do so. She was evil, and the lives of Billy and me were irrevocably damaged. We said our goodbyes and I wished him well. I left the prison with a heavy heart. That damn Carla.

Closure. I could now put it all behind me. If you really think I could put all the mental trauma and lasting effects of Carla's torment behind me, well, you know. The Arizona waterfront property deal.

Kyle and Katie were having a tough time dealing with the sudden loss of their mother. There were some rough edges in their relationship with their mother, but the fact remains, Carla was their mother. Maria and I ensured they knew we were always available to help them, to listen, to do whatever was necessary. We got them both into counseling, which was extremely beneficial. But to their credit, they found ways to help themselves cope. Kyle joined the college rugby team, a club sport, and was able to vent a lot of emotion through that physical activity and its social events. And Katie became a volunteer at the local SPCA, working with animals that needed companionship and love. It was truly remarkable, and I was proud of them. They each took different routes to achieve the same, peaceful place in their souls.

I spoke to Jim a few times after the ordeal. He was taking it pretty well considering Carla was his sister, but then, he had reminded me that he "lost" his sister years ago.

Maria and I had by that time bought a nice little cabin at a lovely place called Lake Gaston that straddled the Virginia/ North Carolina border. Beautiful area. Fingers of blue waters stretching everywhere as far as the eye could see. Thick forests of pine and hardwood trees. The sounds of the lake and forest animals reverberating after nightfall and before sunrise. The cup of java on the deck in the still dark morning hours made especially enjoyable. The cabin was just large enough to meet our needs, and it was affordable without having to rent it out to a bunch of strangers.

We purposely planned on taking a long holiday weekend at the cabin shortly after the conclusion of Billy's trial and sentencing. It gave me an excellent opportunity to reflect on two decades of life largely ravaged by Carla and to really think through what had happened. Katie had stayed behind at a girlfriends.

Maria joined me on the deck that first morning at the cabin. We kissed and I rubbed her back a little. I was still keyed up.

"Maria," I said, "I'm going to take my cup of coffee and hang out on the dock for a while."

"Okay, hon," she responded. "I'm sure you have a lot on your mind."

"Yeah. And I'm sure you still need to come to some closure from your ordeal."

It was about sixty degrees outside, with no humidity or wind, so it was pleasant weather. It was still early so I heard the birds chattering and an occasional squawk of a larger bird, and heard the occasional fish jumping out of the water for food. The setting was bucolic. The lake was calm. It again reminded me of Einstein's comment that a calm and modest life leads to happiness. I was working on that.

I wasn't going to torture myself with trying to recapture all that had happened since those fateful days when I met the cute little brunette and later said, "I do". Rhetorically, oh, if I could have turned back the clock. I certainly wish I never met Carla and let my incurable romantic tendencies shape the early part of the relationship. Inertia built in, and we were married. It didn't take long to see Carla's dark side, which became progressively worse. Her vicious verbal attacks came out of nowhere and left mental scars. The hotel stays and knife incidents should have been enough for me to say, "I've had it, I'm filing for a divorce." But my feet were set in stone for many reasons. I could not get myself to make that move. Keep the family together.

There were so many unanswered questions. How did I let myself fall for and marry her? I do know one thing. In hindsight, I was not ready for marriage, especially to her. Why didn't I push aside all the reservations about filing for divorce when things got really ugly? Why didn't I push her into medical treatment? After the divorce, why did I allow her to relentlessly call and verbally assault me? One would think that a good lawyer could have created some space for me, but then, there was the children. And she kept right on going, with terrible accusations about Maria, along with the threats and crude language to me and her.

What sort of person was this? Why was she this evil, vicious person that in Gatling gun fashion took repeated, countless, perverse pleasure in pummeling me? And the "I'll kill you" threats! Are you kidding me? There were serious mental issues. Post-partum syndrome? Bullshit. Bipolar disorder? Maybe, to some degree, but there was something bigger, something overarching and more defining that shaped her behavior and persona. I'll tell you what. I really do think she was a sociopath. It was somehow reinforced as she grew older. She did not know right from wrong, and could not discriminate. She played people like puppets on strings when and where she could. She even told me so, that her goal was to torment me. She was manipulative. Controlling.

Strong-headed. Demanding. Ask Billy. You don't have to ask me. You know my story. I could not help but reflect on a statement made by John Kennedy. He said, "Anyone who believes there is fairness in this life is seriously misinformed." How about that? I also thought about the lethal combination of Billy and Carla, a toxic mixture for sure. And to Carla? Your deliberate, conscious program to unceasingly torment me was largely a success, I must admit. Taking it to another level with Maria was destructive. You thought you were going to outsmart everyone, but your obsession about Maria lead you astray and was your downfall. It didn't work out as planned, and in fact backfired on you. Is this what you really wanted? Maybe the outcome was what you had intended. We'll never know. Your demise reminded me of a commanding officer I had in my very early years working for the Navy. When he retired from the Navy he actually had the gall to write in our employee newsletter, "I will miss you, but not very much and not for very long." I had to wonder how many people that knew Carla thought to themselves, "I will miss you, Carla, but not very much and not for very long."

No more phone calls from Carla.

THE END

ABOUT THE AUTHOR

Dick Carlsen was born in and grew up in the San Francisco Bay Area. He attended Chico State College and completed his graduate studies at Indiana University. He is retired after a 44-year Navy civilian career, during which he travelled extensively to Navy activities worldwide. He lives in Virginia Beach, Virginia, with his wife Cathy and their two dogs, Missy and Woody. He and his wife enjoy spending time on the beaches of South Carolina and the North Carolina Outer Banks.

Made in the USA
Middletown, DE
03 November 2018